Fortissimo

Fortissimo

Backstage at the Opera with Sacred Monsters and Young Singers

WILLIAM MURRAY

CROWN PUBLISHERS
NEW YORK

Library of Congress Cataloging-in-Publication Data

Murray, William, 1926–2005

Fortissimo : backstage at the opera with sacred monsters and young singers /
William Murray.—1st ed.

1. Singers—United States.   2. Opera—United States.   3. Lyric Opera Center
for American Artists.   I. Title.

ML400.M94 2005

782.1'0973—dc22   2005006406

1-4000-5360-9

Printed in the United States of America

Design by Lauren Dong

10 9 8 7 6 5 4 3 2 1

First Edition

To the memory of my maternal grandmother,
Ester Danesi Traversari,
who first introduced me to the glories of great singing

I know only the stars in heaven.

—ARTURO TOSCANINI

What time is the next Swan?

—Tenor LEO SLEZAK onstage in *Lohengrin* at the Met

When you sing you give everything . . . It is wonderful.

—MONTSERRAT CABALLÉ

Contents

Fortissimo

The Golden Age of La Puma

I WASN'T AT ALL SURE that I was up to singing my first Edgardo, but Madam Josephine La Puma harbored no doubts about me. "You have a nice voice," she said. "A little light for the role maybe, but this is not a big theater and you will be good." I trusted Madam La Puma's judgment. She knew opera singers, having been one herself, and she was the artistic director, as well as the business manager, spiritual mentor and general factotum of the Opera Workshop, a nonprofit educational institution devoted heart and lungs to the year-round public performance of opera in New York City. The year was 1960 and the workshop was then the only place in town where young singers could go to try out leading roles in front of paying customers. Sure, there were the conservatories and music schools, such as Juilliard and Mannes, but their opera programs were for students; the Opera Workshop was for young professionals. At least that's what we told ourselves.

As for me, I no longer considered myself a professional opera singer. I had studied voice for years in Boston, New York and Italy, had sung professionally in musical comedy, but I finally had come to the conclusion that I didn't have a big enough instrument in my throat to fill a major opera house. What I had was a nice light tenor suitable for the smaller parts known as comprimario roles—

the unhallowed stalwarts who appear at some point in the action, usually to make brief announcements of one sort or another or convey information designed to advance the plot—but those assignments were not for me. Besides, by that time in my life I had had some success as a journalist, had written a couple of well-reviewed novels and was working at *The New Yorker* as a fiction editor. I hadn't abandoned singing, however, and had been enjoying myself performing around New York, mostly in Gilbert and Sullivan operettas, and over the past couple of years for the Opera Workshop. I had sung a couple of Alfredos in *La Traviata,* a Nemorino in *L'Elisir d'Amore* and several Rodolfos in *La Bohème*—all roles I could handle, at least to my own satisfaction. (I had also sung in a *Barber of Seville* over WNEW and a *Bohème* on WNYC, local radio stations, as well as a *Fledermaus* with the amateur City Symphony in Central Park.) I was having a lot more fun singing than when I had been obsessed with becoming the next Caruso. So when I was asked if I wanted to tackle Edgardo in Donizetti's *Lucia di Lammermoor,* I found I could be persuaded, even though I thought the part might be heavy for me. Nominally a bel canto opera, *Lucia* depends for its success upon the coloratura bravura of its leading lady, but it also poses a formidable challenge to the tenor hero, Edgardo, especially during the last act, in which he has to sing a difficult aria and a death scene with a very high tessitura, which means a great cluster of high notes in quick succession. You can't croon them and you can't just belt them, as even some quite celebrated tenors do. I had in my head the way the scene should be sung from having listened to the great Italian lyric tenor Beniamino Gigli do it and I knew I could never even come close to that performance, but then who expected me to? This was the La Puma Opera Workshop, after all, not the Met. I agreed to take on the role.

Madam La Puma, who was called simply Madam by her staff and artists, was a large, heavyset, gray-haired woman in her early sixties with incongruously small hands and feet; delicate, rather aristocratic features; and the black, placid, resigned, slightly cynical eyes characteristic of her native Sicily. She was only in her middle twenties when she first came to New York in 1924 as a budding coloratura soprano who had already put several seasons of opera behind her. With her father and teacher, Giuseppe La Puma, a well-known comic basso, she had been touring Argentina, Chile and Peru with the Bracale Opera Company, singing the major light soprano parts. Prior to that she had sung all over Italy, from her native Palermo to Milan, then the opera capital of the world. Giuseppe knew more than a hundred roles, had sung with all the great stars of his day—Caruso, Bonci, Schipa, Tetrazzini, Chaliapin, Gigli, Galli-Curci—and he was much in demand. "If we weren't singing ourselves," Madam recalled, "we were listening to somebody else sing."

Like most Sicilian families, the La Pumas functioned as a tribal unit, with Amalia, Giuseppe's wife, managing the establishment. In the United States, Giuseppe and his daughter toured that first winter with the San Carlo Opera, one of several such companies, but like its competitors it was already in difficulty. Costs were rising and public taste, according to Madam, was being corrupted by the movie industry. "The critics didn't say anything about our singing," she said of her American debut, "but they all said we were too fat." Fat, Madam felt, was almost essential to the production of golden tones, and to criticize an opera singer for his avoirdupois was a frivolity bordering on the sacrilegious. Fortunato Gallo, the impresario, however, bowed to the new decadence in taste and canceled the La Pumas' contracts, temporarily stranding them in New York.

Giuseppe was then fifty-four and for some time had been talking about quitting and going into teaching. The family rented a furnished apartment in Brooklyn, bought a secondhand grand piano and began to advertise for pupils. Within a few months the school had about thirty-five aspiring singers, and Madam, whose own career had been cut short by her father's retirement, accompanied all of the lessons. "After a while we were making so much money I never even thought about going back on the stage," she recalled.

Giuseppe dubbed his school the Mascagni Center of Culture, after his favorite composer. He moved it to Manhattan in 1936, to Room 506 in Steinway Hall on West Fifty-seventh Street, where the more advanced pupils would give concerts of operatic excerpts or entire scenes, without costumes or props, for small invited audiences. The center's main concern was teaching bel canto, the production of the pure, open-throated tone that characterizes the best Italian singing. It was a tiring and often unrewarding task. "Most Americans lock their voices up in their throats, letting maybe just a little of it come through the nose without moving the lips," Madam once explained. "With Italian you have to use the lips to talk and the stomach muscles to make the pure vocal sounds. That's the whole secret of singing right there." Madam remembered that her father saw no reason why even the most frozen-lipped, adenoidal American couldn't be taught to produce a round, beautiful sound, and he spent the rest of his life in pursuit of this ideal.

After Giuseppe died, in 1940, Madam decided to broaden the center's activities by putting on public performances of complete operas. Her daughter, Alberta, from a short-lived marriage to an opera singer named Ottavio Masiello, had already graduated from Juilliard, gotten married and struck out on a career of her own as a mezzo-soprano, eventually becoming an assistant conductor at the Met. Madam was free to become a full-time impresario. "When we did our first opera, a *Barber,* at the Jewish Community Center on West Eighty-ninth Street, everyone was so enthusiastic that we decided to keep going," Madam told me. "Soon that's all I was doing. From a voice teacher I became an impresario, but it's been some job."

The job required raising money, acquiring physical properties (costumes, sets, vocal scores, orchestrations) and bringing enough people into her orbit not only to cast entire seasons of operas but also to staff a chorus, an orchestra and a backstage crew. Somehow she always managed, year after year, to keep going. "She never lost her temper, raised her voice or took no for an answer," one of her singers from the early years assured me. "She'd sit at the telephone sometimes until two or three in the morning, calling up people and getting them to do things for her. If somebody told her about a good chorus tenor in New Jersey, she'd call him up and get him to come to New York for rehearsals. If she heard of an amateur violinist in the Bronx, she'd go to the phone and add him to the orchestra. If some company announced a sale of surplus jerkins, Madam would buy them. She was like a jolly, amiable spider single-mindedly pulling everyone and everything into her web. Once you had said yes to Madam, you were caught. She was so nice and patient, no matter what happened, that you felt obligated."

Between September 13, 1942, and August 29, 1943, the renamed Mascagni Opera Guild put on sixty-six performances of eighteen different operas, a total that compares favorably with the seasonal repertories of the most important opera companies in the world. Madam was able to cast from a nucleus of forty-three leading singers, and provided for every performance an orchestra of about thirty pieces as well as a chorus of comparable size. Not a single performance was ever sold out, but singers, instrumentalists, directors and conductors had begun to seek out the company as a place to launch themselves and gain experience. Participating artists paid ten dollars a month to rehearse a part, twenty to fifty dollars to perform it at least once in public. Members of the chorus and orchestra sang and played for the sheer cooperative love of the thing, while the backstage crew was made up of singers who couldn't afford to contribute anything to the venture but their time. It was an admirable system, from which Madam never made a nickel for herself. "If there were any profits after all expenses had been met, she'd spend them on new costumes or scores or sets," remembered one of her colleagues from those early days. "What she cared about was opera, not living like a queen."

She persisted with her seasons year after year, but it became increasingly difficult to survive. Rents went up at the various auditoriums the company used; the state and federal governments demanded larger shares of the ticket money; the price of everything, from a simple prop to an orchestration, doubled, tripled, quadrupled. "They got me good," Madam recalled. "I couldn't raise my prices because the young singers couldn't pay more. And when I tried to get more admission, the unions jumped up and down on me. They said I was unfair, I don't know to who. Anyway, they made me stop selling tickets."

A slightly less dedicated visionary than Madam La Puma would have thrown in the towel, but she persevered, putting on a minimum of two performances weekly, playing in whatever small auditoriums she could afford. To free herself from harassment by craft unions and tone-deaf bureaucrats, she dissolved the Guild and reorganized it as the Opera Workshop, incorporating it as a nonprofit educational institution. Unable any longer to afford costume rentals, she borrowed some books on costume design and made her own. She copied out chorus parts by hand. She got her students to build a simple unit set, consisting of a few flats, platforms and standing cutouts, that would fit any stage and be easily transportable. Then, in 1957, about the time I became aware of her company, she found what she hoped would become a permanent theater, the auditorium of P.S. 75, on West Ninety-fifth Street, which she rented from the Board of Education and where she put on her performances on Thursday and Friday nights. "Since we got a regular theater," she told a reporter, "it's been easier. At least the people don't have to hunt for us all over the city every week." It also conveniently happened to be only four blocks from the workshop's headquarters, a large, rambling nine-room apartment on the second floor at 250 West Ninety-first Street, with windows looking out on Broadway.

WHEN I ARRIVED at the workshop late one Monday afternoon for my first rehearsal of *Lucia,* the first person I met was Joan Dorne-mann, a cheerful young woman then employed as a music teacher at a private school, but who seemed to be spending most of her time coaching and accompanying singers. She also had begun to play at rehearsals and in performance, which took some of the pressure off Madam, who had so many other chores to attend to. Joan was waiting for me upstairs with a battered-looking score of the opera under her arm. There was a pay telephone at one end of a long hallway and a bulletin board on which were posted re-hearsal schedules as well as exhortations to participants behind in their fees to pay up, all the notices scrawled in ink or pencil across plain sheets of notebook paper. The noise was deafening. In addi-tion to the singing coming from behind the closed doors of various studio rooms, several resonant conversations were being carried on by a handful of loiterers in the hall. They were all singers and they projected their dialogue, bouncing their words off the walls and at one another as if performing on a stage.

On our way to our own rehearsal room, Joan and I looked in on the kitchen, where Madam La Puma, dressed in a loose, faded blue house robe, was sitting at a worktable placidly sewing a pair of tights, impervious to the hubbub in the hallway. Directly be-hind her, embedded in the wall, was another pay telephone, which rang almost constantly. Madam answered every call in a calm, resigned voice, never allowing it to interfere with her work or the conversation in the room. People came and went on various errands, sometimes merely to say hello or good-bye. A plump, cheerful woman named Bessie Jones, a permanent member of the ménage, presided over the stove, where a pot of coffee and a caul-dron of pasta were bubbling merrily. Beyond the stove and the sink, which was piled high with unwashed dishes, was a small bedroom containing a cot, a TV set and several piles of books and vocal scores. Amid this whirlpool of activity Madam sat as imperturbed as the Sphinx.

When Joan and I arrived at our rehearsal room at the very end of the hall, I found the other members of our cast waiting for us. Our soprano—upon whose gymnastic vocal agility in the coloratura singing of the Mad Scene the success of the opera usually depends—was a young, perky Bostonian with a small but pure voice who had been in New York for a year, was employed as a keypunch operator at IBM and was saving her money to make her professional debut in Europe. The baritone was a real estate agent from Queens who had a well-trained lyric voice, had once sung in nightclubs and vaudeville and had retired from the pop field to devote himself exclusively to opera. The bass part of Raimondo was being sung by Andrij (Andy) Dobriansky, a La Puma regular with a dark, well-focused tone and an authoritative stage presence. I had sung with him before, in *La Traviata* and *La Bohème*.

The room, like all the others in the apartment, was bare, uncarpeted, free of drapes and other sound destroyers. It contained a scarred upright piano, a few plain wooden and metal chairs and some rickety music stands. There was also a large bookcase crammed with scores, sheet music, old programs, scrapbooks and bits of costume material and props. On the walls hung photographs of past productions. Joan sat down at the piano and began to lead us through the score.

The rehearsal lasted about two hours. Very little attention was paid to musical nuance or dramatic interpretation. Our main concern was getting through the piece without committing any major blunders. Occasionally, Joan would correct a mistake or one of us would ask for a repeat of some particularly troublesome section, but for the most part it was the sort of run-through that the cast of a Broadway musical would have early on in the process, long before the director or conductor would make any serious attempt to block the action or set tempi. We didn't have time for anything but the basics. We were going onstage that Thursday night, but none of us was concerned. As our baritone put it, "Tomorrow night or Wednesday we'll walk through it once and that's enough. Half the props won't be there the night of the performance, so we'll have to improvise as we go along. We just have to get through it; that's what matters."

I was worried, however, especially about the soprano, whose Italian was mostly nonexistent; she was singing in a language all her own. When she couldn't remember a word or phrase, she'd just invent one. "She says she's going abroad to audition," I told Joan after the others had gone. "If she sings like that in Italy, they'll throw stuff at her."

Joan sighed and nodded. "You know, they all come here to learn a part and to get through it at least once in front of an audience, no matter how," she said. "It's the only way they can get themselves ready for a career, because no opera company in the world can afford to waste time teaching a singer a role. All a manager wants to know when you go to audition is what parts you've already done. The more performances you've had, the better your chance of being hired. As for little matters like stage direction and interpretation, it's pretty basic everywhere, except in the very top houses. If you've done one Rodolfo, say, chances are you can do another one somewhere else, even on a few hours' notice. That's why these singers come here and are willing to perform. That's what the Workshop is all about for them. As for Madam, I don't think she cares about the practical aspect. This has been her whole life."

OUR *LUCIA* TURNED OUT to be one of the workshop's more successful productions that year. Perhaps it was because, modesty aside, the cast was able to sing it quite decently, if not spectacularly. This was not always the case with Madam's productions. Occasionally, to make ends meet, she would have to put on performances featuring, as she once put it in private to me, "a whole lot of dogs and goats." These were singers who would pay quite a lot to appear onstage and who included, most notably, Olive Middleton, a once well-known diva long past not only her prime but her ability to sing at all, who financed performances of herself screeching through the lead roles while members of the audience either fled in horror or rolled about in the aisles in helpless hilarity. These occasions helped to keep the Opera Workshop financially afloat, even in an era when it would cost Madam only about a hundred and fifty dollars a night to put on most operas. She could count on recouping about two-thirds of that amount from the lead singers, who paid for the opportunity to perform, the rest of it from audience contributions, which, in 1957, rarely amounted to more than twenty dollars a night.

The workshop's basic repertory consisted of forty-seven operas, all but nine or ten of which Madam expected to put on every year. She tried to line up her casts and schedule her operas several weeks in advance, but there almost always had to be last-minute changes and substitutions. "People get sick," Madam once explained, "or they go away or they decide they're not ready yet or they get paying jobs. Or they get mad and quit. I once almost had to cancel a *Carmen* because the mezzo got mad at the conductor half an hour before the curtain and walked out. Luckily, there was someone in the audience who could fill in."

Madam also had to supply a chorus and orchestra. "I got about thirty people in the chorus and maybe fifty on the orchestra list," she once complained, "but you can't get them to turn out for every opera. That's because they're in this for the fun or maybe they're young students who just want a chance to play through a whole score. After you've done maybe five hundred *Traviatas*, you got to work hard to find anyone who *wants* to do still another one for any reason." Persuading people to do things they didn't particularly want to do was Madam's forte, however, and it kept her on the telephone for several hours a day. She almost never had to cancel a performance.

The fact that most of us who appeared in the Opera Workshop's productions had to pay to do so was not considered compromising, even though most Americans find it difficult to understand this. Writers who pay to have their own books published, actors who produce plays starring themselves or painters who own their own art galleries are not taken seriously in the United States, by either the public or the critics. Many of the young opera singers who joined the workshop, therefore, began by regarding it with suspicion, so Madam would have to explain the economic realities to them and make sure they coughed up the very modest fees. She was aided immeasurably in this by being able to cite a number of established artists who had once participated in her productions: Nicola Rescigno, Maria Callas's favorite American conductor; Julius Rudel, then the general director of the New York City Center Opera, who conducted for Madam under the name of Rodolfo Di Giulio; sopranos Rosalie Maresca and Josephine Guido and mezzo-soprano Corinne Vozza, who had all launched careers in Italy. (As for my own colleagues from the 1950s, Klara Barlow, with whom I sung a *Bohème,* went on to a career in Germany and Switzerland before being hired to do an Isolde at the Metropolitan; Andy Dobriansky sang comprimario parts at the Met for many years and Joan Dornemann is on the Met's musical staff today as a prompter and an assistant conductor.) Confronted by a list of such luminaries, the new members of the workshop would usually agree to pay at least some of what they owed, though Madam never banished them from her company if they failed for any reason to do so. The only thing that mattered to her was putting on her season.

The auditorium at P.S. 75 was a barren, high-ceilinged room with light yellow walls and rows of plain wooden seats that marched down to an open space just below the level of the stage, where the orchestra sat. The room could easily accommodate five hundred people, and its institutional austerity, so in keeping with the dull, square, redbrick structure that housed it, made the room seem vaster than it was; on ordinary performance nights, when there were fewer than two hundred people in the audience, it could look frighteningly empty. On Madam's gala occasions, however, when word had gotten out that her cast on that particular evening might be one of her best, the place would begin to fill up early and the room would echo to an excited anticipatory buzz. For our *Lucia* we had what amounted in the La Puma world to a sold-out house: more than three hundred people, including many members of the workshop and the usual primly dressed, slightly ill-at-ease knots of cast relatives and friends. There were also several large, noisy groups of young people, many of them clutching scores, the sort of fanatics one encounters standing at the rear of any opera house, as well as quite a few solitary, astute old buffs, shabbily dressed, foreign-looking, leaning on their canes and umbrellas, waiting stolidly for the lights to dim.

We had a good-size orchestra that night—twenty-two pieces—mainly because our conductor had agreed to pay the musicians out of his own pocket in order to guarantee something approximating what a real opera orchestra should sound like. (Madam's usual complement of players rarely numbered more than ten or twelve, with Madam herself thumping grandly away at the piano and cueing all the singers.) We had never had an orchestra rehearsal or any kind of run-through with either a stage director or the conductor, a stocky, gray-haired dentist with glasses who had prepared himself for what he considered his professional debut by beating time to gramophone records.

I had always suffered from stage fright and was, as usual, extremely nervous, a condition that usually disappeared only after I'd sung my first few bars. When I made my entrance this time for my opening scene with the soprano, she was looking for me to arrive from stage right. Unfortunately, I appeared unexpectedly from stage left. Startled, she whirled around to face me, just in time to hear me blow my opening phrases, in which I found my-self battling a sudden onslaught of catarrh, the singer's curse. I don't know how I got through the rest of the duet—especially since the soprano seemed to be singing in Romanian—but I must have, because the audience applauded.

The rest of the opera went along well enough, even though we had to struggle over tempi with the conductor, who never once looked at us. When we arrived at the famous sextet, "Chi mi frena," however, with all of us facing straight out, the dentist stopped beating time. White-faced and perspiring, he clutched his podium and stared at the score as if trying to decipher the Rosetta Stone. Luckily for us, the first violinist, an old pro who had once played for the NBC Symphony under Toscanini, rapped on his music stand with his bow to gain our attention and led us through the rest of the tricky ensemble piece.

With my first-act difficulties behind me, I had begun to sing with confidence. The soprano, still lost somewhere in outer lan-guage land, had done herself proud in the Mad Scene, interpolat-ing a lot of "la"s where she couldn't improvise any words at all. She had at least hit all the right notes, keeping her attention firmly focused, as we all did, on the first violinist, who conducted us the rest of the way while the dentist simply stood there, feebly going along with him. When we got to the last scene, I bounded onstage to address the tombs of my ancestors in "Tombe degli avi miei." To my dismay the first two tombs, painted cardboard cutouts, slowly folded over, causing some audience members to laugh. Never mind, I told myself, sing the damn aria. Which I did, better than I'd ever sung it before. When it came time for me to die, with Dobriansky and our full chorus of eighteen onstage to sympathize, I discovered I'd forgotten my dagger, the prop with which I was supposed to stab myself. What could I do? I turned away from the audience clutching my stomach, sank to my knees and perished, presumably from an acute attack of gastroenteritis.

I never sang another Edgardo. I remember fondly a lot of

smiling and laughing backstage, friendly greetings from people I'd never met, embraces from old pals, and a small, intense little girl of about twelve who thrust a scrap of paper at me and asked for my autograph. I walked over to say good-bye to Madam La Puma, who was sitting offstage left counting the audience receipts, a total of eighteen dollars and thirty cents. Before I could say anything, she fished a bulging little black notebook from inside the bosom of her dress and began flipping rapidly through the pages. "Listen, Adele," she called out to one of her volunteers, "my Radames is sick. Call up Louis right now and see if he can fill in tomorrow night, otherwise we have to move the *Tosca* up a week or cancel. If Louis can't, try Aldo. He won't pay, but he knows the part."

1

The Cell

THE STUDIO GIANNA ROLANDI refers to as The Cell is a long, rectangular room with a grand piano at one end and a full-length mirror along one wall. In a corner is a large, yellow rubber ball on which Rolandi sometimes asks her young artists to sit as they sing; it forces them to adopt a correct posture—feet planted solidly on the floor, torso erect, shoulders straight—to support the tone. On a typical day early in November 2003, I stopped by The Cell to see what might be going on that morning at Lyric Opera Center for American Artists (LOCAA), in Chicago. Rolandi, with the help of one of the company's staff accompanists, was busily at work on Siébel's aria from *Faust* with Lauren McNeese, the young mezzo-soprano about to sing the role for the first time on the Lyric stage a few days later.

McNeese is a slender, strikingly beautiful young woman with blond hair and green eyes. Three years earlier she had been accepted into the LOCAA program for young singers, after auditioning with arias from the heavier mezzo repertory. Once in, however, she was told that she had to make changes; it was much too early in her career for her to tackle the big dramatic parts. Rolandi and her colleague Richard Pearlman, who had been running the Opera Center since 1995, put McNeese to work on arias by Rossini, especially the coloratura passages that require breath control and vocal agility. McNeese labored with Rolandi several times a week. "I'm famous for making her hoarse when we first started," McNeese told me. "She was demonstrating all these things she wanted me to do, all these difficult methods, so we worked for hours." Having been a coloratura soprano diva herself, at the Metropolitan Opera and elsewhere until her retirement fourteen years earlier, Rolandi was just the person to teach McNeese; but it wasn't easy for the young mezzo. "My voice was placed farther back and darker then and this new technique was very difficult for me. I had to place my voice forward, make it lighter." Nevertheless, by the end of that first year in the program, McNeese found herself singing not only Rossini but also Bellini and Mozart. "Gianna lets you know there are no barriers," she said.

At this session, no sooner had McNeese begun to sing the opening phrases than Rolandi stopped her. "You need to get your words smaller," she told her. "You need to think in terms of funneling the sound." After the second attack on the aria, Rolandi exclaimed, "This is good! There you go!" She then asked McNeese what she was doing onstage as she sang, which consisted mostly of gathering up flowers to make a bouquet. "It's really pretty, Lauren, but you also need to think about the words." She asked the young mezzo to speak the words of the aria in order to get the right French vocal sounds: "Lean into that word *bénie.*" She made McNeese hold the tip of her nose while singing. "Better! Better! There it is!" she said. "You know where it is; the other won't carry." McNeese put on a nose clip before singing a soaring climactic high note on the difficult vowel sound *ee.* "Lauren, don't be discouraged," Rolandi said at the end of the hour-long session, "I'm being really picky here. When's your next rehearsal?" It was scheduled for one o'clock, McNeese told her. "You've been singing a lot," Rolandi said. "Be sure to mark." (Marking is the operatic term for not singing full voice.)

"I don't think that'll be possible," McNeese said, smiling as she gathered up her belongings and score, then quickly left.

The rest of that morning I sat there watching and listening to Rolandi work with three more of the young singers in the LOCAA program. Lauren Curnow, a tall, handsome, short-haired blonde with the strong-looking jaw characteristic of many opera singers, was preparing arias from Mozart's *La Clemenza di Tito* and Meyerbeer's rarely performed *Les Huguenots*. Curnow, a first-year LOCAA member listed on the Opera Center's roster as a mezzo, sounded more like a soprano to me and was much less self-assured than McNeese. Before Curnow had even finished singing an opening phrase, Rolandi bounded out of her chair to move in on her. "Lauren, it's the right idea, but you've got to sing every note. You have to sell each one." The whole thrust of her coaching was aimed at getting Curnow to move her voice forward into what the Italians call *la maschera* (the mask), which is the upper jaw and the nasal passages above it. Standing close together now, Rolandi and Curnow faced the mirror. "You have to get all that extra gunk out from under there," Rolandi said, "out of the back of the throat, otherwise your voice won't carry." Most pop singers never get out of their throats, but stick mikes up against their teeth to make any kind of sound, she explained, grinning at me. She made Curnow sing now while holding both hands up to cradle her neck. "That'll help move it forward," Rolandi said, then looked at me again. "All these mezzos fall in love with that darker sound." After a few more phrases, she went to work with Curnow on making sure her tongue was in the right place. "Right, Lauren, you're getting it," she said. "Just make sure your tongue feels like a piece of liver." Tongues, if not properly aligned, can almost literally strangle a singer; mostly they should be lying flat behind the lower teeth.

As Curnow continued to work on mastering not only her vocal technique but also her dramatic approach to what she was singing, Rolandi kept moving around behind, beside and in front of her, energetically dispensing advice, admonitions and always constructive criticism, making her repeat phrases over and over until she got them right. It was an amazing performance, not unlike that of a great coach coaxing a well-trained but inexperienced athlete into mastering his sport.

As I LISTENED to and watched Rolandi work with her charges that morning, I found myself marveling at how different an experience these young singers were having from the one I'd had during the years I'd been hoping for a career and then later hanging around Madam La Puma. The twelve young singers currently in the LOCAA program were not students but already well-trained vocal artists. In addition to McNeese and Curnow, the roster included sopranos Erin Wall and Nicole Cabell, mezzo Guang Yang, tenors Patrick Miller, Roger Honeywell, and Scott Ramsay, baritones Levi Hernandez and Quinn Kelsey, and bass Christopher Dickerson. Before coming to Chicago they had all graduated from prestigious conservatories or university opera programs, they'd studied for years with private teachers and most had sung professionally for various American opera companies. LOCAA was just the sort of career launching pad that hadn't existed back when I was studying, or for many years thereafter. In the fifties, sixties and well into the seventies, young American opera singers, even the best-trained ones, had nowhere to go but Europe to begin their careers. The conservatories and universities that had opera programs were largely unsatisfactory training grounds due to the absence on their staffs of good singing teachers and the requirement that students master other musical disciplines, such as music history and sight-reading, that had little directly to do with training the instrument in your throat. No one at the New England Conservatory of Music, in Boston, or at the Manhattan School of Music, in New York, where I studied, ever explained to me how the vocal cords worked, what the larynx looked like or how the tone should be supported on a column of air by the diaphragm muscles. Then there were the private teachers, who were prohibitively expensive (ten dollars for a half-hour lesson back in the mid-forties), especially if they had been great opera stars themselves, and who were mostly as incompetent as the earnest pedants in the conservatories. Great singers don't necessarily make great teachers; singing comes too easily to them or they've forgotten how they got there.

In Boston, while establishing a reputation as a goof-off through five terms at Harvard, I studied with a middle-aged ex-soprano who made me learn a half-dozen classical Italian songs without telling me anything about breathing or how to sing anything above an F, the last note an untrained tenor can sing without having to go into what is usually called a passage note, which leads into the so-called head tones any tenor has to master to sing in his upper range. In New York I studied with two great Wagnerian baritones, Friedrich Schorr and Herbert Janssen. Schorr hadn't a clue what to do with me and saw me only once a week. Janssen, who was still singing at the Met and elsewhere, taught all of his students to funnel the sound by pursing the lips to make it look as if we were sucking bananas. Not a word from either man about breath support. Matters didn't improve much when I finally left for Italy in 1948 to pursue my studies there. My first teacher in Rome was a celebrated baritone named Riccardo Stracciari, a famous Rigoletto and the singer who persuaded Ruggiero Leoncavallo to let him interpolate a high A-flat into the Prologue, the opening aria of *I Pagliacci*. Stracciari would sit at his upright piano in his apartment in Rome dressed in his pajamas and bathrobe while belting high notes off the walls in an effort to show me by example how to do it. Eventually, I wound up at the Calcagni School of Music, off the Corso, in the heart of the city, where, as one of about thirty aspirants, I showed up every day, five days a week, to sing solos, duets and ensembles with my fellow students. Countess Calcagni, who had been a successful lyric soprano herself, taught the women; the Count, who couldn't sing a note and sounded when he tried like a fishmonger hawking his wares, supervised the men. Still, the lessons cost only the equivalent of fifty American cents and simply by trial and trial and trial and sometimes useful advice from my fellow students I was finally able to figure out approximately how to sing without cracking my high notes—no mean accomplishment. At my first *saggio musicale* (a sort of school concert), given in a small church on the outskirts of Rome, I did break on my first sustained high note, in an aria from *Mignon,* but I managed to get through the Love Duet from *Madama Butterfly,* though to this day I don't know whether I managed to get up to the high C at the end of it. I had my mouth open and I was straining every muscle I had, but my Butterfly, standing next to me, was Caterina Mancini, a jolly young Roman soprano with a voice like a cannon, who went on to sing later that year at the Teatro dell'Opera in Rome and at La Scala. All I can be sure of today is that *she* hit the high note.

I wondered, as I thought about those years, whether these bright-eyed kids working that morning with such a talented coach as Gianna Rolandi had any idea how favored they were.

THE TWO OTHER YOUNG SINGERS who followed McNeese and Curnow into The Cell that morning were sopranos Nicole Cabell, a second-year member of LOCAA, and Erin Wall, then in her third year and about to make her debut at Lyric in a major role, that of Marguerite in *Faust.* Cabell, elegantly dressed in beige slacks and a fuzzy white sweater, is a tall, willowy brunette with long, curly brown hair and a luminous smile who radiates confidence and optimism.

Because Cabell wanted to practice her runs, she immediately went to work on "Bel raggio lusinghier," a fiendishly difficult bel canto piece from Rossini's *Semiramide,* an opera about a Babylonian queen who is raised by doves and murders her husband; the opera survives only because of its gorgeous music for soprano and contralto. Despite a number of stops and comments from Rolandi about the need to get "a little more into the tube" and to beware of "widening the sound," Cabell sang ravishingly. She has a very beautiful lyric voice with a solid coloratura top. I first heard this aria sung by the great Catalan soprano Montserrat Caballé many years earlier and had never heard anyone sing it nearly as brilliantly since, even though I'd been listening to Cabell work through it only in stops and starts that morning. Cabell was just twenty-six years old, but judging only from what I'd just heard, she seemed more than ready to embark on a professional career. Instead, after finishing the aria, she told Rolandi she thought she might be too old to qualify for the Metropolitan Opera regional auditions by the time she got around to applying. The yearly Met auditions, held all over the country and culminating in a final contest for the survivors at the Met itself, are the most prestigious in the nation. They are widely promoted in the opera world and can launch a career. The singers who win them have a chance to be signed to Met contracts, and all the finalists receive cash awards and recognition. "Don't worry about it now," Rolandi told her. "Next year I want all you guys to do it. Now, let's do this again, exactly what you've been doing, only a thousand times more."

As Cabell went back to work, Erin Wall walked into the room and sat down to listen. When Cabell paused to express some frustration over her ability to master the runs, Wall called out, "You can do it, you can do it. I can do it."

Rolandi turned to her. "No, you can't," she said. "Not while you're doing *Faust.*" Singing Rossini and tackling a romantic role like Marguerite are conflicting disciplines, and Wall knew it.

Rolandi proceeded to sing one of the Rossini runs herself. "Like that or something like that," she told Cabell, grinning. "Anyway, this is impressive, Nicole. You can do this. It'll be ready in a week. Now that you're in your place, your runs sound really good."

Before Cabell left, she and Wall spent a minute or two horsing around for my benefit, singing some phrases the way they used to do them, parodying the big hollow tones set way back in the throat that some singers use. Such tones can sound huge in a room, but, as Rolandi never fails to point out in her coaching sessions, they won't carry in an opera house, especially one as big as Lyric, with its thirty-six hundred seats.

After Cabell swept cheerfully out the door with a wave and another one of those brilliant smiles, Wall and Rolandi went right to work on the Jewel Song, the showpiece aria that has launched the careers of a thousand lyric sopranos. In it, while Marguerite is draping herself in the baubles Dr. Faust has left at her front door to woo her into his arms, and admiring herself in the mirror he cunningly included with his gift, she showers the audience with cascades of brilliant trills and high notes culminating in a high B that, sung correctly, never fails to bring the house down. The minute Wall began to sing the aria, I hadn't the least doubt that I was listening to a major talent. Her voice, especially the top range, sounded enormous in this room, perfectly focused, thrilling as it rose to each climactic moment in this familiar old chestnut. As I watched her, she also struck me as the embodiment of what an opera singer should look like. She's tall, beautiful and strongly built, with long legs and square shoulders, her looks accentuated that morning by a long black skirt, a black jacket and high heels, her long blond hair pulled back into a ponytail. Being a lyric soprano, she'll almost certainly never sing a Brünnhilde or any other of Richard Wagner's Teutonic goddesses, but she'd look better in those roles than any other singer I've ever seen in them.

Rolandi allowed Wall to finish the aria before she began to break it down for her, making her redo it the first time while holding her thumbs against Wall's neck muscles below the jawline. From time to time as she sang, Wall would stop herself to explain what she was supposed to be doing onstage at the time. She was a bundle of energy, always in motion in time to the music, bouncing on her toes, arms swinging. It was as if there was so much music inside her that it wanted to burst out of her. After they'd finished working on the piece, Wall said, "I'm trying to blow out on it."

"Go ahead, blow out on it," Rolandi said, then asked her if she'd get an orchestra rehearsal before having to sing her first Marguerite, scheduled for December 9. When Wall said she didn't think so, Rolandi told her she'd heard the first orchestra run-through and had found the tempi slow. "Some sections are slow, others are really fast," Wall replied. Rolandi reassured her there'd be adjustments made and Wall shrugged. It didn't seem to concern her. She had told me earlier, at our first meeting back in October, that she'd been waiting so long for this chance that she couldn't wait to get to it.

After Wall and the accompanist left, I lingered behind to chat with Rolandi, who, despite four hours of bouncing around The Cell, seemed as fresh and happy in her task as when she'd begun. She was wearing a dark red pantsuit that perfectly matched her cropped red hair and bright lipstick and was sporting elegant high-heeled pumps. In fact, she looked spectacular, the image of the opera star she had once been. I had heard enough already in these coaching sessions to know that she easily could have still been singing herself, but she told me she had stopped after the birth of her son and also because she was married to Sir Andrew Davis, the music director of Lyric and a world-famous conductor. "You know conductors," she said, with a wry smile. "They're everywhere. It makes it impossible." She speaks with the soft southern accent of her native Spartanburg, South Carolina, and like most of the southern women I've known she seems to be impervious to bullshit in a profession that thrives on self-delusion. "You tell them what you know; you have to be straightforward with them," she continued. Her job, as she saw it, was to listen more to the technical stuff, while Pearlman paid attention to the dramatic context. "Once a week we try to get all the singers together," she said, "so they can critique each other." She nodded and gave a little smirk. "You wish you could put your fifty-year-old knowledge into those young bodies."

These coaching sessions are typical of the care and concern for its young artists' welfare that distinguish the Chicago Opera Center's methods. Other American opera companies—most notably the Met and San Francisco—have had similar noteworthy programs for young singers, but none as strikingly successful as Lyric's. Even the Met, with its vast resources and international reputation, is far more rigid in its selection of singers and less nurturing in its treatment of them. Some of the artists who have come out of that program have described the coaching there as often being catch-as-catch-can and have spoken of the intimidating atmosphere for first-year members. In the past few years Lyric has acquired an outstanding reputation for training and then dispatching out into the fiercely competitive world of opera the best-prepared young vocal artists anywhere. Since the 2001–2002 season, a number of LOCAA singers have already launched successful careers. Becoming a successful opera singer—stepping out on a huge stage to try to fill the house with your voice, to bring an audience of thirty-six hundred people to its feet and to bask in the applause and bravos of the fanatics who may one day follow you around the world to worship at your feet—is as risky in its own peculiar way as embarking on a career as a matador. You can triumph, you can struggle to survive or you can perish from your wounds. So when I decided to write a book about a group of young singers and follow them through a whole season, I found myself repeatedly being urged by most of my friends in opera to go to Chicago. It was very sound advice.

2

Chasing Down the Talent

ICHARD PEARLMAN IS A lovely man. Ultimately, he's the reason I came to Chicago in the fall of 2003. No one was better at working with young singers and nurturing them through the difficulties of operatic careers than he, I was told. No one had had more experience, no one knew more about opera in general, no one was more responsible for the success of the Opera Center. His background includes stints as a director at the Met, the Washington Opera, San Francisco Spring Opera, Santa Fe, Wolf Trap and Spoleto USA. He has worked with Gian Carlo Menotti, Franco Zeffirelli, Lucchino Visconti, Tyrone Guthrie—all legendary directors—and his own productions of musicals and operas have invariably been highly praised by critics and audiences alike. For eighteen years he ran the Eastman Opera Theatre at the Eastman School of Music, in Rochester, New York, where he put on several productions a year, tailoring his choice of repertory to the talents of the student singers available to him—everything from *La Bohème* to a musical named *Reaching for the Moon,* based on an unproduced P. G. Wodehouse script that was dug out from the RKO Studios archives and featuring songs by George Gershwin. I also soon discovered that he was a walking encyclopedia on all matters operatic and would answer any question from anyone on his Web site, www.operaman.com.

No sooner had I walked into his office on my first day in Chicago that November than we began to talk about famous old opera singers. Pearlman is a middle-aged, trim-looking, bearded man with receding curly brown hair, a strong nose and keenly observant dark brown eyes set in a sensitive, intelligent face. He is witty and strongly opinionated, but disguises it by being unusually soft-spoken and kind. He was sitting in a comfortable-looking leather armchair behind a desk facing a wall with two windows that looked out onto the street. His desk, the sofa, the low-lying table facing it and the good-size room as a whole were cluttered with all sorts of papers, books, scores, sheet music, filing cabinets, pictures, plants and mementos of one sort or another. I pushed a pile of stuff to one side and sank into the sofa. Before I could ask him a question about the Opera Center, he told me he'd attended an opera concert the evening before in the old auditorium at Roosevelt University, where ninety-three years ago to the day a performance by a touring European opera company had been held. The event recalled for him the glory days of great European singing, as opposed to the American version that came into fashion later. The main difference between the two, he said, was "charisma and style," and he cited Maria Callas, whose voice was not conventionally pretty but who had an abundance of both. Then there was Leyla Gencer, a great soprano who never made a professional recording of an opera but who became famous as the "queen of the pirates" because so many of her live performances were illegally recorded and sold to aficionados everywhere. "She never made a lira from them," Pearlman said, going on to compare Gencer's career to the more locally illustrious one of Zinka Milanov, for many years the Met's reigning diva. "She was a potato onstage and never had a career in Europe, where singers like Callas and Gencer flourished." Even the great Jussi Bjoerling—the Swedish tenor who preceded Pavarotti as the "King of the High Cs" and was frequently compared to Caruso—wouldn't have made it as big in Italy as he did in the United States, Pearlman maintained, "because his Italian diction was less than perfect."

I told him I found that hard to believe, if only because I had heard Bjoerling sing many times at the old Met and treasured recordings of his, particularly the arias "Che gelida manina" from *La Bohème* and "Nessun dorma" from *Turandot.* "No one has ever sung those better," I said. "And besides, Italian audiences especially love tenors who can sit on top notes till the chandeliers shatter."

Pearlman sighed. "Bad Italian diction causes me physical pain," he explained, "one reason being that the language is so beautiful and so conducive to good singing."

Every would-be opera singer, no matter how talented, he pointed out, soon discovers that it's a long, often painful road from having a beautiful instrument in your throat to being able to compete in one of the world's most demanding and difficult professions. Pearlman has fifteen hundred names of singers in his computer, and he auditions an average of five hundred potential applicants a year. The Opera Center receives applications from all over the globe, and often singers come to Chicago to audition. Pearlman tours the country to find what he wants, holding auditions and teaching master classes, attending spring and summer festivals, popping up here, there and everywhere to hear anyone who fancies himself a potential star. He often hears singers several times over the course of two or three years, keeps track of their progress or lack of it, follows their careers, encourages them if he believes they have real potential. Some show real progress but are not ready yet, others fail to advance and fall by the wayside and then inevitably there are the many hopefuls who simply can't cut it. Pearlman, sometimes accompanied on his quests by Rolandi, hears them all—the good, the bad, the beautiful, the ugly, the mediocre, the hopeless. He prays they will not audition with what he calls "the bladder busters"—the Letter Scene from *Werther,* Zerbinetta's aria from *Ariadne auf Naxos,* pieces that if sung incompetently can seem as long as an hour in a dentist's waiting room—but ultimately he accepts whatever they insist on singing for him. If they're really comically incompetent, to keep his composure he allows his imagination to stray to images of

dead puppies. "The first thing you have to ask yourself in auditioning singers," he said, "is whether this is a sound people would
pay money to hear. If they don't have that, what is the point?"

Who ultimately gets into the program is determined by a
final audition held in early September in the Lyric theater itself.
These hopefuls have to sing onstage in this 3,563-seat house, intimidatingly empty except for the few people who will decide
their fate. In addition to Pearlman and Rolandi, usually present
are Andrew Davis and general director William Mason, who, I
soon found out, was on top of everything going on in the opera
house. A very influential and forceful opinion is that of Matthew
Epstein, who became the company's artistic director in 1999 and
involved himself deeply in every decision made regarding the
young singers—from what roles they should prepare to sing and
understudy during the seasons to their audition repertories. I
found myself wondering, as I talked to Pearlman that first morning, if Epstein's active involvement might cause problems, because he can be overruled only by Mason. Epstein, an ex-manager
and long a powerful and controversial figure in the incestuous
world of grand opera, is no blushing petunia about expressing his
opinions, and he has been known to intervene forcefully, even
brutally, to get what he wants. This can cause resentment and
even havoc on occasion. He has his enemies, but his admirers
point out that essentially he's an opera groupie. At performances
he's a one-man claque for his singers, his enthusiasm is enormous
and his influence is often vastly beneficial. "You don't always
agree with him," Rolandi, an ex-client, has said of him, "but he
was the only agent I ever knew who could build a career."

Usually no more than four or five singers are admitted every
year into the LOCAA program. This is because, although singers
sign on at first for only one year at a time and have to audition
again to be readmitted, they almost always remain for a second
and sometimes a third year if, as Pearlman explained in a program
interview, "it's mutually decided by the company and the singer

that they're on the verge of some kind of breakthrough, vocally and artistically. If staying on for another year is going to facilitate that breakthrough, *and* if there's enough here to keep them usefully employed, it makes sense to keep them for a third year. After all, from the company's point of view, they're a known quantity and we can depend on them." Of the current group of twelve whom I was about to spend time with, only four were new members and four had been held over for a third season.

They were not going to become rich from what the company was paying them. They'd all signed a contract for a minimum of about thirty thousand dollars based on twenty-four weeks of work during the Lyric season, from late August through March, and would be paid extra for any major roles they performed, as well as for overtime (i.e., more than thirty hours a week, or more than six hours a day). Under American Guild of Musical Artists (AGMA) union rules, they'd enjoy full benefits and be free to take outside engagements, as long as those engagements didn't interfere with their work for Lyric.

The singers would almost certainly find themselves so busy, however, that they'd have very little time for anything outside of LOCAA. The work begins for the new arrivals in late March and for everyone else about ten days later. They immediately embark on an intense schedule of coaching sessions to learn their roles, dramatic interpretation, language meaning and pronunciation, movement—every conceivable aspect of becoming complete operatic artists. They're also expected to eat a proper diet and engage in regular physical workouts. The fat lady singing, her mouth open wide over a triple chin, is not the image today's opera management wants to project. If you have a truly magnificent voice—one that can soar above a heavy Wagnerian orchestration or cut through the bellowing of a Verdian chorus—you can still get away with looking like a small mountain in fancy dress, but young singers today are expected to look the parts they're interpreting. It's hard work and it gets a lot tougher in the early fall,

when the Lyric season kicks off and the singers are actually performing in small roles, covering bigger ones, working on their
repertories and auditioning for the managers, agents, impresarios, conductors and artistic directors who come to Chicago to
hear them. What they all hope for during the course of the season
is a chance to show what they can do, especially if they're second-
or third-year members. Stepping suddenly into a big part, having
to go on maybe at the last minute for an ailing principal, could be
the opportunity of a lifetime. The old Hollywood legend about
the chorus girl in a big musical suddenly being given a chance to
go out there for the ailing star and tap dance her way to immortal-
ity can actually happen in the world of opera—not often, but often
enough to enchant. It can also mean quite a lot of extra money for
young artists living on very tight budgets.

A big problem affecting the selection of singers for the Opera
Center is the protracted audition period. "If you hear someone
early on whom you may want, by delaying you can lose that person," Pearlman said. The previous year, he and Rolandi had heard
a tenor and a coloratura soprano they wanted, but lost both—the
tenor to another young singers program, the soprano because her
manager had persuaded her to reject the opportunity in order to
launch her career. Being part of the Opera Center, Richard had
pointed out to her in vain, meant that she'd be heard by top opera
managers and other artists.

During the nearly two hours I spent in Pearlman's office that
first day, our conversation was interrupted several times by long,
cheery phone calls with Rolandi, whom Pearlman described to me
as his soul mate. They almost always found themselves in perfect
agreement, he told me, about everything connected with the program. "Her influence has been critical in the formation of these
artists," he said, "this being the best young group of singers we've
ever had." For the singers it's a critical time in their development as
artists. "They have to leave wherever they are to come to Chicago,
leaving their voice teachers behind." This used to worry Pearlman

in the past, when there was no funding in the program for voice lessons. "They'd periodically have to go back to see their teachers." Before Pearlman took over the program, an ex–Metropolitan Opera star, contralto Margaret Harshaw, was teaching in town, so there was someone of stature the young singers could turn to locally. "After her, though, there was no one, and having any vocal instruction is better than none." Singers, after all, are like ballet dancers: they need to work out and have someone around technically able to guide them through their exercises. It takes a lot of muscle to be an opera singer. You have to develop a diaphragm as hard as knotted rope and you have to be able to move around gracefully under the weight of heavy costumes and with big, clumsy props such as swords and shields—the cloaks that opera singers often have to wear would have weighed down Dracula—and all this frequently on raked stages that threaten to topple you into the orchestra pit, on elevations such as balconies or on long flights of stairs from which you'll sometimes tumble. Whatever happens, you'll have to keep singing. Audiences will forgive anything except a poor sound and cracked high notes. Since Rolandi's appearance on the scene, Pearlman assured me, the quality of the singing in the program had vastly improved. Neither Rolandi nor Pearlman will ever push a singer forcefully in a direction he might not want to go. Very often singers may want to learn roles they're not suited for or ones that at an early stage in their development could damage their voices—such as the heavier Wagnerian and Verdi leads. But the singer may also be reluctant to tackle a part he feels uncomfortable in; he shouldn't be pushed too hard. "I never tell a singer you *should* do this, but rather I think you might *consider* doing this," Pearlman said. "It's a difficult decision for any young singer to make, especially if you're suggesting changing their vocal category or repertory."

Pearlman's constant companion is a bulky black leather briefcase on wheels that he keeps stuffed with what he calls "my whole life"—papers, scores, contracts, correspondence, notes, gewgaws, bits of this, that and the other. It accompanies him wherever he goes and no one has ever seen him without it. In fact, he reminds me of King Kaspar, the comprimario tenor in Menotti's Christmas opera, *Amahl and the Night Visitors,* who sings a charming little song that begins, "This is my box, this is my box, I never travel without my box." When we walked out of his office together at around noon that day, Pearlman zipped up the briefcase and tugged it along after him. I asked him if he was taking it to lunch with him. No, he informed me; he had a meeting to go to. Besides, he'd had "a huge breakfast" and didn't eat lunch. He also worked out regularly, walked a lot, and rode his bicycle on weekends, five to fifteen miles a day. This impressed me because all I do is play a few leisurely sets of tennis a couple of times a week, watch baseball games, bet on race horses and read a lot. And, of course, listen to opera.

I was soon to discover that nobody at Lyric Opera of Chicago ever eats lunch. (Well, to quote W. S. Gilbert, hardly ever.) They nibble at their desks on food brought from home or on takeout, or they rush across the street to one of several accessible fast-food emporiums, including, I was appalled to see, a McDonald's. "Lunch is not in Lyric Opera culture," is the way Richard Pearlman put it to me. It wasn't long before I found out why: they're much too busy to take the time.

3

State of the Art

ACCORDING TO *The New Grove Dictionary of Opera,* "From the beginning, Chicago has had an audience for opera that in its enthusiasm and dedication is unlikely to be surpassed anywhere in the world." No one knows why this should be. The city has had a long, well-established reputation as a rough, tough, brawling sort of place run by a series of corrupt municipal governments and as the site of some of the bloodiest crime wars ever fought. It is also still one of the most racially divided communities in the country, politically partitioned into wards pretty much along ethnic lines. There is very little love lost between north and south, east and west, as anybody can attest who has followed the fortunes of the city's two baseball teams, the blue-collar White Sox and the darlings of the north, the hapless Cubs. When *The New Yorker*'s A. J. Liebling wrote *The Second City,* his three-part classic put-down of the town in 1952, not only didn't he write a word about opera or much about the arts and culture in general, but as a dedicated and passionate gourmand, he reported not being able to find a good place to eat. After eviscerating all things Chicagoan, his conclusion was that "Chicagoans are left in the plight of the Greeks at the beginning of history, when the gods commenced ceasing to manifest themselves."

It's too bad Liebling didn't live long enough to spend some time in Chicago today. I knew him fairly well from my years at *The*

New Yorker and I'm guessing he'd have loved the place. For one thing, Chicago now teems with excellent eateries. For another, it has one of the most vital, passionately dedicated cultural lives of any American hub. Its municipal government may still be corrupt, but somehow it works. Compared with New York and Los Angeles, the Third City is spotlessly clean—at least downtown and along the lakefront—and it has a public transportation system that is refreshingly efficient. And nearly everyone knows that Chicago has long been the architectural capital of the country, with more innovative and structurally splendid public and private buildings than anywhere else in America. All of which still doesn't explain why Chicago has long flourished as an operatic mecca.

The first opera ever to be performed here, on July 29, 1850, was Bellini's *La Sonnambula,* a trifle about a sleepwalking virgin who wanders into the wrong man's bedroom. It does spin some very lovely arias, however, including a spectacular closing rondo for coloratura soprano that can bring opera maniacs shrieking to their feet. (I once heard Maria Callas sing this role in Milan and I thought the audience might tear the auditorium apart in ecstasy.) Put on by a touring company accompanied by a pickup orchestra and a hastily recruited local chorus, this initial effort still wowed the public, but unfortunately didn't survive the second night, when the theater caught fire during the performance and had to be evacuated.

After that, the history of opera in Chicago was for years pretty much one of touring opera companies from abroad and New York, when the Met offered seasons of a month or so, including, in 1889, the first local performances of Wagner's *Ring* cycle and Verdi's *Otello,* starring the great tenor who created the role at La Scala in 1887, Francesco Tamagno. Attempts at forming local companies failed, primarily because they couldn't compete with the outsiders.

Everyone connected to opera in those days still believed it would be possible to show a profit, but even then the form had become so expensive it couldn't make it on its own. Nevertheless, impresarios, usually blinded by adoration for some great diva, persisted in trying. The most notable effort was made by financier Harold McCormick, who created the Chicago Grand Opera Company, with Italian conductor Cleofonte Campanini as musical director. The first season, in 1910, featured American soprano Mary Garden as its starring attraction. Garden, a beautiful woman who could chirp like a nightingale, was the first authentic so-called sacred monster to appear on the Chicago scene. Sacred monsters are bigger than mere stars. Like a Domingo, a Callas, a Pavarotti, they are personalities who are always stage center, who command everyone's attention, who bask in the love of an adoring public and on whom the success of the entire incredibly cumbersome and costly production of an opera depends. As the term implies, sacred monsters can be overbearing and childishly willful, and only the bravest of impresarios and general directors will risk challenging them. Mary Garden, fresh from artistic triumphs all over the world and in New York, was the attraction McCormick counted on, and for the next twenty-one years she dominated the operatic scene in Chicago. Nobody had ever seen or heard anyone quite like her and not everybody approved of her.

That first year in Chicago she appeared in Debussy's *Pelléas et Mélisande,* Charpentier's *Louise* and Richard Strauss's *Salomé,* all sung in French. But it wasn't only her singing that made an impression. Garden was a woman with very strong opinions on a variety of subjects and she was not at all shy about airing them. Her appearance in the title role of *Salomé*—the neurotic Biblical princess who in her famous Dance of the Seven Veils strips for the delectation of Herod, the Tetrarch of Judea, in order, ultimately, to kiss the severed head of John the Baptist—caused the same sort of uproar that greeted the opera when it was first produced in New York, at the Met three years earlier. "I am a normal man," fulminated the president of the Law and Order League, "but I would not trust myself to see a performance of *Salomé.*" "Anyone whose morals could have been corrupted by seeing *Salomé,*"

Garden fired back, "must already have degenerated." To the police chief who considered her prancing about the stage dropping veils disgusting, she declared, "I always bow down to the ignorant and try to make them understand, but I ignore the illiterate." By her presence on the scene, the power of her art and the strength of her convictions Garden set the standards by which opera in Chicago eventually established itself, also under the dominance of two other very strong and talented women.

That didn't come about, though, until long after Garden's time. Opera ventures and companies came and went, presenting mostly performances from the standard nineteenth-century romantic and verismo repertories. Between 1947 and 1953 there were no local companies of any stature in the city, and Chicago's opera buffs had to depend, like those in most other American hubs, on visits from the Met and the New York City Opera. The irony was that by then the time was totally ripe for the creation of a great local company, and the splendid building, long used mainly by visiting opera and dance companies, touring operettas and musicals, was there waiting to house it.

Samuel Insull (1859–1938) was a local tycoon who speculated in utilities and real estate, a typical Midwestern capitalist who hurled himself with gusto into every venture that captured his imagination. The monstrous Merchandise Mart office building on the north bank of the Chicago River is typical of what he envisioned for his city, and to spur further downtown development he backed the construction of the elevated lines that became known as the Loop. The trains ensured that people would be able to get around where he wanted them to be—especially the opera fans he envisioned flocking to the grand new theater he was building for them inside another of his ambitious projects: a forty-five-story skyscraper beside the river on North Wacker that locals nicknamed Insull's Throne because, with its twenty-two-story wings cradling a central tower, it looked from the west like an enormous armchair.

The skyscraper took only twenty-two months to build, and its distinguishing interior feature was its auditorium and backstage area, which occupy about a third of the total space. For sheer grandiosity, the Civic Opera House matches up to every other major opera venue in the world. A colonnaded portico runs the entire length of the structure and, at the south end, enormous bronze doors open onto a spacious foyer "whose gilt cornices glitter beneath the sparkling lights of Austrian crystal chandeliers and elaborately stenciled ceilings," as the Lyric's press release so eloquently describes it. Other features are "a floor and wainscoting of pink and gray Tennessee marble, and fluted travertine columns and pilasters topped with carved capitals covered in gold leaf." Designed for Insull by the local architectural firm of Graham, Anderson, Probst & White, it was meant to symbolize "the spirit of a community which is still youthful and not much hampered by traditions." When it was completed, however, what it mainly recalled was the old Paris Opera House designed by Jean-Louis Garnier, with its happy blend of rococo and functionalism.

Insull told his designers that in the auditorium itself he wanted "safety, excellent sight lines, comfortable seating, gracious surroundings and premium acoustics." He got these and then some. Inside the huge shoebox, with its 3,563 seats, mezzanine boxes and two additional balconies, audiences can admire a fire curtain depicting the triumphal march from *Aida,* painted by American artist Jules Guerin. In 1993, after Lyric bought all of the theater and backstage space, the company began a $100-million technical and artistic restoration project that took four years to complete. The money came entirely from private sources, a testimony to Chicagoans' enthusiasm for and commitment to the arts. I venture to guess that even Liebling would have been impressed.

The premise behind the construction of the Civic Opera House was that any deficits from putting on regular seasons of such expensive entertainments as grand operas could be made up from renting office space in the rest of the structure. Unfortunately for Insull, his timing was disastrous; the opening of his theater, with a performance of *Aida,* took place exactly six days after the stock market crash of 1929. His company, the Chicago Civic Opera, nevertheless managed to limp along for three seasons until it, too, was forced to dissolve. As for Insull himself, his financial empire collapsed and his great theater languished for twenty-three years, mostly as a temporary shelter for doomed local operatic ventures and big touring musicals.

This all changed in 1954 with the creation of the Lyric Theatre, which two years later was renamed Lyric Opera of Chicago. Its creators were Carol Fox, a socially prominent ex-soprano, businessman Lawrence V. Kelly and conductor Nicola Rescigno. In February of that year they put on two performances of *Don Giovanni* that were so successful that the company was able to proceed with a fall season of eight works. Fox understood that to establish itself on the operatic landscape the company would need a star, and it got one—a true sacred monster—by engaging Maria Callas to make her American debut in Chicago, of all places. Already an international celebrity, Callas showed up mainly because she was going to be paid higher fees than she'd have received even at the Met. She debuted on opening night, in November 1954, as the eponymous heroine in Bellini's fiendishly difficult *Norma* and followed that triumph up with others, in *La Traviata* and *Lucia di Lammermoor.* She came back in 1955 in *I Puritani, Il Trovatore* and *Madama Butterfly,* the only time she ever sang the role.

Despite its immediate artistic success and the notoriety Callas brought to that first season, the company almost went under after 1955, when it produced twenty-five performances of fifteen different works, a recipe for financial disaster. At that stage of its development a much more prudent number would have been three or four. After a reorganization that put Fox in sole control, with Kelly and Rescigno leaving to pursue operatic careers in Dallas, matters improved, even though in 1957 Lyric staged fourteen operas, still far too many to make balancing a budget feasible. Fox's basic approach to keeping the company afloat through ticket sales and contributions was to hire from Europe the most famous singers and conductors available. By the late 1960s, Lyric, with 70 percent of its seasons devoted to the Italian repertory, became known as La Scala West. Under Fox there was glamour and chic and a lot of great singing, but little innovation or experimentation. Stage directors then were not expected to do much more than move people around and make sure they made their entrances and exits on time.

After her death, Fox was succeeded by her associate Ardis Krainik, another powerful personality who had her own ideas about what the company should be doing. Not only did she have a far more adventurous approach to the repertory than her predecessor, but she also introduced supertitles, which enabled audiences to follow the action and to understand why the people onstage in their funny costumes were behaving so bizarrely. Thousands of new subscribers were signed up. By that time, Lyric had settled comfortably into a routine of putting on between eight and ten operas a year, and by the mid-eighties the more popular operas could be put on for ten or more performances each, with about 60 percent of the budget being generated by ticket sales. By the 1988–1989 season, with the company's usual complement of great singers, subscribers made up the vast majority of ticket buyers and 60 percent of the yearly budget still came from ticket sales. For the first time, Lyric sold out its entire season, achieving 103 percent of box office capacity, what it rightly called "a historic achievement."

Mortally ill with cancer, Krainik announced her retirement in 1996 and died the following January at the age of sixty-seven. Like Carol Fox, she had become the heart and soul of the company that she had transformed from a sort of museum of great singing into a vital artistic entity open to new music and modern innovations.

She had also overseen the stabilization of Lyric's finances. Her death marked the ninth consecutive year that the company sold above capacity, an achievement no other North American opera entity has been able to equal. In fact, only once in the past fifteen years, the 2002–2003 season, has Lyric failed to finish the year in the black, a testament not only to an excellent administration but also to an operagoing public now used to seeing and hearing only the best and willing to pay for it. The United States is, of course, the only supposedly civilized nation in the world that doesn't support the arts with generous government grants, which may not be too bad a thing. Maestro Arturo Toscanini, the greatest of Italian conductors, was against all forms of scholarships and subsidies because he maintained that they only guaranteed mediocrity; real talent would establish itself. Well, maybe. But without financial support from somewhere besides ticket sales, opera would disappear overnight. What we all have to hope for is that the rich don't run out of money.

IN 1997, AFTER KRAINIK'S DEATH, William Mason became the general director of Lyric, the post he had been preparing for his entire career, having been with the company for more than thirty years. Like so many people in opera, he began as a singer, performing in children's choruses and with various amateur groups. As a boy alto at Lyric in 1954 and 1956, he sang the little shepherd's offstage solo that opens the third act of *Tosca,* but after his voice changed it eventually became evident to him that his future in opera lay elsewhere. While still studying for a degree in voice at Roosevelt University in 1962, he asked Krainik, whom he'd run into on various occasions, if there was anything he could do backstage. That September he went to work as an assistant to Pino Donati, who, with conductor Bruno Bartoletti, served as co–artistic director of the company. This was the Fox era, when everyone either was Italian or spoke it fluently. Donati, who operated out of a small backstage office, was from Verona and spoke no English. "I crammed like crazy," Mason recalls, "and by the end of the season I was speaking passable Italian." Donati became like a second father to him, taught him everything he knew about crucial matters such as scheduling and gave him work to do even after the season had ended. In those days the company was putting on an average of eight works of three to four performances each over a span of about two months, from late September or early October through November.

In 1968, Mason became an assistant stage manager and continued to rise through the ranks until by the time of his appointment as general director, he was the company's director of operations, artistic and production. With the exception of brief hiatuses to work for the San Francisco Opera and to do other outside gigs in Cincinnati and New York, Mason, a native Chicagoan, has stayed put. Even though he had to survive what was called at the time "an extensive search" for a successor to Krainik, he was clearly the right person to step into her shoes. Nobody knew more about the inner workings of the company and no one was more dedicated to maintaining the high performance standards set by his formidable predecessors in the job. Those two early productions of *Tosca* in which he sang featured sopranos Eleanor Steber and Renata Tebaldi and tenors Giuseppe di Stefano and Jussi Bjoerling, all great stars, with the superb baritone Tito Gobbi in both casts as the villainous Baron Scarpia, perhaps his finest interpretation. From his boyhood as an aspiring singer, Mason has heard on the stage of Lyric practically every legendary artist from the past fifty years of opera.

Opera seasons these days have to be planned years in advance, but it wasn't very long before it became clear exactly how Mason intended to run his company. Since 1980, Matthew Epstein, still employed as a top agent at Columbia Artists Management, Inc. (CAMI), in New York, had been working as an artistic advisor to the company. Mason now brought him into the fold, beginning in 1999, as artistic director, with an iron-bound contract negotiated with CAMI that gave Epstein a great deal of power over repertory and the young singers program. In 2000, after the retirement the year before of Bruno Bartoletti, who had been with Lyric since 1964, Mason appointed Sir Andrew Davis as music director and principal conductor. Like Epstein, Davis had been deeply involved with the company for some time, having conducted five productions since 1987. Recognized in the United States and abroad as among the finest opera conductors, he brought added cachet to the roster. His hiring was in keeping with Lyric's by now well-established tradition of settling only for the best and not cutting corners where talent was concerned.

When cuts did have to be made after the deficit incurred during the 2002–2003 season, Mason was forced to take a second look at the 2003–2004 rep, which included two operas that risked putting Lyric into the red two years in a row. Italo Montemezzi's *L'Amore dei Tre Re* is a rarely performed, gloomy melodrama that is revived from time to time for a great bass—in this case Samuel Ramey, long a Lyric stalwart. To celebrate the centenary of Hector Berlioz's birth, the company had also scheduled a new production of his *Benvenuto Cellini,* like all of the windy master's works a great sprawling tapestry of a piece absolutely certain to disperse a great chunk of capital. "Our budget last year was forty-eight million dollars," Mason told me. "We had to take between two and three million out of it." To do that and keep Ramey, whose Mephistopheles is one of his bread-and-butter roles, Lyric chose to produce *Faust,* but substituting for the Berlioz was more complicated. "We had to find out what major artists were available," Mason explained, "because these days singers are hired years in advance and may already be committed elsewhere." They decided to pick a lighter piece—perhaps a *Fledermaus* or *Merry Widow*—but then they took a look at Gilbert and Sullivan. "We'd talked about *Gondoliers* and *Yeomen of the Guard,* then we hit on *Pi-*

rates. We knew some of our subscribers might be disappointed, but it wasn't as if we'd exchanged the *Cellini* for it. Besides, people have seen bad high school productions and so they don't realize how good these operas are. Also, you cannot have artistic integrity without fiscal integrity." This is the delicate balancing act that all major opera companies have to achieve to survive. Lyric today is a far more adventurous enterprise than the Met, which puts on nearly three times as many works yearly and has to concentrate on perennial favorites such as *La Bohème* and *La Traviata* to sell tickets. The general rule is that the smaller the enterprise, the more experimental it can afford to be.

Bill Mason is a tall, gray-haired, balding man with an affable manner that immediately puts one at ease. I came to think of him as a typical Chicagoan, mainly because of his outwardly relaxed, unpretentious attitude toward his job. None of that steely-eyed, suspicious, paranoid defensiveness that characterizes so many of the bigwigs in this often weird—at least to outsiders—world of lyric drama. Many of the great impresarios of the past had the same egos and grand mannerisms as the most sacred of sacred monsters who strutted across their stages. (One thinks immediately of Rudolf Bing, who during his elitist regime at the Met had the effrontery to fire Callas.) The job is conducive to ego-enhancement, since the general director of any major opera house finds himself wielding almost absolute power over an enclosed fiefdom rife with rivalries, rumors, gossip, jealousies, grievances, disappointments, turf wars, confrontations and outbursts of temperament. To get some idea of how complicated and cumbersome the management of an opera company can be, it was hard for me even to get an exact count of how many people Lyric employs. There are about a hundred in administration, another twenty to twenty-five hired part-time. In 2002, the company mailed out eleven hundred W-2 tax forms to staff employees and between seventy and eighty 1099s to independent contractors. The basic orchestral complement is 78 players and there are 48 members of the chorus, between 90 and 110 stagehands and 60 other people in production and wardrobe. Except in administration, they are all represented by labor unions whose leaders are often entirely unsympathetic to fiscal realities and who fiercely guard their prerogatives. "I could run any opera company in the world," Richard Pearlman told me one day, "except for having to deal with the unions and having to go out every year and raise money." Two very important qualifications, which made me admire Mason's cool all the more.

At our first meeting I told him I was grateful he was allowing me to hang around the company—with practically unrestricted access to all performances, rehearsals, coachings and auditions—and to interview everybody connected with the Opera Center. Reporters are usually not given that much freedom by a major opera company. I had originally approached the Los Angeles Opera, which under its artistic director, Plácido Domingo, used to have a young singers' program and now sponsors an international competition called Operalia, but I was turned down. I hadn't even considered approaching the Met, which is harder to get into than the Pentagon. Mason smiled and told me that Lyric was proud of its program. "It's gone from strength to strength," he said. "People want to come here. Word has gone out that this is a program that will launch them. We try always to find the best voices, look for good strong singers for supporting and leading roles. The talent has gotten so much better, also because we have a better selection process. If you had come here ten years ago, you'd have heard two or three singers who could make it. These guys we have today will all have careers. Although sometimes they think they're going to make it, but then they decide they don't want to spend their lives in hotel rooms."

I could relate to that. The last time I auditioned for a professional singing job was in 1954, in New York, shortly after I came back from Italy. I'd heard from a friend that a producer of touring musicals was auditioning performers for a bus-and-truck tour through the Midwest of Cole Porter's great musical *Kiss Me*

Kate. My friend had been signed to sing the baritone lead, performed on Broadway by Alfred Drake. I auditioned for the show with a ballad from *Brigadoon*. "Can you sing high?" the producer asked. I then sang the aria "Questa o quella," from *Rigoletto*. "Higher?" he asked. I told him the aria had a healthy number of B-flats. How high did he expect me to sing? "Oh," he said and then offered me the role of Hortensio, who has exactly one number in the show, a trio called "Tom, Dick or Harry." "And, of course, you'll sing in all the chorus stuff," the producer said. Plus I'd have to help move the scenery on and off the truck. We'd be on the road for six months and I'd be paid $150 a week, out of which I'd have had to cough up for a hotel room and meals. That was the end of my professional singing ambitions.

4

Coming Out a Star

$\mathcal{T}$ HE 2003–2004 LYRIC OPERA season began for the singers on Monday, August 25, with a rehearsal in Room 200, a huge space that exactly duplicates the size of the main stage, for the cast of Mozart's *Le Nozze di Figaro.* The opera was scheduled for September 20, opening night, always a gala occasion for any major opera company. Despite having had to substitute for two of the eight operas originally announced, Lyric powers were looking forward to another successful season. The budget had been trimmed, the total number of performances had been reduced from eighty-six to eighty-three and, as an article in *Opera News* proclaimed, the repertory trumpeted "enough star power to make opera-lovers wonder why they'd ever live anywhere else." Catherine Malfitano, a veteran diva and local favorite, would sing the title role in Marc Blitzstein's *Regina,* a chicken-fried musical rendering of Lillian Hellman's famous play *The Little Foxes.* Patricia Racette, perhaps America's finest singing actress, was to interpret Marguerite in *Faust* opposite Ramey and Texan Marcus Haddock, a rising tenor star fresh from his debut at the Met in the title role. Olga Borodina, the Russian star with the creamiest sound in the mezzo category, would treat Lyric audiences to her first local Dalila in Saint-Saëns's *Samson et Dalila,* with the Argentine José Cura, a dramatic tenor with a voice almost as big as his ego, as her Samson. The petite French soprano

Natalie Dessay would tackle her first *Lucia* in Italian, and Sir Andrew Davis would preside at the podium over Wagner's *Siegfried,* with bass-baritone James Morris in his signature role of Wotan, the would-be sire of the superman, and England's Jane Eaglen, the heir to the winged helmets of Kirsten Flagstad and Birgit Nilsson, blasting through the orchestra as Brünnhilde. Other opera companies in the world put on more works every year than Lyric, but none can outdo it in quality. The only unease I sensed, when I first began making my rounds inside the administrative offices on the seventh and eighth floors of the Insull Building, was whether *Pirates,* considered an unworthy trifle by some subscribers and outside commentators, would draw enough people. But inevitably, opera being the chancy, disaster-prone activity it has always been, that was not to be the first crisis to confront the company that season.

On August 12, two weeks before the start of rehearsals, a press release announced that mezzo Angelica Kirschlager had asked to be allowed to withdraw from her engagement to sing Cherubino in *Figaro,* "for personal reasons" and that the role would now be taken over by Lauren McNeese. During her first two years at the Opera Center, McNeese had sung a number of small roles, ranging from the Second Nursemaid in *Street Scene* to a Flower Maiden in *Parsifal,* not exactly the kind of parts that set one's pulse racing. Her upcoming Siébel in *Faust* was to be a step up into a more rewarding assignment, but singing a Cherubino would make real acting, as well as vocal, demands on her. It's a so-called "trouser" part in which she would have two arias of her own and would be asked not only to sing well, but to caper about the stage as a young buck with hot pants dying to bed any woman he can get, from the Countess Almaviva to the lowliest peasant girl on the estate, Barbarina. And because this opera is considered a masterpiece by most opera lovers, and has been recorded many times with internationally famous casts, anyone who sings in it is immediately compared with her more illustrious predecessors and contemporaries who have appeared in it. McNeese was initially terrified.

It wasn't as if she hadn't prepared for it. Originally asked to be a second cover for the part, she'd already sung it in an excerpted concert version put on outdoors by the Opera Center that summer, at the Grant Park Music Festival. In addition, she'd been studying and singing opera for years, first while still in high school in her native Tulsa, Oklahoma, and then at the University of Cincinnati, which has a strong student opera program. Every year, she'd performed leading roles, one of her favorites being Lucretia in Benjamin Britten's *The Rape of Lucretia,* which she told me she'd do again "in a heartbeat." McNeese radiates enthusiasm and commitment and prefers not to single out any one part as her favorite. "My favorite opera is the one I'm working on at the time," she said. "At the moment I know lots of arias, but only a handful of roles." She tends to get totally caught up in whatever she's working on. During the previous season's production of *Die Walküre,* in which she appeared as Rossweisse, a minor Valkyrie, she'd linger in the wings every night to hear James Morris sing Wotan's closing farewell to his favorite daughter, Brünnhilde, one of the great climactic moments in all of opera. "I love Wagner," she said. "Every night I'd be crying backstage during that scene."

She knew she was ready for Cherubino, but actually doing it onstage at Lyric would be a challenge. No sooner had she started working with director Sir Peter Hall, however, than she managed to get a grip on the part. Hall is another in a long series of distinguished Brits who have been ennobled by the Crown for their efforts in the arts. He first directed *Figaro* in 1973, at Glyndebourne, one of the world's best-known opera houses, where he was artistic director from 1984 to 1990. He's directed not only operas, but also plays, movies and TV shows, and he's written books about the theater. His approach is mostly traditional, but also inventive. Unlike many modern opera directors, Hall doesn't think his vision of the work at hand is more important than the composer's. In the case of *Figaro,* he understands the larger implications of the piece and why it was considered revolutionary at the time Mozart and his librettist, Lorenzo Da Ponte, wrote it.

Hall has a charming, soft-spoken, suggestive way of getting his ideas across to his cast. His manner was immediately reassuring to McNeese. "I was afraid of Cherubino for a while," she said, "but now he's like an old friend. Once I got into rehearsals, I realized that his problems were real problems. I mean, he's always in somebody's room at the wrong time."

At her first performance in the role, on September 20, she admitted to being the most nervous she'd ever been in her whole life. As she headed for her dressing room an hour before curtain, she felt herself almost lost in the hectic backstage comings and goings of everyone else in the production. This was the opening night of the whole season and everyone had his own concerns to deal with—from all the other cast members to the chorus, the instrumentalists, the backstage crew, the wardrobe and makeup people and all the administrative types clustered in their offices. Seeing her name posted on her dressing room door gave McNeese an immediate lift, but also rammed home the responsibility that had been entrusted to her. An unknown singer in her first big part at a major opera house, she felt for a while as if she were carrying the weight of Mozart and all operatic history on her back.

When she shut herself inside her dressing room and began to warm up, however, she started to feel better, and by the time Rolandi and Pearlman showed up to lend their support she was feeling more confident. "Once I got onstage," she recalled, "I calmed down. I was able to identify totally with the character. Now it's wonderful. I feel fine. My first big role and I had so much love and support." She tackled the part with the same light mezzo I'd heard her work at with Rolandi, sporting a nice even range from top to bottom. She also acted well, bouncing perkily about the stage as that frantic oversexed teenager, though I had a hard time believing in her as a boy, only because she's so obviously a beautiful woman.

What this break basically meant to her was that chance all young performers hope for: the opportunity to show what they can do. Perhaps major engagements might now begin to flow her way; the season was young, the critics had found her pleasing and the managers, artistic directors and impresarios of other companies would be coming through Chicago to hear her. She felt she had a lot going for her.

So, it turned out, did one of her colleagues at the Opera Center, bass-baritone Wayne Tigges, who, halfway into the second night of the run, had to step cold into the leading role of Figaro, the wily barber who is the motivating force in the comic drama. As one of the local critics described the moment, "confusion and concern ensued . . . as a gentleman calmly announced" that Ildebrando D'Arcangelo, the Italian star engaged to sing the part, was indisposed and would be unable to continue. Tigges was in the audience, having decided to attend the performance with his mother, and had been hurriedly summoned to fill in.

Such last-minute announcements are not uncommon in opera. A bad cold can be enough to knock a singer out of commission for days, sometimes weeks at a time. D'Arcangelo turned out to be suffering from a persistent bronchial infection, which forced him to cancel the rest of the run. Veteran opera audiences are used to seeing representatives of management appear in front of the curtain to convey these dismal tidings. At some houses it's the general director who faces the public, but in Chicago it's a member of the public relations staff, Jack Zimmerman. A middle-aged, stocky, bald, bearded citizen with a calm, unassuming manner, who always wears for the occasion either a dark or a pinstriped suit, Zimmerman stoically endures the groans and moans that inevitably greet his every appearance from the wings. I asked him one day how he happened to be chosen for this unhappy duty, to which he answered, "I was born Catholic. I'm supposed to suffer."

Audiences are usually told before the curtain rises on act one that there will be a substitution that night, but it's not unusual for indisposed artists to be replaced during a performance. Early in Birgit Nilsson's career at the Met, she sang an Isolde to three different Tristans on the same night, each worse than the one before. Often an indisposed star on whom the success of an evening depends will ask a representative of management to inform the public that despite suffering from some undisclosed ailment, he, for the sheer love of his adoring fans, will continue and begs the audience's indulgence. Such announcements are always greeted with applause and shouts of encouragement, especially in Italy, where fans tend to be more raucous in their reactions. I once attended a performance of *Rigoletto* at the Teatro Bellini in Catania starring a celebrated Italian tenor named Giacomo Lauri-Volpi as the nefarious Duke of Mantua. Lauri-Volpi marked all through the first act, using a barely audible mezza voce, even in the aria "Questa o quella." As the curtain fell on act one, there were rumblings, hisses and scattered whistles (the Italian form of booing). Out in front of the curtain stepped a portly gentleman in a dark suit to announce that the *"commendatore,"* an honorary title created by Mussolini, was suffering from a bad cold but would do his best to continue if, of course, the public would kindly permit him to. A roar of acclamation and much clapping ensued. The curtain rose on act two, during which the Duke reappeared in the Garden Scene, this time in full voice. Volpi was getting on in years and had developed a noticeable wobble, but he had a trumpet in his throat that could shatter plate glass. He belted the rest of the way through the evening and brought the house down. I remember men standing on their seats to shout their approbation. It isn't only artistry that makes a sacred monster.

Like McNeese, Wayne Tigges was more than up to filling in

as Figaro, even though he hadn't had a single rehearsal with the opening-night cast. A second-year member of LOCAA, he had been assigned to cover the role after having sung both of Figaro's arias at a master class given the year before by Andrew Davis. I heard him several performances into the run, by which time he'd obviously settled comfortably into the part. Hall's direction stressed the comedic aspects of Figaro, and Tigges's barber dominated the action—which is as it should be. Figaro is smarter and faster on his feet than anyone else—except possibly his intended bride, Susanna—and is the master of the games being played in and out of the bedrooms of Almaviva's palazzo; he's the character the audience should most identify with and root for. I had grown up in opera hearing a number of great basses sing this role, most notably Ezio Pinza, so at first I found Tigges's voice a bit light for it, but here he was, performing it well and confidently, in a major opera theater and with well-established stars in the other leads— Ruth Ann Swenson as the Countess, Isabel Bayrakdarian as Susanna, the extraordinary Swedish baritone Peter Mattei as the Count. He had every reason to feel that "this was like the final stamp of approval for the larger houses."

Tigges was born in Dubuque, Iowa, the youngest of ten children in a musical family. "My mom raised the brood," Tigges recalls. "She used to put a great bowl of food in the middle of the table, which is why today I still eat so fast." His father, an electrician, sang in a barbershop quartet and made his youngest teenage son sing in it as well, even though he remembers hating it. Later, the father formed another quartet, called the T-Tones, with three of Wayne's brothers, to sing old barbershop tunes. In high school, Tigges was in a heavy metal rock band and was also a jock. Tall, powerfully built and graceful, Tigges played basketball and football, then went on to Iowa State, where he began studying voice. "The college had a very small musical program," he said, "so I was this big fish in a very small pond."

Eventually, he transferred to the University of Cincinnati, where he acquired a master's degree and began to sing in all sorts of student and professional productions in the Midwest, while also competing in the Met's regional auditions and other contests. Richard Pearlman, ever on the prowl for a promising talent, heard him and asked him to come to Chicago to audition for the Opera Center. While waiting to go onstage for his audition, with the set of the company's opening production that season of Verdi's *Otello* looming behind him, Tigges retreated into star tenor Ben Heppner's dressing room to warm up. "I was freaking out," he remembers, but then he calmed down, walked out onstage and sang a handful of arias, including one of Figaro's. He was immediately admitted into the program.

With this *Nozze di Figaro* behind them, Tigges and McNeese felt they'd proved what they could do. They both had more comprimario and understudy assignments ahead of them, but they could now also think of themselves as established artists. They were confident that offers would materialize and agents would come calling.

5

Letting It Fly

T HE OPERA CENTER occupies a corner suite on the seventh floor of the Civic Opera House. The L-shaped quarters include a reception area, six offices, a conference room and a lounge. All day long the Center bustles with young singers going to and from rehearsals, coaching sessions and auditions; photocopying parts; working at computers; munching on takeout meals; often just communing and gossiping with one another. When I began to hang around there, the atmosphere struck me at first as mildly chaotic, but I soon became aware of something I had never noticed in any other opera company before—a feeling of friendship and united purpose among the twelve young artists engaged for the whole season. Though their bios reveal that they come from widely divergent backgrounds, they behave like schoolmates. One of the aspects of their participation in LOCAA, which Pearlman stresses from day one, is that an unkindness to or a disparaging remark about a colleague will not be tolerated—a far cry from the days at the Calcagni School, when a bunch of us used to hang around the back of the house during performances at the Teatro dell'Opera in Rome knocking not only most of the singers onstage but also one another. "What a dog! What a goat!" we'd mumble or whisper, delighting no one but ourselves. Opera singing is such a competitive art that insecurity can breed contempt and success envy.

One important factor in all this ongoing Chicago camaraderie is that the LOCAA singers are working so hard they don't have time to be temperamental or difficult; there's so much going on that it's in their own best interest to be gracious to one another. "We throw a lot at them," Dan Novak, who administers the Opera Center, told an interviewer, "but it needs to be only what they can absorb. Their greatest challenge is simply to keep up with everything. If you're in this program, the secret is figuring out when you've hit your saturation point. Some people learn that the hard way, but it's a lesson well learned."

Novak is a tall, lanky, scholarly-looking man with short dark hair. As the person in charge of the Center's finances, he spends a lot of time staring at a computer screen and hustling for money. LOCAA's budget is $1.4 million, about $900,000 of which has to be raised through contributions. But what Novak likes best about his job is being personally involved with the development of the company's young singers. A French horn player who grew up in a Chicago suburb, he planned to become a band director, then later hoped he'd end up with the Chicago Symphony, perhaps in administration. "I always thought I'd wind up in orchestral music somewhere," he said, but after graduating in 1989 from Northwestern, he received a call from Lyric. They put him to work in fund-raising, and he's been there ever since, moving into his present job four years ago. "I'm now part of backstage life," he declared cheerfully when I descended on him one day in his office next to Pearlman's. "The opera bug has definitely bitten. It's been so interesting to me as an instrumentalist to see how singers develop. Instrumental musicians nail down their basic technique early; not so with singers."

No matter how pleasant the surroundings or gentle the atmosphere, it can be intimidating for young singers to show up and suddenly be thrust into the world of a major opera company putting on a season. They have to learn the roles assigned to them—small parts and large, in the case of those who understudy the leads—attend rehearsals and perform, while going to lessons, classes, auditions and meetings of all sorts. They even have social obligations, having to meet with the company's most generous financial supporters and especially those who have agreed to sponsor individual singers. This program, initiated by the Development Department, has become an important source of financing for the Opera Center, and the young artists are encouraged to bond with the people who pay for part of their training. It's been a notable success, but it also takes time out of the singers' lives. "Above all, there's music, more music and still more music to learn," Roger Pines, the company's dramaturge, observed in a program article. An unfailingly enthusiastic, bubbly sort who knows more about the history of opera and singers than anyone I've ever met, Pines would also like the young arrivals to delve into the past. "Even though these young singers are much better prepared than they were twenty years ago, most of them have no idea what anybody sounded like before 1960. Of today's stars only a few—like Fleming, Hampson and Jerry Hadley—are interested in the continuum of singing and are totally committed to their predecessors."

I found this astonishing. The great singers of the past, immortalized on recordings, should be an inspiration to all young singers. You can almost hear them breathe, note the way they attack or conclude a phrase, spin out a long legato, handle the most difficult coloratura and above all interpret what they're singing. The idea is not to imitate, but to learn from precedent.

Pines also likes to point out that by the time most LOCAA members show up, they have a solid vocal foundation and have sung professionally, even if only in the smaller houses. Some have appeared in Santa Fe or St. Louis or Central City and they think they know what they want to accomplish; they have the tools and the savvy. "A singer can come in and step into a role he may have done before somewhere else," Pines declared and cited the case of Stacey Tappan, a coloratura soprano from the Opera Center group of 2002–2003, who had already sung at Wolf Trap and other major venues. "You come out of a program like that already at a very high level. Then they come to Lyric and find themselves working under conductors like Davis or Mark Elder—the highest international standards—and after working with our coaches here you're that much more ready to go. What Gianna and Richard can do is take somebody who's already together and make him even better. Stacey has now developed this elegance in her phrasing, added so much refinement that her singing is spectacular. She's comfortable on a stage anywhere."

Not all the new arrivals are that well prepared. "For those whose only prior experience has been an academic environment," Pearlman has said, "the amount of material they have to learn can temporarily overwhelm them. When they hear the level of LOCAA colleagues who have been here for a year or two, I suppose that could also be intimidating—but I hope it's inspiring, too!"

THE PRODUCTION of Marc Blitzstein's *Regina* that opened at Lyric on September 29 restored to the American opera repertory a piece that had been pretty much ignored for nearly half a century. Originally produced on Broadway in the fall of 1949, it couldn't make up its mind whether it wanted to be an opera or a musical, with the composer himself wavering back and forth during the rehearsal period in a general effort to make the show a popular hit. *Regina* was savaged not only by some of the critics, but also by Lillian Hellman, the author of the play on which it was based. It limped along at the box office for fifty-six performances before expiring, and has only infrequently been revived. Still, it has its passionate adherents, especially among a coterie of aging sopranos who are always looking for a juicy, scene-chewing role like that of the eponymous lead. Regina Giddens is a scheming, ruthless ex–southern belle who outwits her equally unsavory brothers in their struggle over inheritances and shady money-making ventures in Bowden, Alabama, in the spring of 1900. Despite an uneven score that varies from pure operatic melodrama to touches of jazz, the piece, as recently revised and restored, can be dramatically effective. "A near-masterpiece of American musical theater," the critic for *Opera* magazine wrote in his review of Lyric's version, "filled with memorable moments as well as some lengthy stretches of tedium." He and the other critics praised John Mauceri's conducting and the staging by Charles Newell, of Chicago's Court Theatre; *Regina* was Newell's first attempt to direct a lyric drama. Critics also praised the cast, though the *Opera* reviewer found Catherine Malfitano in the title role to be "vocally uneven and a little too fluttery to be entirely credible."

I hadn't seen a production of *Regina* since 1958, when the New York City Opera put it on with Brenda Lewis as a memorably hammy doyenne of the Giddens clan, but I thought Malfitano was terrific in the role, not vocally outstanding, but entirely into the character and well matched by a strong supporting cast, including Scott Ramsay as a would-be southern charmer. Other LOCAA members on hand were Levi Hernandez, Roger Honeywell and Christopher Dickerson, in typically tiny comprimario parts. While wandering around backstage after the performance, I came across Mason and asked him what he thought. He indicated that he was pleased with the production but didn't believe the opera would be worth reviving too often. His reaction and that of the *Opera* critic reminded me of Rossini's famous remark after having attended the premiere in Paris of Richard Wagner's *Tannhäuser.* "It has some very beautiful moments," the sage of Pesaro reportedly declared, "and some very long quarters of an hour."

I had been told by Magda Krance, the tall, dashing-looking woman who manages media relations for Lyric Opera, that Malfitano had been working with young singers recently, particularly with soprano Maria Kanyova, another graduate of the Opera Center, who would be starring that spring at Lyric in several performances of *Madama Butterfly,* so I decided to interview Malfitano.

She received me late one morning in her suite high up on the forty-seventh floor of one of the four Presidential Towers, an enormous skyscraper where many visiting artists stay, mainly because it's only three blocks from the opera house. Malfitano, who has been around a long time, doesn't fit the definition of a sacred monster, but she is definitely a diva. She received me in full drastic makeup, with dark red lipstick and heavily outlined dark eyebrows, her black hair pulled back into a bun, and wearing a loose-fitting magenta dress with a light-green scarf draped around her neck and long jeweled earrings. She struck me at once as a life force, often smiling broadly as she recalled her long career, talking about it in a big, dark voice that seemed to bounce off the walls. Regina is her twentieth role with the company, where she has sung in all the main repertories except the French, though she feels there's no reason she couldn't have tackled any of the Gallic parts. "A wonderful gallery of heroines," she called her interpretations. "I go toward them gleefully. You have to embrace them, to try to understand where these tragic characters come from. You have to justify what you do to form a complicated character."

I asked her how she went about doing that. "You never know what contributes most to the creative flow of an artist, whether it's composer or performer," she said. "You have to reflect the character's humanity." Sometimes she takes into consideration what might happen to the character she plays after the opera's story ends, but she doesn't worry too much about it "because most of them wind up dead." I asked her about Regina. "I love her," she answered quickly. "I love her. I'm honored to play this character. One of my missions in this opera business is to present these characters, to stimulate, to provoke, to reveal them.

"When I began there weren't any programs for young singers," Malfitano reminisced, "but back then, in a way, it was easier to get started." Especially if you had a big, well-trained voice and the right connections. Malfitano likes to claim she was born in a trunk. Her father was a violinist with the Met orchestra and her mother was a ballet dancer who was only eighteen when she married him. "I was actually born in New York City, one of three kids," Malfitano said, "and I got it all through my genes." She studied at the Manhattan School of Music, where she sang Suzel, the soprano lead, in her first opera, Mascagni's *L'Amico Fritz,* a wistful little opus about an Alsatian landlord who falls in love with the farmer's daughter. She followed that up with Pamina in *The Magic Flute,* a much tougher part, requiring Mozartean delicacy. Both performances were favorably reviewed by the New York critics, so she was well known even before she got out of school. Matthew Epstein, then already a powerful agent, quickly signed her up, and her career was launched. "Today," she pointed out, "young singers can be in their late thirties before they break through. By the time I went to the Met at thirty-one I was already established."

She had never considered working with young singers until Epstein and Pearlman asked her to take on Kanyova, who they felt was highly gifted but needed some technical help to make her already beautiful soprano more expressive. Within a year of beginning to work with Malfitano, Kanyova began to attract attention for her performances in a variety of roles. "It was an experiment for me and we've had an extraordinary relationship," Malfitano said. She still works with Kanyova, and the experience has spurred her to teach master classes. "I didn't know I had this in me, wanting to share," she said. "It was like falling into a bath of warm water, something I really enjoy doing." She adopts what she calls a "holistic approach, getting them to use their voices, to speak as they sing, to use the whole instrument, creating what I call a safe place. You can never stop searching and exploring away from the pressure of critics, people making judgments."

In July 2004, Malfitano celebrated her thirty-second year of singing major roles, a remarkable achievement, technically as well as artistically. "Loving it passionately is a great help," she declared, going on to point out that she was inspired by the great lyric tenor Alfredo Kraus, who sang well into his seventies and died in full career. "Rysanek, Evelyn Lear, Marilyn Horne—these are all singers who had long careers and never stopped evolving. The only way you can have a long arc in a career is never to stop being a student."

Every great singer or performing artist in any field has to go on practicing and staying in shape, but there is such a thing as too much study. "Eventually these young singers are going to have to take risks," Malfitano said, sweeping her scarf about her like a cloak in a grand gesture worthy of a true diva. "They can be too coddled. They need to know it's all there in the music."

The singer who had impressed me the most in the cast of *Regina* was Dale Travis, the bass who played the role of Ben, Regina's cunning and ruthless older brother. I couldn't recall ever having seen or heard Travis before, even though he's had a long and successful career singing character parts. I could have, however, because he's one of those performers who disappears so totally into a role that he becomes that person. In fact, when he emerged from his dressing room backstage after the performance and I was introduced to him, I didn't immediately recognize him. Not only did he look different, but he moved and spoke differently, with no trace of a southern accent or the physical mannerisms he'd adopted to portray his character.

Travis was also staying on the forty-seventh floor of a Presidential Tower. When I dropped in on him a few days later, I found him informally dressed and sprawled out on the sofa watching a football game, the typical middle-aged American sports fan. He immediately told me that he'd much rather work in Chicago "than anywhere else on the planet" and that over the years he'd performed twenty parts at Lyric. In his first season alone, he was in three productions, including Menotti's *The Consul,* in which he played the Secret Police Agent, a character so vicious that he was booed every night. He now knows about eighty roles and sings them everywhere. "That's the life of a bass," he said. "There are so many parts, large and small, that we'll always have work. You come in as the complete package—that's how you separate yourself from the masses—and everybody is impressed."

Travis came out of the University of Cincinnati opera program and studied with the great American baritone Sherrill Milnes, who is famous for his acting as well as his singing, and then later with the Italian bass Italo Tajo, who taught master classes at Lyric for many years. In his early years, Tajo sang the leading roles, but in his later ones he became a master of the character parts and an exquisite interpreter of classical songs. He proved to be an inspiration to Travis, who said he was now writing a manual for singers on how to prepare for a role. "One thing is that kids are lacking in good operatic character preparation and how to go about doing that," he said. "I've learned my notes and here I am and they think that's all they need to do. Maybe that's the way it was years ago, but today you have to tear it down brick by brick before you can build up a character. There's a handful of singers who can just stand there and let it fly, but most others can't do that anymore."

Among the let-it-fly singers I'd heard, both in person and on recordings, were some of the greatest names in opera—Caballé, Nilsson, Stignani, Gigli, Bjoerling, Merrill, Ruffo, Bechi—the list is nearly endless, but also, I realized, not pertinent. There would always be exceptions to today's rule—another Pavarotti or Carreras—but the competition is now so extreme that it's increasingly difficult to build a career on voice alone. "American singers today are very well prepared in the mechanical aspects of singing," Travis observed, "but don't know that the key is to react, to find a way to listen to what is being said to you by others onstage, also to listen to what the composer is saying to you. The music has to speak to you, and lots of people have a hard time listening. The whole reason we are here is that somebody wrote the music and the words and that's why we can make a living doing this wonderful stuff."

I told Travis that I thought the *Regina* had worked very well onstage purely as a drama, quite apart from the quality of the score. "That's because this director, Newell, didn't try to impose anything on us we'd be uncomfortable with," Travis explained. "He'd never directed an opera before, but he asked the singers for advice." Travis has appeared in other productions in which the directors were so intent on imposing their own particular visions that "they succeeded in raping the work and got a rise out of the audience. To explain what they've done they write twenty pages of footnotes in the program. It's crap."

Another hazard for young singers to worry about in this era in which directors, even more than conductors and sacred monsters, wield the power. It's not one the kids can do much about, though; they're not the ones wielding that power.

6

The Director Also Rises

*I*T'S HARD TO PINPOINT exactly when the stage director became the dominant force in most opera productions today, at least in the States. In the so-called golden age of great singing, between 1900 and World War II, it was mostly the great divas and sacred monsters who bestrode their world like colossi, yielding only in the face of a few acclaimed conductors such as Toscanini and Wilhelm Fürtwangler. You scan the reviews of important performances at the Metropolitan during this era and rarely is the director even mentioned as an important contributor. His job, mostly, was to move the chorus about and make sure the principals made their entrances and exits on time. (When George Bernard Shaw was writing opera reviews back in the 1880s, this figure wasn't even called a director but a stage manager.) The singers' interpretations of the great roles were praised for their individual artistry, not because they had benefited from the insights and guidance of a talented director. Even when I was singing around New York in my modest way in the 1950s, I can't remember ever being helped by the direction, except, in a *Bohème* put on at the Brooklyn Museum, for such routine instructions as, "Okay, now when Mimì holds out her arms to you, move down left and sink to your knees by the bed." This was the same director who suggested that when I go up to the high C in Rodolfo's act-one aria, I should turn, walk upstage and indicate the moon's rays flooding in through the skylight. I had to explain to him that

I'd be lucky to hit the high C at all without having to stroll any-where, especially away from the audience with my right arm up-raised. He complained that I didn't understand his concept of the scene. I sang it in the performance front and center, straight out.

The revolution in the status of the director in the United States can probably be traced back to the Rudolf Bing regime at the Met, in the 1950s, when he lured such legit stage luminaries as Sir Tyrone Guthrie, Margaret Webster and Garson Kanin into the opera house. Their names were too big to ignore, and for the first time the reviewers had to pay attention to what the direction was all about. After the Bing revolution came the enormous suc-cess of Franco Zeffirelli, who is not in any way an innovator but whose specialty is creating a whole world in which his characters can fulfill themselves. His first opera in Chicago was a *Lucia* that opened the Lyric season of 1961, with Joan Sutherland singing three performances as Donizetti's pathetic heroine. Sutherland is a big woman with a lantern jaw who looks about as fragile as a Bradley Fighting Vehicle, but she had a huge dramatic coloratura, seamless from top to bottom, and enough breath control to swim underwater the length of an Olympic-size pool. She was the sort of performer around whom Zeffirelli could structure a whole production—which he did, even though it was Richard Pearlman, then working as his assistant, who did most of the blocking. De-layed in Italy by another project, Zeffirelli arrived just in time to garner the kudos. Pearlman, who worked with him from 1959 until the mid-sixties, admired him and understood him. "What-ever was good about his direction came from his being in touch with Western civilization," Pearlman said. "He created beautiful stage pictures. And if the performers were great, he could make a cornice for them."

The first time I saw Zeffirelli in person he was sitting alone halfway up the ground-level seats of the huge Roman Arena at Verona, supervising a brushup rehearsal of his *Carmen.* The or-chestra was tootling away; the principals were in full voice;

several hundred choristers and supers were milling about the stage, singing and carousing; there were Spanish flamenco dancers, ballerinas, horses, donkeys, geese, dogs, even a goat. A typical Zeffirelli production. The director raised a finger, somebody shouted, minions scurried about, the conductor stopped beating time, the whole vast enterprise ground to a throbbing halt and waited, eyes focused on the monster. Holding a mike in one hand, he walked toward the stage. "Children," he said, "for the love of God this is *not Rigoletto*! *Look* at the beautiful woman!" More instructions, more scurrying about, more changes, then the whole thing again from the top. Now *that's* power.

Sacred monsters are hard to pin down. I'd been chasing this one around for a month. Like Figaro, he was up, down, here, there, everywhere—London, Paris, Rome, Sicily, New York, Verona—except where I'd been told he might be. He's famous for being elusive, especially when it comes to something he really doesn't want to do. If he does want to do it, his friends say, he'll get to it, but always at the last minute. He's an improviser, but so charming, so generous, and so talented, says a screenwriter who's worked with him, that "he makes you forgive him for everything." He has summoned people to his sumptuous villa in Positano to work on various projects, but kept them waiting around for weeks and never appeared. Playwright Christopher Hampton reportedly showed up to work on a screenplay with him, and sat around for two weeks. He was wandering through Zeffirelli's house one day when he chanced upon the novel *Dangerous Liaisons,* which he had never read. And so a play and a movie were born, but not the one Hampton and Zeffirelli were supposed to collaborate on. Writers, especially, are welcome, but often never see him. A would-be biographer dropped in on him one year, hung around for weeks, then left, never having talked to him. Actors, too, celebrities even, all are kept waiting. Bring something to read, old friends warn everyone.

Actually, I was surprised he kept putting me off, because

everybody knows he's publicity-mad; he secretly adores journalists, and there isn't one he can't con into loving him. As for photographers, no one is more photogenic, and he cunningly strikes poses for them like a movie star. "If he has a single ruling passion, it is for wanting to be in the headlines," an old colleague warned me. "You will see. You will be summoned to Verona in time and dragged along behind his chariot like a slave in *Aida.*" He was right; that's exactly what happened.

Franco Zeffirelli was born in Florence, on February 12, 1923, the illegitimate son of a businessman who acknowledged him and made sure he learned fluent English, a useful gift. His mother was a seamstress who died when he was six. She had wanted to give him the surname Zefiretti ("little breezes"), from an aria in Mozart's *Così Fan Tutte,* but a clerk at the registry misspelled his name. He was raised by an aunt, who took him one night to hear *Siegfried.* He was stunned, he has recalled, and the next day he threw away his puppet theater and began to invent "fantastic scenes" for himself from an illustrated Sunday newspaper. That's one story he tells, but there are other equally romantic ones, all with at least some measure of truth in them.

He claims, for instance, to have been a Partisan toward the end of World War II, when he and a group of friends took to the hills in order to avoid being caught by the retreating Germans, but whether or not he actually fired a gun, nobody knows. What is sure is that he was adopted as an interpreter by a regiment of Scottish soldiers, several of whom he has stayed in touch with ever since. He was very young, very good-looking, with blue eyes and reddish blond hair, and already had a formidable gift of gab.

The defining influence in Zeffirelli's life was movie and opera director Lucchino Visconti, for whom he went to work as an assistant on the film *La Terra Trema* in 1947. Visconti was a true magnifico—a dashing Milanese aristocrat, a devout Communist and a seducer of beautiful young men. But he also recognized and rewarded talent. Zeffirelli learned much from him before he took off on his own—into theater, movies and plays, as well as opera. "Visconti was the first great director to treat romantic opera seriously," maintains Masolino D'Amico, a well-known Italian writer and critic. "Franco also has that gift, the taste for opera. That is where he is at his best."

Some critics, especially lately, have found Zeffirelli's productions to be overloaded, so cluttered that the central action tends to disappear into the mass, but few have questioned his genius as a set designer, his ability to evoke not only a specific place and time, but also an entire society and way of life. I've seen dozens of *Carmen*s over the years, but never one like that staged in Verona. With Zeffirelli you are in the world he creates—in Spain, in Seville, part of the whole exotic scene—not merely watching the singers strike poses while holding high notes.

I stuck around for three days in Verona to watch him work. Of course I had now been swept up into his entourage and was being treated like a long-lost relative. This was because his assistant, a cheerful, supremely efficient young woman named Sabrina, had been prodding him daily to talk to me and reminding him that I had to leave for home. "*Caro,* what is your name?" were his first words to me. "Ah, Bill—you are not the son of Natalia? But I knew your mother very well. Why do you have to leave? Come, sit here." And so there I was, suddenly beside him, front row center during the rehearsal, with his driver-bodyguard, Luciano, on one side, Sabrina on the other and Blanche, the queen mother of his pack of Jack Russell terriers, on my lap, while we all tried unsuccessfully to keep her from barking at the horses.

At first, apart from his status as a sacred monster and an occasional intervention, Zeffirelli didn't seem to be contributing very much of anything. It was his assistants who were pushing and prodding and shouting, moving great masses of people about, correcting positions, instructing the singers, running the errands, scampering here and there for this and that. Always, however, they kept an eye on him, to look for his approval, or came scrambling offstage to where he was, seemingly unconcerned, alone or with us, and sometimes standing with Blanche tucked under his arm. These were, after all, touch-up rehearsals for a production he'd mounted for the Arena the year before. Not all of the principal singers had even arrived. What else was there to do? But then, two days before the dress, with almost the entire cast of four hundred people onstage for act one and with everything apparently going smoothly enough, at least for an opera rehearsal, the director suddenly took charge.

One more puff on his omnipresent cigarette, one last swig from his pocket flask full of straight whiskey, and here he came again, mike in hand, heading straight for the stage.

He stood by the orchestra pit for a moment, surveying the scene, then began to talk and wave his hands about, indicating where he wanted everyone onstage to be. His assistants jumped into action as he made corrections for every soloist and group of performers in the scene. "This is not a solemn High Mass," he admonished them. "You are not all members of some squalid political movement. . . . Supers, make groups, little groups! . . . Mind your own fucking business, don't look around at the others! . . . Don't laugh at Carmen! She's making fun of the police! . . . Chorus, with the music, eh? You have to make these movements always with the music! . . . Talk it over, eh? Discuss it! It's a big event, yes? . . . Now, again!"

Conductor Daniel Oren picked up his baton and the action resumed. "Beautiful, like this it's beautiful!" Zeffirelli called out as Carmen began to dance. "Look at her, she's fascinating! You want her! . . . Very good, *cari,* not more than that!" But soon he saw something else he didn't like and bounced up onstage himself to correct it, acting out every part in the whole scene. Then he retreated to floor level and called out more comments through the music until the end of the act. "Look at him," Oren said when we were on a break and Zeffirelli was off to one side conferring with his assistants and members of the backstage crew. "Franco can put us all to shame. He can give us all lessons."

If he has any weaknesses as a director, they are not evident in the opera house. This is because in opera he's limited by the text and the score. "He is not an inventor, an *auteur,*" according to D'Amico, who has worked with him on a number of film projects, "but that's not bad. In Shakespeare, too, he is wonderful."

In movies his improvisational style can be troublesome to actors, especially those with intellectual pretensions or who favor the Method and like to brood over psychological nuances. On the set of *Jane Eyre,* for instance, there were memorable clashes with William Hurt, who thought Zeffirelli wasn't up enough on Charlotte Brontë. "Franco likes to act out himself what he wants his performers to do instead of telling them," recalled one crew member. "That can lead to feelings of loneliness and abandonment. There were also big issues of control."

This almost never happens to him in the opera house, where there is no time for such foolishness and territorial byplay. Among true sacred monsters there is at least mutual respect. One of Zeffirelli's closest friends was Maria Callas, who was unjustly maligned, he feels, for her temperamental excesses. And he has worked happily with many other stars, including most notably Plácido Domingo.

During the last rehearsal break of my last night in Verona we were sitting alone, with a full moon rising dramatically over the thousands of empty seats behind us in this great ancient Roman amphitheater. People were bustling about onstage, changing the set, and half the cast had gone home. It was after midnight, and everyone looked exhausted except Zeffirelli, who seemed as fresh and alive as he had six hours earlier. Even with all his assistants and helpers doing the bulk of the physical work, it was a remarkable performance.

He was seventy-three years old at the time, and his celebrated beauty had faded, though he still looked fascinating on film. (He tries to make sure that no photographer ever catches him unawares.) He was plump, wore glasses and had a small bald spot at the back of his head. He smoked heavily, but Sabrina informed me that he had regular physical checkups and was always found to be in excellent health. His memory was prodigious, his culture and erudition vast, his attention to detail legendary, and he was always looking toward the future, though he was saddened by the fact that so many of his contemporaries were dying around him. "You have always to fight, to fight, never to give in," he told me, "until they take it away from you."

At 2:00 A.M., when the rehearsal finally ended, I was hoping to go off for a late snack with him and his intimates, but he was through with me. "Remember, *caro,* one thing," he said. "The opera is a river that carries you forward." He repeated the phrase to make sure I got it down exactly as he had said it, then switched off the charm and dismissed me with a suddenly formal handshake.

7

The Sources Inside

AT ELEVEN O'CLOCK on the morning of November 12, three days before the premiere of *Faust,* the director, Frank Corsaro, held a master class in Room 200 for all LOCAA members. The atmosphere was resolutely informal, with the singers sitting in an uneven line facing the grand piano and the accompanist. Gianna Rolandi was perched at the far right and Pearlman at the left, with Epstein slumped into a seat well behind them all. Corsaro, who is short and stocky with long, curly white hair, presided from a seat between the piano and the singers. He was wearing olive green slacks and a light-tan sweater and looked as relaxed as a beloved college professor secure in his tenure. A long-established member of the Actors Studio, he has been around forever and has made a good career for himself in both legitimate theater and opera by not crushing his performers under the weight of the Method. This production of *Faust* was a revival of the one he had directed for the 1995–1996 Lyric season, and he had done little to an already conventional staging of the piece but tweak it here and there to add a bit of life to it. I had watched him a couple of days earlier working with his cast through act two without doing much of anything at all except to make sure that everyone could be seen. Mezzo Judith Christin, in the role of Marthe, and Samuel Ramey were accomplished veterans who had long since made these parts their own. Lauren McNeese was bounding about the scene looking adorable.

Marcus Haddock, the Faust, moved stolidly around the set in typical tenor fashion, blasting tremendous high notes out into the auditorium. The only singer seemingly totally concerned with credibility and interpretation was the Marguerite, Patricia Racette, who marked throughout but questioned every movement and bit of business until Corsaro accommodated her. Not for nothing is this American soprano considered one of the finest pure artists in opera today.

On this particular morning Corsaro had no defined agenda. He asked for a volunteer to sing first and informed everyone present, "I want you all to feel free to comment." Patrick Miller was the first to step forward. Miller is a tall, graceful-looking man with a thick shock of dark hair, who looks ten years younger than his real age of thirty-four and handsome enough to play a Hollywood leading man. I had already heard him rehearse the balcony scene from Gounod's *Roméo et Juliette,* with Nicole Cabell, for a concert to be given at the new Harris Theatre for Music and Dance, downtown, and had admired his clear, ringing lyric tenor. After the duet, Pearlman, who was with me, said, "If you were casting a play on looks alone, you'd cast these two." Though only a first-year member of LOCAA, Miller had considerable professional experience and had been a finalist in the Metropolitan regional auditions. My only negative feeling about his performance during the duet with Cabell had been that it lacked passion, but then it had been only a rehearsal, after all.

Miller grew up in Minneapolis, the youngest of three children, and heard a lot of music; both his parents were teachers in dramatic arts at the University of Minnesota. All through his education Miller had been singing, but his parents were skeptical about the possibility of a career in the arts because they knew how tough it could be. They believed that if he had some degrees, he wouldn't have to wait tables while trying to break through, so for a while he was slated to become a counseling psychologist. As he looked back on that period of his life, he couldn't believe he was going to become a singer. But all along he'd been taking voice lessons, was singing every day, and, with all of his college friends in music, was pushed toward a music career. When he finally told his teacher, tenor Tim Sawyer, that he wanted to become a professional singer, Sawyer answered, "It's about time. Do your parents know?" When he did tell them, they thought he was crazy. They grilled him, but he assured them that if he had to wait tables to be in music, that's what he would do. After which, unlike most parents, they became very supportive, because they wanted to see him happy and successful.

Miller was in New York in February 2002 with his girlfriend, Veronica Mitina, a Russian-born soprano, when he auditioned for Pearlman. Three weeks later he was summoned to Chicago to sing for Epstein and Mason. Since then, Miller had also auditioned for producer-director Baz Luhrman, who had offered him one of the Rodolfos in his Broadway-bound version of *La Bohème*. But when Chicago accepted him, Miller opted for the program most likely, in the long run, to advance his career.

When I met Miller he struck me as a very smart, very cool customer, securely focused on his career, and it didn't surprise me in the least when he informed me that he never gets stage fright when he performs. What he loves best, however, is the process—the rehearsing, the working through a part with other people. "In rehearsals," he said, "you don't have to be perfect." The only time he ever remembers being nervous was when he was singing an Alfredo in *La Traviata* in San Antonio. Suddenly, just before going on, he found himself wondering what would happen if he forgot his part, what if something were to go wrong. But he quickly got over it once he set foot onstage. "How weird it is," he said to me, "how wonderful and crazy at the same time."

Now, standing firmly in place and facing his peers, Miller launched into Lenski's great aria from Tchaikovsky's *Eugene Onegin*. Lenski, a poet, knows he is going to die in a duel that very morning and so he sings of his past, his youth and his one regret, losing Olga, the woman he loves. It is one of the most pathetic, moving scenes in all of opera. Miller sang it well, with a nice free, open sound and easy top notes, but without moving anyone. "All right, Patrick," Corsaro asked, "what's the song about?" Patrick recited the basics, about life flashing by, Lenski's love for Olga. "But the question always comes up, 'What am I saying, really?' " Corsaro responded. "We're left here not knowing where you live. Look, I'm being told something I haven't heard before. You've told me the general story, but not what moves Patrick. The notes are not enough, the words are not enough. It's what's in here that counts." The director patted his chest. "You need to get underneath all that wonderful music. Now, you've told me exactly what's in the story, but what about Olga? Do you still see Olga?"

Corsaro wanted Miller to dig more deeply into himself, so he continued to prod him about Lenski's feelings for Olga. "This girl that you love," he said, "has this girl ever done you wrong? And what about Lenski?" He turned to the other members. "We need to know what's going on in Lenski's mind." He looked at Miller. "Lenski is a difficult character. What you've said about Lenski doesn't define him." He paused, then asked, "Have you ever felt everything was falling apart?" Miller said yes, when he was in college. "Hear that? The bitterness?" Corsaro told the group, then turned to Miller again. "Everything that happened then is still living inside you."

Miller told the class about a love affair he'd had in college that went wrong, when the girl broke off the relationship. Corsaro asked him to describe her physically, which Miller did very flatteringly. "Nevertheless, despite all that good stuff, she turned you down," Corsaro said, going on to relate Miller's rejection by his girlfriend to Lenski's being alone in the forest before the duel. "We could go further, but let's concentrate on this. Forget about other aspects of the aria." He asked Miller to recall physically the moment of rejection. After Miller told him he was sitting alone when it happened, Corsaro made him take a chair and sit on it, hunched forward, hands clasped. As the tenor sang the aria again, the director continued to prod him verbally about what he was thinking and feeling. "People might say Lenski can't just sit on a stump in the forest," Corsaro said when Miller had finished. "Well, he could, but that's not the point anyway. You see how this is quite different now?"

Roger Honeywell, a second-year member of the group who has a vast classical stage background, spoke up to talk about the historical context in which the piece is set, but Corsaro immediately shot him down. "You're giving me the history of the aria," he said. "I can get that better out of the library, from many sources, but this is the way you really get it. How would you play the King of Sicily? Would you wear a pizza on your head? Why do we go to five hundred revivals of *Hamlet*? Because we want to see what this particular actor will bring to it." He recalled recently hearing a soprano audition with "Una voce poco fa," Rosina's spicy and self-revealing opening song from *The Barber of Seville,* and being totally unimpressed. "She sang the notes, but there was nothing there," he explained. "You are all millionaires, you have all this richness inside you."

During the general discussion that followed, Corsaro also warned the singers about adopting clichéd operatic gestures, one of which he defined as "the misplaced vagina," when a female singer holds her hands cupped together in a V in front of her. "What is that person trying to tell me?" Corsaro asked.

Pearlman recalled what he terms "the tenor arm," in which the singer stretches out or crooks his arm like a sommelier waiting for someone to drape a towel over it. And then, of course, there was Pavarotti's famous handkerchief, omnipresent at the tenor's every concert performance and some operatic ones. "Those gestures are all to cover tension," Pearlman declared, going on to point out that one disadvantage American singers face is that most of the time they are singing in a language they don't understand. "It's one thing to know it intellectually, but it's another thing to have it in your bones."

Before going back to his seat with the others, Miller said that he found it much easier to sing onstage in front of an audience rather than for people he knew well. "The audience is that rare thing, Patrick," Corsaro assured him. "You live for them! Okay, as a beginning that's fine. Thank you very much."

"It's very important," Pearlman added as Miller sat down, "for each singer to examine very carefully the sources inside."

No sooner had Miller returned to his seat than Roger Honeywell, also a tenor, bounded to his feet to replace him. At thirty-six, Honeywell was the oldest of the group, but he had been singing opera for only three years. Until then, he and his wife, also an actor, had been earning a living on the legitimate stage, mostly in his native Canada. With their two small children, the couple had moved to Chicago so Roger could master his newly chosen art. So far, it had not been easy for them, especially financially.

Now, for Corsaro, Honeywell launched into Macduff's last-act aria in Verdi's *Macbeth,* "Ah, la paterna mano," in which the character mourns the murder of his children by Macbeth and swears revenge. Honeywell is tall and strongly built, with a full head of flaming red curls, and he cuts an impressive figure onstage. He stood in front of the piano, feet set wide apart, and simply belted out Verdi's elegant trumpet call to action. His voice sounded huge inside the rehearsal studio, with clanging metallic high notes, but he sang fortissimo throughout, without subtlety or grace.

Corsaro immediately called him on it. When he found out that Honeywell was himself a father, he said, "You have all the information in you to draw on here." He proceeded to explain to him that his problem was to channel the emotion of the piece in a more elegant way. He made Honeywell analyze the aria. In the first verse, the father expresses mourning for his dead children; in the second, he calls for action against a tyrant. "You go from inaction to action," Corsaro pointed out and asked the tenor to sing the aria again.

This time Honeywell sang the first verse very softly, the second even louder than before. "No, now you're caught betwixt and between," the director said. He asked Honeywell to sit down, sing while seated, and to concentrate more on the emotions being expressed. This third time through, Honeywell found a better balance, singing the first verse seated, then brought to his feet by the call to action in the second. The tenor's singing seemed effortless this time, but still filled the room without the strain evident earlier. "What do you think of that?" Corsaro asked through the applause that followed.

"I quite like the dreamlike state this causes," Honeywell said, smiling.

Corsaro complimented him on his presence and the contrast he'd achieved between the opening verse and the second. "Earlier, the tension was showing in your body," he pointed out.

Scott Ramsay, the other tenor in the LOCAA program, piped up that Verdi gave you all the clues you needed in the music itself, but Corsaro quickly contradicted him. "The music will not do it for you," he said. "Without emotion, this aria will not do it. It becomes just another Verdi *oom-pah-pah.*"

From the rear of the room Matthew Epstein suddenly spoke up in a booming baritone. "I've never heard Roger sing with such emotion before."

"You gave us the raw stuff and I wish I could see that more often," Corsaro commented as Honeywell returned to his seat. "In your case it's how do you start from a state of relaxation."

Erin Wall jumped up and indicated she was planning to sing the Jewel Song from *Faust,* which she'd soon be performing as Marguerite for the last four performances of the run on the Lyric main stage, but Corsaro asked for something else. "I want to take the burden of *Faust* off you," he said. Wall sat down again and began to shuffle through her music, while Lauren Curnow replaced her and launched into "There Is a Garden," a sweetly sentimental piece from Leonard Bernstein's *Trouble in Tahiti.* She sang it very well, but broke off toward the end, overcome with emotion. "Were you too emotional?" Corsaro asked.

"No . . . yes," Curnow admitted, wiping a tear from her eye and looking a bit dismayed by her lack of professionalism.

Corsaro suggested she drop all intensity, then asked the other singers for comments. Miller observed that until the breakdown "it was so beautiful." Corsaro then compared the problem here with the Verdi aria. "Where does the singer allow himself to go?" he said. "Being caught up in an intense emotion can interfere with conveying that emotion to the audience. It can also tie you up technically. The work must be looked at in terms of pleasure. You can use the emotions you feel to find pleasure in the music, technically use the emotions to provide the element of pleasure."

"How and when you get to that place," Epstein called out, "is something you do in rehearsal. Onstage, in performance, you can take it as far as you can without breaking. This is what rehearsals are for. It's great!"

"You need the mixture of the two," Corsaro said.

When Erin Wall got up again to sing, it was Donna Anna's difficult aria from Mozart's *Don Giovanni,* "Non mi dir," in which Anna, ravished by the Don and incessantly courted by her boob of a boyfriend, Don Ottavio, basically begs the latter for time to make up her mind. No sooner had she finished singing it than Wall said, "It felt awful."

"In what way?" Corsaro asked.

Wall explained that she hadn't connected what she was singing to anything going on inside, so she and Corsaro discussed the relationships in the opera. Corsaro pointed out that Anna is a very complicated character. "You were talking to a wall," he said. "He wasn't there. What is she after here?"

"I think she's trying to buy herself some time," Wall said.

Corsaro questioned Anna's relationship with Don Ottavio. "Does she love him, for instance?"

"I think she feels affection for him."

Corsaro asked her to sing the aria again for him and placed a chair directly in front of her. "Sing to that chair," he suggested. Wall began to sing again, then she, too, broke off and ran to her seat to grab a couple of tissues from her bag. "You mean you got emotional?" Corsaro said. "Good! This shows more vulnerability."

Again Matthew Epstein from the back of the room: "Oh yes!"

Corsaro proceeded to give Wall a long analysis of the character's conflicting emotions. "What would happen if she let herself go?" he asked. "Would he accept it? No? But she would. Why?"

The discussion of Donna Anna's character and emotions continued for another twenty minutes, till the end of the two-hour class, which, I realized, seemed to have passed very quickly. Corsaro was a superb teacher, just the person to conduct a master class, too many of which often degenerate into dogmatic pronouncements and inattentiveness to each artist's individual needs. Corsaro listens closely, he pays attention to nuances of interpretation, he knows what the technical problems are, he understands the characters, he's willing to probe motivations, but he also has a sense of humor. No one leaves his presence unenlightened.

Frank Corsaro is no longer considered in some quarters to be in the front ranks of today's opera directors, probably because he has made the mistake of having been around too long and not having been experimental enough for the companies, especially those in Germany, which fancy themselves on the cutting edge, mostly by staging outrageously ill-conceived updatings of the classics. But then, as Richard Pearlman observed one day, "There's nothing as old-fashioned as last year's avant-garde."

8

Getting Through It

ON THE OPENING NIGHT of *Faust,* Saturday, November 15, I went backstage an hour before the performance and hung around just to get a feel for what was going on. The dressing room area is stage left, just inside the stage door. A short corridor leads past a bulletin board filled with various announcements about rehearsal schedules and other matters, then immediately opens up into a spacious lobby off of which two hallways of singers' dressing rooms extend to another, narrower space between them that functions as a rest area for the costume makeup and wig people. It's furnished with comfortable chairs and a long table on which are laid out cookies, snacks and soft drinks. A humidifier puffs into the atmosphere the damp air singers like, while speakers in the wall pipe in the muted noises of whatever is happening onstage.

The nerve center and heart of the backstage scene is the Rehearsal Department, a glass-enclosed room that contains half a dozen desks, computers, another bulletin board, mail slots, filing cabinets, coat racks, a water cooler and shelves full of all sorts of documents and mementos. It is staffed by six people and presided over by two women, Marina Vecci and Josie Campbell, whom Pearlman describes as being capable of running any major corporation in America. They take care of the singers' needs, coming and going; handle visiting celebrities; do the management's bidding and improve on it; deal with every crisis, large and small, with self-effacing but ruthless efficiency and are adored by everyone who knows them. Sometimes they are both present, but on performance nights at least one of them is always there. On this particular night it was Campbell, a sturdily built woman who looks to be in her late thirties or early forties, has brown hair flecked with gray, wears glasses and a touch of makeup and likes to sport gaudy outfits designed to entertain. That night it was a black dress spotted with sequins, devil-red Mephistophelean tights and a wristwatch heavy enough to break a child's arm.

Across the way from the Rehearsal Department are several smaller rooms, one of which functions as backstage quarters for Mason, Epstein and Davis, all of whom showed up well before curtain time. The singers were mostly in their dressing rooms—each of which is equipped with an upright piano—either warming up, putting final touches to their makeup and costumes or simply communing with themselves. The general atmosphere was decidedly cheery, with confidence exuding from every pore. *Faust* is vocally demanding, but it's such a familiar piece that it poses few challenges artistically or technically to any top company. There were going to be no surprises sprung on the audience; all they had to do was sit back and enjoy the performances of some very good singers, including Haddock, who made up for his limited dramatic skills with an outpouring of pure lyric tenor singing that was likely to melt even the critics.

The most active person backstage was Pearlman, who had two of his LOCAA members in the opening-night cast, Lauren McNeese and the young first-year baritone Quinn Kelsey. Kelsey was singing the small role of Wagner and understudying the big one of Valentin, Marguerite's unfortunate brother, who gets to sing the most beautiful aria in the opera, "Avant de quitter ces lieux." Pearlman never fails to talk to his young singers before every performance, not just to wish them luck, but also to reassure them by his presence. From what I had seen and heard so far in Chicago of both McNeese and Kelsey, they were going to be fine. In fact, Kelsey had an instrument in his throat that had the potential to make him a very great star and my only regret was that I probably wouldn't get to hear him sing Valentin during the run.

During the first two acts, which were played without intermission, I spent most of the time in the wings, where I could watch the action from the side and also keep an eye on the TV monitor showing conductor Mark Elder in full energetic action. By prudently moving about I managed to stay clear of stagehands pushing set pieces on and off. I watched the flats rise and fall into the flies; the armorer supervising his weapons; the prop people making sure everything was in its proper place; the stage manager, Caroline Moores, a bundle of supercharged energy, supervising with her assistant the singers' entrances and exits and all the cues for sound, lights and action. There are hundreds of things, big and small, that can cause trouble, sometimes even derail a performance, but on this night it was going off with the precision of a rocket-launching countdown.

TWO DAYS EARLIER, after the *Faust* dress rehearsal held at 1:00 P.M. on Thursday, November 13, during which everyone in the cast except Racette sang full voice, I had wandered across the street to what Lyric calls a preview lecture. Several hundred ticket holders had gathered in a lecture hall on the second floor of this nearby office building to listen to two members of the production, usually including at least one of the principal singers, discuss the work about to be premiered. The audience was encouraged to ask questions or make comments, and the sessions usually last about an hour. When I arrived, I found Ramey and Elder seated facing a good-natured crowd of fans and flanking the moderator, Carl Grapentine, a jovial, heavyset man with a booming baritone voice whose task it was to move the proceedings along. Elder and Ramey, who had just come from working hard for four hours, were informally dressed and looking totally relaxed. Grapentine picked on Elder first, asking him about conducting in general.

Elder is a fiercely energetic, youthful-looking Brit who approaches music as if it is a challenging sport. He began as a choirboy and discovered opera in the school library, after which he made it a point to listen to an opera a day. He has conducted all over Europe and the United States, has held key positions with a variety of opera companies and symphony orchestras and was awarded a CBE (Commander of the British Empire) by the Queen in 1989. He admires Gounod for his "poetic sensitivity" and the "theatrical skill of the music." Now, in answer to Grapentine's question, he defined conducting as an essentially athletic profession. "I do a lot of stretching and light exercise before going on," he said, "so I make sure my body is at my disposal." He also concentrates mentally, because "if you don't start right, it's very hard to put it back together."

Elder is a witty man, full of ideas and anecdotes about his conducting experiences, and the audience lapped him up. He tried from time to time to be serious. "Experience is so important," he said, "the division between heart and brain, which is really a division inside the conductor's head." Nobody seemed to be quite sure what he meant by that, but it didn't matter because he kept right on talking. "I never take my eyes off the singer," he continued. "It's sort of like playing the finish at Wimbledon. You always have to be aware of the form of the singer and what he's doing and you look out for the unexpected." He recalled conducting a *Salomé* during which the baritone singing John the Baptist was informed he'd just become a new father. "He was so ecstatic about the birth of his child that he wouldn't get off his F-sharp."

After Elder, Ramey came on at first like a straight man, with the gravitas that his deep bass voice conveys. He grew up in a small town in Kansas, "which sure didn't help much," and went to college intending to become a teacher. A member of the faculty there, however, suspected he had a voice and taught him to sing "Non più andrai" from *Le Nozze di Figaro*. He enjoyed it so much it inspired him to go to a record store, where he bought an old LP that featured "some guy named Ezio Pinza," the great Italian lyric bass who for a generation set all the standards for the category at the Met and later on Broadway as the romantic lead in *South Pacific*. That started Ramey off on his career, though he'd never been to an opera until he found himself actually singing in one, a *Don Giovanni*. Ramey then talked about how hard he'd had to work on his languages. He studied Italian and German in college and for his French roles went to work in Paris with a vocal coach there. Divorced from his first wife and recently remarried, he told the delighted audience that he was also a new father and had become a Chicago resident partly because "living here is so central to traveling anywhere in the world to sing."

Among men, deeper voices tend to last longer than higher ones, and it occurred to me as I sat there that Ramey had been around a very long time. Recently his voice had begun to show portents of wear and sometimes, when he pushed too hard, ominous signs of developing a wobble, but during the *Faust* rehearsals, in all of which he'd sung out full voice—I was told he never marks—there had been no trace of trouble. Over the years the devil roles have become Ramey's specialty, not only in Gounod's opus, but also in those of Berlioz, Auber, Boito and Offenbach. He's never made an exact count of how many Gounod devils he's sung, but guessed that this *Faust* was probably his twentieth, for a grand total of some two hundred performances.

Like every other established star, Ramey has had his share of misadventures, especially with stage directors. "You always know you're in trouble," he said, "when at the first rehearsal the director says, 'Would you mind just singing through this for me?'" Directors who haven't done their homework can be exasperating. Ramey also recalled having to fly to Munich to fill in for an indisposed Mephistopheles at the last minute only to be told when he got there that this *Faust* would include the Walpurgis Night scene, a sort of balletic orgy in which Dr. Faust and Mephistopheles party on a mountaintop with a gaggle of famous courtesans, a scene that is usually omitted. "Nobody told me," he said, "that I was going to be in the middle of twenty-five naked women."

The discussion, with its relaxed give-and-take, was highly entertaining, with none of the tension that can surface when a production is in trouble or the opera in question has to be sold to a possibly indifferent public. *Faust* has been a staple of the American operatic repertory ever since its first performance in Italian at the Academy of Music in New York, on November 26, 1863, and this Lyric complement of artists was expected to bring in sell-out crowds and garner the usual splendid reviews.

BEFORE THE SECOND ACT was over I went back to the Rehearsal Department, where I found Racette, who had just come offstage, sitting in full costume at one of the computers checking on her forthcoming travel schedule. Marguerite has very little to sing before act three, but I had expected that with the Jewel Song about to come up after the intermission, Racette would be holed up in her dressing room getting ready. Evidently she was ready, because she seemed entirely unconcerned. She looked stunning, every inch the diva. Nothing in this role was going to prove much of a challenge for her, I figured.

When the act ended, the chorus and supers came pouring offstage and headed upstairs to their communal dressing rooms. McNeese sped past me, looking radiant; her little aria had earned her warm applause, more, she told me later, than she'd ever received for her Cherubino, a much tougher role. Kelsey strolled past, his evening over, since his character dies after his one scene. He seemed cheerful that it had gone well—in fact, so well that the audience had responded strongly to his outpouring of sound and there was astonished approval on the faces of several of the stagehands who had heard him. Wagner, with just the beginning of a song to sing before he's interrupted by Mephistopheles, is not the sort of part anyone can make a lasting impression in, but in just those few phrases Kelsey had served notice that he was potentially a major talent.

Erin Wall now also showed up. Dressed in a pink sweater, black slacks and black pumps, her blond hair somewhat untidily pulled back off her face, she was full of excitement and cheer. "It's great," she announced to no one in particular. "So much more energy than at the dress. I love opening nights!"

So, apparently, did everyone else in the cast, because the whole performance—the rest of which I saw from a good seat in the orchestra—was strongly applauded, with everyone receiving his share of bravos. Both McNeese and Kelsey were also subsequently singled out by the critics for their contributions to the sort of evening of grand opera that big companies such as Lyric are expected to put on for their audiences. Of *Faust,* "it may be treacly and sentimental," concluded the reviewer for the *Chicago Sun-Times,* "but it's great entertainment, a devil's bargain that cannot be resisted."

After the performance, there was the usual opening-night party given in the Graham Room, a luxurious dining suite on the second floor that is usually open to members only. It was crowded this time with everyone involved in the production, including some backstage and administrative staff, and the production sponsors and their guests. There was a lavish buffet, a bar serving wine and soft drinks and a sea of round tables for the guests to sit down at. The evening had gone well and everyone was resolutely cheerful, with congratulations and compliments flying in every direction—which they always do, even if an evening hasn't gone well, the order of the day in all such affairs being positive thinking. I noted that a few key figures were not present, most notably Matthew Epstein, who, I was told, never attends these functions.

The most impressive moment of the soiree came when Bill

Mason rose to speak. He stood at a small lectern and began a recitation of names, beginning at the top and working his way down to each member of the company present, thanking everyone personally by name, with encomiums for all, including, not least, the donors who had contributed to the cost of putting the opera on. Not even the few chorus members present were overlooked. Amy Bishop, a cheerful young woman who works in the Rehearsal Department, had told me that from her first day on the job Mason had never forgotten her name. The man could run for public office anywhere.

THE FIRST TIME I asked Gianna Rolandi how she felt about one of her charges, Erin Wall, stepping into such a big, demanding role as Marguerite, she said, "It makes my palms sweat." Having been an important singer herself, she could all too clearly identify with the hazards of being suddenly thrust front and center before a demanding public used to hearing great singers in the part. The first time I asked Wall herself, however, she said, "I can't wait." She felt that as a third-year member of the Opera Center she had paid her dues. Besides, she had already proved to herself that she could step into a situation without any rehearsal and succeed. It had happened to her on New Year's Eve 2002, when Jonita Lattimore, the soprano soloist scheduled to sing that night with the Chicago Symphony Orchestra, had been forced by illness to cancel at the last minute. The CSO contacted Wall in mid-afternoon, found out that she knew three of the four arias on the program, two by Mozart and one by Franz Lehar, and booked her to perform them. "It was all sort of a blur," Wall told a reporter later, though her performance was a triumph. "She had fifteen or twenty minutes' preparation," an official of the CSO said afterward. "She came onstage and was a complete pro."

Even so, performing a role on the Lyric main stage in full costume while not only singing but also interpreting a character had posed a much bigger challenge. During all of the *Faust* rehearsals I had kept track of how much actual time onstage and with the orchestra Wall received, and the answer was almost none. Her best chance had come when a rehearsal in the theater ended at 4:30 P.M., a half hour before it was scheduled to. Wall rushed down from a coaching room to step out in front of the drawn curtain to face Elder at his podium over the pit, with a smattering of an audience in the seats behind him that included Epstein and Mason. Wearing jeans and a white pullover, she launched into the scene of the Jewel Song. It was thrilling. Her rich soprano soared effortlessly over the orchestra, with a great trill and explosive top notes that caused several of us to cry out, "Brava!" Afterward she complained that she couldn't hear herself because the curtain behind her deadened the sound, and she felt she was pushing all the time, but by then I'd learned enough about Wall to discount her sometimes quirky self-questioning. It wasn't insecurity, which afflicts many singers, even the best; basically, she was a perfectionist. On the day I first interviewed her, after a three-hour run-through rehearsal of the role in one of the studios, she was going to attend that evening's performance of the opera because she wanted to make notes on Racette's interpretation, breathing, bits of business, vocal shadings and emphases.

Wall's parents were from the Houston, Texas, area but moved to Vancouver, Canada, where she grew up. Her father played the French horn, her mother the cello, and as a child Wall played the violin, then studied piano before going on, at the age of eleven, to the flute. "It fell out of my closet the other day," she told me, "but I can't play it for long anymore; the muscles are not in use. I always felt passion for the music, but with piano and flute the lightbulb never came on. It was such great training, though. It gave me a great education, which not all singers get."

By the age of ten, in the fifth grade, she was singing in the choir and the school chorus, but her early vocal ambition was to become a jazz singer. She worked all the way through college at the University of Western Washington in Bellingham, Washington, and studied voice with Virginia Hunter, a soprano who had had a career in France and whose specialty was French art songs. When Wall first went to college and began singing, it was as an alto. "They put me in the alto section," she recalled, "so I thought I must be an alto." The top of her voice didn't begin to flower until her last year there, but she went on singing in the chorus, mainly because she always had. It wasn't until she came to the Opera Center that she was told absolutely to stop doing so. Choral and solo singing are two entirely different disciplines, if only because a true solo voice will not blend well in a chorus and a soloist will inevitably be required not to be outstanding in any way, which can be damaging to a singer's development and technique.

After college Wall spent a summer in the Aspen, Colorado, opera program, then went to Rice University—back in Houston, where she had family—for two years to get a master's degree in music. It seemed the best place for her to be, because it was a small program. "I don't think I'd have done well in a conservatory," she said, "because I knew I wasn't there yet. It wasn't fear of performing, but I didn't want to sing in front of people yet. Besides, I don't like competitiveness." It was one of the things she liked best about her years at the Opera Center. "I enjoy listening to my colleagues," she said. "You get so proud, so excited. You've taken this journey together."

In the summer of 2000 she went to the Music Academy of the West in Montecito, California, where the retired great mezzo Marilyn Horne runs a sort of finishing school for young singers. This was where Pearlman first heard Wall, and where she also sang, separately, for Epstein. Both men wanted her in the LOCAA program, with Epstein in particular determined to take her under his wing. In his long career as a manager he had had much to do with launching and nurturing the career of Renée Fleming, the reigning American diva, with whom Wall has since often been

compared. From Wall's first day in Chicago, Epstein has personally hovered over her, guiding and advising her while also steering her toward representation by his old agency, Columbia.
"Matthew wants to make sure I've got someone who'll take care
of me," Wall explained. Presumably a successful debut as Marguerite would serve as the launching pad for a major career.

On December 8, the day before her first performance in the
role, Wall was supposed to benefit from a 9:30 A.M. run-through
with Mark Elder, but it was canceled because the conductor had
thrown his back out. There was even a question as to whether
he'd be able to conduct the following day, in which case the
baton would pass to his cover, Philip Morehead, the head of the
musical staff, a fine maestro in his own right but one with whom
Wall had never rehearsed the part. The change didn't seem to faze
her. When I caught up to her in the Opera Center lounge later in
the day, she appeared relaxed but eager, like an athlete poised to
meet a challenge. As it happened, Elder did show up to conduct
the next day, but it probably wouldn't have mattered much one
way or the other.

Backstage on the night of the performance, the members of
the Lyric Opera chorus arrived to find a notice posted on their
bulletin board. It was addressed "To the Amazing Lyric Opera
Chorus" and it read: "It is a thrill and an honor for me to be onstage with you tonight for my very first Marguerite! Hearing and
seeing you every night has been a treat, and I'm so excited to do
these four *Fausts* together. Your support and encouragement
throughout this process has meant so much to me and I feel very
lucky to know you all & to perform with you! You guys rock!
Knock 'em dead tonight!" It was signed "Your new Marguerite,
Erin." Very few leading singers at any stage of their careers ever
bother to acknowledge the chorus, much less thank them for their
contributions. I think I fell in love with Wall that night, and I became so eager for her to succeed that I lost all objectivity and
wandered around backstage like a twiddly parent. I was only

slightly reassured by Pearlman, who emerged from Wall's dressing room a few minutes before curtain to inform me that she was looking beautiful and brimming with confidence.

It was not misplaced. From her opening entrance right to the end of the opera, Wall not only sang like a goddess but also was even more convincing in the role than Racette, which both the major local newspaper reviewers noted. As Pearlman commented afterward, "Her gawky innocence in the role is more like the character than Racette, whose performance, though excellent and also beautifully sung, had a more calculated, cerebral quality." As for Wall herself, after I was able to get to her through the throng of people wanting to congratulate her, she said she was disappointed with her performance of the great closing trio, where the soprano's voice is supposed to soar fortissimo over the singing of both her colleagues and the playing of the orchestra. She said she'd spent herself in the opening scenes and had had to struggle later. It reminded me of a remark she'd made earlier about singing. "You can be sick, you just may not feel like it," she said. "That's when your technique gets you through it."

Erin Wall, ever the perfectionist.

9

A Cornucopia of Characters

THE LYRIC PRODUCTION of *Siegfried,* which opened on December 5, was extraordinary even by the most exacting Wagnerian standards. Not only was the singing and the playing of the orchestra beautiful and deeply moving, but the whole concept of how to present the work struck a delicate balance between old-fashioned realism as it affected the relationships of the characters to one another and the adroit use of symbolism to suggest the cosmic requirements of the composer's vision. The stage director, Herbert Kellner, was basically entrusted with re-creating the original production conceived by the late German director August Everding for Lyric's first *Ring* cycle in 1996. At the time, Everding had commented that the saga was "about money, sex and power that leaves us with the idea that the redemptive power of love is greater than all of them." He also pointed out that no theater could possibly compete with TV and the movies to create the magical effects Wagner demanded, so he chose an approach that suggested rather than depicted them. It wouldn't have worked, of course, without the first-rate singing of the leads—John Treleaven in the title role, Jane Eaglen as a vocally splendid Brünnhilde and James Morris in his signature role of Wotan—and the presence at the podium of Sir Andrew Davis conducting the inspired orchestra.

That didn't tell the whole story of the evening, however. The critics were uniformly impressed because *Siegfried* is rightly regarded as the most difficult and demanding of the *Ring* dramas, but what also caught their attention were the contributions to the performance's success of all the artists in the smaller roles, from the rich alto sound of Jill Grove as Erda, to the snarling baritone of Oleg Bryjak as Alberich, to the booming bass of Raymond Aceto as Fafner. No current LOCAA members were in this production, but two recent graduates were: Stacey Tappan, as the unseen Voice of the Forest Bird, and David Cangelosi, as the dwarf Mime. Not much is asked of the Forest Bird but to chirp and trill away up there for Siegfried to listen to, but Tappan's sound was clear, pure and true, every trill and top note firmly in place. Why she wasn't already a big star I had yet to figure out, but surely the day would come when she would grace some big stage in a leading bel canto part. As for Cangelosi, his Mime was amazing.

The opera is supposedly about Siegfried, the fearless innocent Wagner envisioned as the ideal New Man, the successor to the tragically flawed god Wotan and his crew of cronies and merry warriors gamboling through the halls of Valhalla. It's hard to be sympathetic to Siegfried because he's such a dope and so unthinkingly boorish, so I found myself this time rooting for poor Mime, the dwarf whose motives are anything but pure but who, in his scheming and lustful desires, is at least recognizably human. Cangelosi was so convincing in his portrayal of the chattering Nibelung, with his outbursts of anger, his complaints and his wheedling of his difficult charge, that he dominated the proceedings, bounding about and swinging from the rafters of his hut like an enraged gibbon. The ordinarily staid reviewer of *Opera* magazine singled out Cangelosi's performance as the most impressive of the evening, "with powerful singing, extraordinary physicality, impeccable diction and mastery of both the comic and the darkly sinister aspects of his character."

Cangelosi is not the kind of opera singer who will ever rise to stardom, because his light tenor, though pure and bright, is essentially that of a true comprimario, destined by its limitations to grace the smaller parts. This is not to say he won't have a very good career. Since the 1996–1997 season he had already sung fifteen roles at Lyric and he was much in demand elsewhere, including at such big houses as the Met and the Paris Opera. He has a thoroughly professional approach to his career and will very likely become as well known in his category as Charles Anthony, who has been singing comprimario roles at the Met for fifty years, and as the current top tenor in such parts there, Anthony Laciura. Comprimario singers are often the unheralded heroes of many opera productions and no first-rate company can do without the good ones.

DURING A METROPOLITAN OPERA season of some years ago, I spent some time hanging around Laciura to get an idea of what it's like to be a singer of character roles. After having been cleared by the administration to come backstage, I met Laciura at the Met stage door at six-thirty on a Thursday evening, an hour and a half before curtain for that evening's performance of Puccini's *Madama Butterfly*. This would give Laciura plenty of time to warm up and get into costume and makeup. He would be singing the supporting role of Goro, described in the program notes as "a marriage broker," the man from whom the feckless American naval lieutenant B. F. Pinkerton has procured himself a house, three servants and a fifteen-year-old bride, Cio-Cio-San. Goro appears in the opening scene and briefly in act two, but, even though he has only a few lines to sing, his presence is crucial to the action. "Without Goro, Pinkerton would never have met Cio-Cio-San," Laciura described the part. "He's the cause of the trouble. To make him live, I need to feel he's as important as the stars, as if the opera was called *The Matchmaker*."

The principal dressing rooms backstage at the Met are located off a long corridor that looks like an interior deck of a cruise ship. Each room is large and comfortable, with a private bathroom and plenty of closet space, as well as an upright piano, a humidifier and a long counter under a wall-length lighted mirror. Laciura's first act was to turn on the humidifier (a dry larynx onstage is every singer's nightmare). Then he undressed, put on a bathrobe, struck a chord on the piano and began to vocalize, warming up mainly on "mio" and "nai" as he moved up and down the scale. "If you do a lot of singing, you don't have to do too much warming up," he said after a few minutes. "And in these roles there's a lot of middle-voice singing. Even so, sometimes you leave your dressing room not knowing what's going to happen and saying to yourself, 'It's in God's hands.' And then you go out there and open your mouth and it sounds great."

At about seven o'clock, a staff makeup artist showed up to help Laciura get into character. The sort of parts comprimari sing usually call for all sorts of visual aids—wigs, false noses, warts, age lines, deformities large and small. "We're usually not the pretty people," Laciura explained. "And to make an impression we need all the help we can get." In the case of Goro, neither Puccini nor his two librettists bothered to describe the man, so it was pretty much up to the singer and the stage director to create a look for him. Laciura, at the time of our meeting a bouncy live wire of forty with a cherubic smile and a shock of dark curly hair, had elected to play Goro as a contemporary, but, in addition to the imposition of standard Japanese features, he added a shortened nose and a slightly crooked mouth. "He's not a pimp, but he's not a nice guy either," Laciura commented twenty-five minutes later, as he surveyed himself in the mirror.

During the final half hour before curtain, which was punctuated every few minutes by the stage manager's announcements over the backstage intercom system, visitors and colleagues popped in periodically on various missions. Fabrizio Melano, the stage director, showed up to warn Laciura not to cross his ankles when he sat down in the first scene, because "it's not Japanese." A young woman from management stuck her head inside the door and asked, "Are you here? Are you dressed? Are you ready to sing?" then disappeared without waiting for an answer. Charles Anthony, who was covering the role that night, dropped by to wish Laciura luck. And in between these visits the tenor went over his part at the piano, checking each line against the text in the score. Just before Laciura went on, a dresser appeared to help him into his kimono and obi. The stage manager called places and Laciura headed for the stage, already in character and ready to sing.

The performance that night went off without a hitch. *Madama Butterfly* is a staple of the Met repertory, a popular favorite that usually moves some portion of the audience to tears. The current production had failed thus far to excite the music critics and was considered typical of the sort of routine spectacles that cause the Met to be considered in the opera world a conservative house dedicated mostly to yesterday's pleasures. Such considerations do not concern Laciura, whose task, as he sees it, is to create each night he performs a living, believable characterization. Goro may not be his favorite part, but—as he shuffled about the representational set that depicted Butterfly's house and grounds, tilting slightly to one side as he pursued his cynical, venal affairs and singing as if out of the side of his mouth—he set a standard of performance that few leading artists even bother to attempt. "A lot of singers think they can just stand there and sing," a colleague of Laciura's named Loretta Di Franco said to me. "There's more to opera than that these days."

After the performance, Laciura managed to get out of makeup and costume in thirty minutes, got dressed and headed for his car, parked in the Lincoln Center garage. Outside the stage door he was greeted by several fans who wanted autographs and to compliment him on his singing, then he drove home across the George Washington Bridge to his wife, Joel, and their seven-year-old son in Teaneck, New Jersey. He struck me as a happy commuter, warbling for his supper several times a week in one of the world's great opera houses and supremely confident in his ability to bring it off night after night, as if opera were as easy as singing in the shower.

MOST SINGERS EXPERIENCE at least moments of panic, especially early in their careers and on opening nights in difficult or unfamiliar roles. Some even well-established performers get the jitters every time and suffer agonies of insecurity until reassured by the sound of their own voices. (Rosa Ponselle, a soprano regarded in her heyday, the 1930s, as one of the glories of the lyric drama, literally had to be pushed out of the wings almost every time she appeared. So did Franco Corelli, the Italian dramatic tenor with movie-star good looks, who used to throw things and scream at people before going on.) Not Laciura. When he first stepped out onto the stage of the Met in *Der Rosenkavalier,* during the opening night of the 1982–1983 season, and looked out at the audience, his first impression was that Maestro James Levine seemed to be conducting from somewhere out on Columbus Avenue. But instead of being awed, as most singers are, by the cavernous void of the huge house, he remembered thinking, "It's home; this is where I belong." And ever since then he had tried to recapture that feeling every time he sang, because he believed it helped him to do his very best. "These people have paid a lot of money and they want you there and you want them there," he explained. "It's my job as an artist to entertain them."

Laciura was then in his eleventh season at the Met. Since that opening night, in which he sang the very small part of Faninal's majordomo, he had sung more than six hundred performances of some thirty roles in six languages. He was already very well known to New York audiences, but even today he is still rarely singled out by the critics, though some of the parts he sings are quite long, with arias and a good deal of ensemble singing. They demand the same level of technical skill as many of the starring roles. Nevertheless, in the world of opera, with its rigid hierarchies and long dominated by prima donnas of both sexes, little distinction is made among the supporting players. "Anyone who sings less than a leading role is a comprimario," is the way Jim Scovotti, Laciura's manager, defined the category to me. "It's a craft," my old colleague Andy Dobriansky told me. "You're there to make the leads look better. You're not there to shine yourself. If the leading singer cracks a high note, you have to keep your expression. The big thing is not to overdo."

Funny things can happen if a comprimario suddenly finds himself for some reason the focus of the audience's attention. A friend of mine recalled a production of *La Traviata* at the San Carlo in Naples in which, at every performance, the young bass singing the bit part of the Doctor was roundly whistled. The problem was that the Doctor, who has only one important line to sing, basically pronounces a death sentence on the heroine, Violetta, who is dying of consumption. "La tisi non le accorda che poche ore," he sings, which translates idiomatically to "She has only a few hours to live." To a Neapolitan audience, this was equivalent to casting an evil eye on the poor woman. The young singer was a Florentine not used to southern superstitions. He became tired of being booed, so on the last night of the run, when it came time for him to sing the fatal words, he remained silent and walked off waggling one hand, palm down, to indicate that the kid had a fifty-fifty chance.

Most comprimari, in the United States at least, would prefer to be described as "character singers." "You just don't come onstage, open your mouth and sing anymore," Scovotti said. "There are comprimari who can't do character parts. You have to change your personality several times a week, and it goes beyond makeup. Anthony's strength is that he can sound like a ninety-year-old man one night and a cherub the next."

This is confirmed by the variety of roles Laciura sings. As Pedrillo in Mozart's *Abduction from the Seraglio,* Beppe in *I Pagliacci* and David in *Die Meistersinger,* he reveals a smooth lyric tenor with bright top notes; as Basilio in *Le Nozze di Figaro,* Monostatos in *The Magic Flute* and Pong in *Turandot,* he produces the quavery tones of citizens well beyond their prime; as l'Incredibile in *Andrea Chenier* and Spoletta in *Tosca,* he provides the sinister, slimy intonations of a police informer and in *The Tales of Hoffmann,* he creates four memorable eccentrics, each one vocally distinct from the other, a tour de force the New York reviewers singled out. "In these roles, you're not on long enough to work gradually into a characterization," Laciura pointed out. "Vocally and dramatically, you have to make your points immediately."

The Metropolitan is almost the last of the world's major opera houses to function as a true repertory theater, putting on performances of several different works a week on successive nights over a period of about eight months. This requires the company to keep on its roster about ten comprimari for the full season and at least two dozen others on a part-time basis, who can not only sing all the small parts but also cover for and step in for one another at a moment's notice. Stars also have understudies, and if they get sick, another leading singer is almost always available or can be rushed in from elsewhere to take over. A character performer, however, is a rarer bird, in his own way as essential to the success of the opera as the leads. An audience will accept the fact that a star can become ill and that, in an extreme emergency, a performance might even have to be canceled, but no one would sit still for a *Tosca* being called off because Baron Scarpia's weaselly henchman was indisposed. "The opera is called *Tosca,* not *The Revenge of Spoletta,* " is the way Laciura put it.

The Met, with its tight schedule of productions sometimes requiring dozens of soloists a week, has provided employment over the years for comprimari who have aged into their parts like casked wine. Tenor Andrea Velis retired after three decades of singing more than two thousand performances in some two hundred different roles. Still actively on the Met roster in 2004 was Charles Anthony, christened Calogero Antonio Caruso, a tenor who changed his name for obvious reasons. Anthony debuted at the Met in 1954 and has a repertory of more than seventy roles. Most comprimari are men, because, as in television and the movies, there are many more parts for males, but the Met also has several women comprimari under contract. Loretta Di Franco, for example, a cheerful woman with a laugh like the boom of a distant cannon, began singing character parts in 1965, making her debut in Tchaikovsky's *Pique Dame.* Though listed on the roster as a soprano, she had a huge range and could produce sounds stretching from coloratura top notes to contralto chest tones. "You can really let go in these parts, be zingy and off center," she told me, "but if you miss one word, your whole role is gone." In Janáček's *Jenůfa,* her entire stint consisted of one line: "She has killed her child." Miss that one and a fairly crucial plot revelation has been eliminated.

No one starts out in the world of opera expecting to become anything but a leading artist. "Like all singers, you see the glamour, you want to be a star," Laciura observed. "You want to be the greatest tenor who ever lived." Becoming a comprimario is a choice made usually out of necessity, after some time spent trying to break into the big roles in the major opera houses. And, as in the theater, the dividing line between stardom and professional competence is often blurred. Some comprimari become character singers after their vocal resources begin to fade, as in the cases of Renato Capecchi and Italo Tajo, a baritone and a bass who sang leading roles all over the world and who ended their careers at the Met and elsewhere in a variety of small parts.

They are the exception, however. Most comprimari come from the ranks of younger singers, who all start out, in their own heads at least, as potential superstars. In 2004, the Met's Young

Artist Development Program, founded in 1980, had ten singers, evenly divided between men and women. Of those, some had already made their debuts in small roles, but none intended to make careers as comprimari. If the Met won't eventually cast them in principal parts, they will probably go elsewhere to sing, perhaps to a smaller company or abroad. The late James Mc-Cracken, a renowned dramatic tenor, became tired of singing the Messenger in *Aida* and departed for Europe, where he quickly established himself as a major artist and eventually returned to the Met as a star.

This is the exception, not the rule. Most conductors and coaches think they know a comprimario when they hear one. "It's in the quality, the timbre of the voice, not its size," maintains Craig Rutenberg, once the head of music staff at the Met and now recognized as one of the best vocal coaches and accompanists of singers in the world. "Hilde Gueden, a great soprano, had a voice about as big as my little finger. It's placement, not size." The great singers, according to Rutenberg, have voices of such beauty and individuality that they make an immediate impression. The Italians have a word for it: *pastoso,* indicating a warm, mellow sound that ravishes the ears. A good comprimario, on the other hand, even if he has a nice voice, has to be able and willing to alter it for dramatic effect.

Laciura grew up in an Italian family in New Orleans and began singing at the age of ten as a boy soprano in the choir of his local Catholic church. By the age of eleven he knew he wanted to become an opera singer. At twelve he debuted as a street urchin in a production of Charpentier's *Louise.* After his voice changed, he studied for seventeen years with a local voice teacher named Charles Paddock, who warned him that he'd have to give up many things. Laciura was such an enthusiastic pupil that he couldn't recall what he gave up; all he wanted to do was sing. In opera he started out in supporting roles, but soon moved to performing leads—Pinkerton in *Butterfly,* Alfredo in *Traviata.* After he moved to New York and began auditioning around, he continued to get jobs, but mostly in small roles or as an understudy in both operas and musicals. He was becoming skeptical about ever being able to break through when he went to sing for Scovotti, a manager with a small but active roster of clients. "You're going to have a career," Scovotti said to him, "but you're going to have to let me decide what you'll sing."

Laciura was living in Brooklyn then and married to Joel, an ex-dancer who had been helping to support them by teaching high school English. They wanted children, and Laciura was willing to listen to anyone who could build a solid career for him. Scovotti unhesitatingly steered him into the character parts. "Tony's very spontaneous and he can change expressions from one moment to the next," Scovotti told me. "Also, he could do great imitations of other singers. It was this talent I wanted to promote." When Laciura finally auditioned for the Met, he sang an aria from John Philip Sousa's forgotten comic opera, *El Capitan,* which called for him to sing soprano as well as tenor and parody the coloratura pyrotechnics of Rosina in *The Barber of Seville.* He was hired on the spot.

THE NIGHT AFTER his Goro, Laciura was back at the Met, preparing to go on this time as Bardolfo, one of the fat knight's drunken cronies in Verdi's *Falstaff.* He lengthened and thickened his nose with the aid of a rubber extension, reddened his cheeks, dirtied himself up and prepared to disport himself onstage as a rascally carouser and petty schemer. "I'm going to have more to sing tonight, a whole little *ariettina,* and a lot more to do dramatically throughout," he said. He was looking forward to the last act, in which he would disguise himself in a bridal costume and get to cavort about the stage like the heroine of a transvestite revue. "What I won't get to do is run a whole gamut of emotions," he said. "But you can't have everything."

10

Mastering It

THE FIRST TIME I heard Michael Mayes sing was on the stage of Symphony Center, on Michigan Avenue, the elegant home of the Chicago Symphony. He was twenty-seven years old, a Texas-born lyric baritone who happened to be married to Lauren McNeese. Mayes is a tall, good-looking man with long, wavy brown hair who sings with a relaxed, confident air and who knows how to sell a song. His first selection that evening was the aria "Sois immobile," from Rossini's rarely performed monster of a lyric drama, *William Tell,* remembered today only for its rollicking overture, which was used on radio to celebrate the ride of the Lone Ranger. Mayes's culminating top note was a dandy, and he sat on it just long enough to wow everyone without distorting the musical integrity of the piece. It was an impressive performance because so much was at stake for him.

The occasion was the central regional auditions finals sponsored by the Metropolitan Opera National Council, whose stated purpose is "to discover exceptional young talent" by giving artists the opportunity to be heard by a representative of the Met and making it possible for the winners of the competition to be admitted into the Met's Lindemann Young Artist Development Program. The audition procedure is incredibly detailed and cumbersome, with two winners each from sixteen regional competitions being summoned to New York in the spring for "several days of musical preparation under the guidance of the Metropolitan's musical staff," after which they compete against one another on the stage of the Met, with piano accompaniment only. From that competition, the ten chosen semifinalists go up against one another a week later, this time accompanied by the full Met orchestra. Five ultimate winners receive $15,000 each, the runners-up $5,000 and $1,500. Who would be chosen for the young singers program for 2004 remained to be seen, dependent mainly on the needs of the company.

The auditorium of Symphony Center was only about three-quarters full that day—it was an invited audience—but the pressure on the nine contestants, who ranged in age from twenty to twenty-nine, had to be tremendous. (The Met doesn't consider anyone over the age of thirty to be a young artist, whereas the Opera Center has no such rigid rule.) The young singers basically had to please three poker-faced judges, and the atmosphere was intimidatingly formal, with all the contestants in evening dress. They walked out one at a time onto the bare stage, followed by their accompanists, and faced the invited guests, most of whom were total strangers to them. They got to choose which piece they would perform during the first half of the audition, but in the second half, after a brief intermission, it would be up to the judges to select what they wanted to hear from the list of four or five arias each singer had submitted to them.

I was sitting next to Rolandi and Pearlman, who were there casually scouting the talent in the hall, but neither of them was at all impressed by any of the contestants who followed Mayes. In any case, they already knew how good he was, because he had already sung for them a number of times, hoping he'd also be taken into the Opera Center with Lauren. Having heard him sing, I found myself wondering why he hadn't been recruited. Not that he was vocally any better than either of the current LOCAA baritones, Hernandez and Kelsey, but he had the edge on them in experience. Of course, oddly enough, that may have worked against him.

Apart from Mayes, the only contestants who impressed Rolandi and Pearlman were the last two on the program, soprano Adelaide Muir and bass-baritone Brandon Mayberry. The latter opened with "Vi ravviso," a bel canto aria from *La Sonnambula,* which he sang smoothly, with no apparent hitches in his technique and an easy stage presence. His tall, dark-haired, slim good looks enhanced his performance, in which, however, Rolandi must have identified some problem, because she whispered to Pearlman, "I'll bet he's fixable." It turned out they were both a bit worried about him. He had already been accepted into the LOCAA program and been invited to drop in on rehearsals of *Le Nozze di Figaro,* but had failed to put in an appearance or to take advantage of any of the invitations to come and preview what would be happening to him beginning in the spring of 2004. Pearlman informed me at intermission that he intended to set up a meeting with him.

The singer who impressed everyone the most was soprano Adelaide Muir, who, at twenty, was the youngest of the contestants by several years. Tall, very beautiful and dressed in a long, sleeveless red evening gown that hugged her body, she moved onstage with the grace of an ex–ballet dancer. Her opening selection was the fiendishly difficult aria "Piangerò la sorte mia," by Handel, a composer who requires from singers the ability to indulge in the elaborate coloratura ornamentation that operagoers of his time insisted on. Muir made a huge impression and generated the only real excitement I'd heard from the audience so far.

During the intermission both Rolandi and Pearlman expressed the hope that she wouldn't win, because they felt she was too young and too inexperienced to risk being swept up into the hype and pressure of being lured to New York to compete against singers probably more advanced than she. Then, even if she did win, she might find herself in the Met's program, where she could easily flounder and get lost. Pearlman thought she still needed to study at a top conservatory, such as Juilliard or the Curtis Institute in Philadelphia, among the better finishing schools for aspiring opera singers. For her second aria, Muir was asked to sing a much easier piece, a sprightly little aria from Donizetti's delicious comedy *Don Pasquale,* which she knocked off very easily but without arousing the enthusiasm that had greeted the Handel. Still, it was an impressive performance, one that Pearlman found "mind-boggling for a twenty-year-old."

At the end of the evening, as we were all hanging around awaiting the judges' selections, Rolandi again expressed concern that Muir was too young for New York. When I reminded her that two famous American coloratura sopranos, Patrice Munsel and Roberta Peters, had both been in their teens when they started to sing professionally and that the history of opera included dozens of sopranos who had begun their careers very early, Rolandi said, "Yes, but it was different then. Singers were more vocally prepared." She attributed this to a dearth today of really good voice teachers. In fact, neither she nor Pearlman thought most of the singers we had just heard were any good. It reminded Pearlman of another such competition years ago, when the veteran soprano star Martina Arroyo found herself serving as one of the judges. "It's like picking the prettiest girl on an ugly block," she said.

This time, when the judges delivered their verdict, one of the winners was Adelaide Muir and the other a contestant none of us had admired. Michael Mayes finished third, which, as far as I was concerned, testified to the difficulty of being a baritone in a world dominated by the higher voices, who perform most of the romantic leads. Muir went on to New York, but did not make it into the Met program.

ON SUNDAY, NOVEMBER 9, five days after the Met auditions, Bruno Michel, the artistic director of the Théâtre du Châtelet in

Paris, showed up to hear some of the Opera Center singers. Also present was John Such, an important manager from New York, who already represented several former LOCAA members. The two were a contrast in style. Michel is tall, handsome, dapper—everyone's idea of a romantic-looking Frenchman, with perfect manners and a suave, relaxed approach to his task. Such struck me immediately as the quintessential agent, frozen-faced and dressed in a dark suit, not the bantering type. He conveyed the feeling that he had sat through many more auditions than he'd have cared to, if he'd had a choice. He and Michel sat at a table in Room 200 facing the grand piano and the singers, while behind them perched Rolandi, Pearlman and Epstein. One of the Opera Center's top coaches, Eric Weimer, a superb musician who had worked with most of the young artists on their arias, had settled himself at the keyboard to accompany them.

The first to sing was Lauren Curnow, who was wearing a chic black pantsuit that accentuated her tall good looks. She launched right into a showy mezzo aria from Meyerbeer's *Les Huguenots,* one of those rarely performed elephantine operatic spectacles characteristic of this now largely unperformed composer. As she sang, Epstein, dressed in his customary funereal black, rocked back and forth in his chair, while Such never looked up from a pad on which he was scribbling away. After Curnow had finished, Michel asked for another piece, then a third one, after which he and Such huddled together to talk things over. When Michel finally looked up, it was to say, "Thank you very much," to which Such added nothing. Curnow smiled bravely and left.

In strode Scott Ramsay, wearing a dark suit and tie, beaming and looking supremely confident. He opened with a difficult aria from Mozart's *Abduction from the Seraglio,* which he sang very pleasingly, easily handling all the difficult coloratura runs. When Michel then asked for something in French, Ramsay sang "Le Rêve," the sentimental piece the hopelessly misguided Chevalier des Grieux sings to his venal girlfriend, Manon, in Massenet's melodic potboiler of the same name. Ramsay handled it with grace and the same ease he'd demonstrated in the Mozart, but received only the customary polite thanks from Michel and no comment from anyone else. Ramsay left at the same brisk, confident pace he'd displayed upon entering, smiling and saying as he went, "Thank you and have a good afternoon."

Lauren McNeese was next, looking adorable in an open-necked black pantsuit. She walked over to the table to introduce herself to the two men, forcing them to rise and shake her hand. She sang "Non so più cosa son" from *Figaro,* then "D'amour l'ardente flamme," a long, very beautiful, serene Berlioz aria she had long had in her repertory. It showed off better than any of her standard audition pieces her ability to handle the sweeping arc of a demanding legato. What she heard upon leaving were the usual emotionless thank-yous.

Nicole Cabell began her audition with Manon's entrance aria, "Je suis encore tout étourdie," in which the naïve young temptress, fresh out of a convent and on her way to Paris, expresses amazed enchantment at the new world opening up before her. I'd never heard anyone sing it better, except perhaps the great Beverly Sills when she was at the top of her form many years ago with the New York City Opera. As Cabell sang, her body and arms moving to convey the passions and meaning of the song, Michel reacted physically to her, as if he were conducting her, which could have proved distracting. Rolandi leaned far forward in her seat, intent on every note, while Pearlman maintained his usual calm demeanor, almost immobile, but with his eyes glued to the singer. Cabell is the kind of artist who, from the first note, commands your attention, involves you in the meaning of the music. When she had finished, Michel smiled and said, "You're enjoying this, aren't you?" She really didn't have to answer; her smile and whole demeanor spoke for her.

Quinn Kelsey stood solidly facing the table and confidently

launched into his opening aria, the lament "Ah, per sempre io ti perdei," from Bellini's *I Puritani.* It's not one of the more demanding numbers in the baritone rep, but its flowing melodic line shows off very well the quality of a voice. Kelsey's huge, dark baritone, with its easy ringing top, and his clear Italian diction elated all of us in the room, because we all knew we were in the presence of a budding major talent. Kelsey was only twenty-five years old and this was his first year in the program; he was the only one of the young singers auditioning that day to bring that level of inexperience into the room. After his second selection, the drinking song from Ambroise Thomas's *Hamlet,* in which he effortlessly belted out tremendous top notes that seemed to bounce off the ceiling and walls, there was much grinning and laughter at the table and from the rest of us. Even Such seemed to be impressed. I was told later that he has a policy of never contacting a singer first; he always waits to be called. This time, however, he reportedly made sure Kelsey was given his card.

The only two other LOCAA singers to audition that day were Erin Wall and Roger Honeywell. Wall, looking gorgeous in another of her long, black pantsuits and high heels, knocked off the Jewel Song, then launched into a seemingly endless aria from Richard Strauss's *Arabella.* Strauss is even more long-winded than Wagner, and this piece is a test of endurance comparable to competing in the Tour de France. As Wall performed, we all sat forward in our chairs, rooting her along, and I sighed with relief when it was over. Arabella is certainly a role Wall will sing one day, but for audition purposes this particular piece teems with pitfalls and I found myself wishing she would drop it.

Honeywell, dressed in a gray suit and tie and looking impressive with his height and full head of thick red curls, launched spiritedly into Pinkerton's farewell aria from *Butterfly.* He was loud and hit all the top notes, but there was little subtlety in his singing. Michel then asked him for the Flower Song from *Carmen,* a famous aria almost all opera tenors know. The start seemed rocky and he cracked his first high note, an A-flat—not a good sign. He was clearly pushing too hard, and in the softer phrases he showed a tendency to croon. Then he cracked a second time, before the climax of the aria—a demanding B-flat, a note the young Caruso had broken on repeatedly when starting his career. Honeywell did not crack it, but got off it very quickly. He seemed very tense, obviously not himself, and departed hurriedly.

After the audition, Rolandi and Epstein left, but Pearlman lingered to ask, "Do you have any questions?"

"No; it all speaks for itself, doesn't it?" Michel replied affably as he gathered up his papers. Such said nothing.

When I found myself alone with Pearlman, I asked him what he thought had happened to Honeywell. Pearlman told me he was planning to meet with him. "He was trying to manipulate his voice," he said. "He's got to open it up and sing." Pearlman likes to stress with his singers what he calls the "Zen-like art of doing nothing," which can be interpreted to mean relaxing, letting the voice flow on the foundation of a solid technique. "I'm confident Roger will get it," he said, "because he's a very intelligent guy. And also he has this vast background and training as a stage actor."

MASTERING A SOLID TECHNIQUE and going beyond it is what only the best opera singers are capable of doing on a regular basis. This point was rammed home to me at the master class given by Jane Eaglen in early December in Room 200. In addition to staff and the LOCAA singers scheduled to perform, there was a small invited audience of about fifty people, who had earned the right to sit in by having contributed a minimum of $7,500 to Lyric that year. Everybody sat on folding chairs, with Eaglen to the right of the piano, where the indefatigable Eric Weimer perched, waiting. After Pearlman had introduced her, Eaglen rose to her feet to address the audience.

To say that Eaglen was a large woman would be an understatement. She is huge, a classic example of the popular perception of a Wagnerian opera singer, the proverbial "fat lady." But she is not so much fat as solid. She is also graceful and womanly, with a round, beautiful face framed by short, dark hair. When she moves, it's with the elegance of a clipper ship under sail. During the last act of *Siegfried* she had chosen pretty much to sit or stand still, which was probably a better idea than trying for a series of passionate embraces with the hero, also a sturdily built citizen. Wagner requires big voices, and big voices require big jaws and big bodies with the strength to support the outpouring of sound demanded. The new trend in opera these days is to give preference to singers whose voices may not be quite up to what their roles call for, but who at least look the part. This is not possible in Wagner, where disbelief often simply has to be suspended in order to put on the work at all. In the opera house, amplification is a no-no, so sometimes, if you've been corrupted by Hollywood, closing your eyes in certain sections may be your only recourse. What Eaglen accomplishes every time she sings is a rich, flowing, dramatic soprano sound that exactly conveys the appropriate emotion, delivered with phenomenal breath control and perfect diction.

She began the class unpromisingly by saying, "I really, really disapprove of master classes. It's very important to remember that in half an hour with a student you can only do so much." Having thus poured a little cold water on the proceedings, she listened to four of the Opera Center singers—Erin Wall, Quinn Kelsey, Lauren McNeese and Nicole Cabell.

Wall led off with the *Arabella,* which I thought she sang more impressively than she had five days earlier, and drew a healthy round of applause. Eaglen rose majestically to her feet and walked up to Wall to demonstrate several key points. Like Rolandi in her coaching sessions, who stresses the tube, Eaglen urged Wall to concentrate on what she defined as "the column" of air flowing up from her diaphragm. She talked to her about posture, about not overdoing the chest, the lower notes that can be quite dangerous. She complimented her on her beautiful top but warned her about spreading it, then stressed the importance of every single note. Also like Rolandi, she made an inverted *L* with her right arm and hand to make sure Wall could visualize what she meant by breath support. Her pupil responded cheerfully to all these pointers, bobbing her head in assent, smiling, laughing, clapping her hands in pleasure—then sang the piece through again, better than before. "It's beautiful," Eaglen told her. "Thank you."

When Kelsey delivered Valentin's aria, Eaglen was temporarily rendered speechless, then said, "Beautiful, beautiful." Her basic advice to him was to relax, so that when he went up for the climactic high G he'd have such control that the muscles would be totally committed. On his second rendition of the piece, she urged him to open it up more, to be more legato in his phrasing, to think of it as a large elastic band he was stretching. After his second run-through, she commented, "I really hate to say anything about this, it's so beautiful," but she again emphasized breath control, the key to all good singing.

Lauren McNeese, wearing black slacks and a white turtleneck sweater, her blond hair flowing free, seemed to bound through her selection, the rondo "Nacqui all'affanno," from Rossini's *La Cenerentola,* one of those fiendishly demanding bravura arias, with cascades of coloratura and trills up and down the scale, that are this composer's specialty. McNeese's rendition of it was a testament to all the hard work she had put in with Rolandi over the past two years. Eaglen complimented her, but suggested she not move around so much. "You need the support," she said. "You have to keep thinking all the time about keeping anchored. It takes a lot of strength to sing coloratura." She told McNeese to relax her jaw more, to think of the vowels as being a little bit smaller in the runs. "Trills," she added, "are a weird thing," then showed McNeese how to start one and get into it. Eaglen's voice effortlessly filled the room. "You have to have confidence and the courage to believe in what you are doing," she resumed. "The more you practice it on your own, the easier it becomes to do it in public, in front of three thousand people." McNeese now knocked off a trill of her own that brought spontaneous applause from the audience, then told Eaglen she found it very hard to stand still while singing this particular piece. "Fine," Eaglen said. "It's okay to move, as long as the body isn't being used to make you do the wrong thing. And keep the vowels narrower." She smiled. "Fabulous, fabulous," she added.

Eaglen gave much the same advice to Nicole Cabell after the latter's rendition of "Signore, ascolta," from *Turandot,* a typically melodic Puccini aria that demands careful phrasing and the grace and feeling I had already decided were Cabell's great strengths. When she sang it through a second time for us, Eaglen said, "That was totally right. Did that feel good?" Cabell smiled and nodded, then, at Eaglen's suggestion, again sang the closing measures, which call for a soft attack, followed by a swelling of the sound, then a diminuendo on the last soaring high note. "That was a beautiful piano," Eaglen said. "Stunning. Keep it at this level. You'll never lose it. Keep rethinking that the sound is never going to stop."

After the young singers had returned to their seats, Eaglen spoke to them in general terms about their whole approach to singing well. "Trust is a big part of it," she said. "If something seems easy, sometimes you should just trust it."

Fear and Trembling

URING MY BRIEF CAREER as an aspiring opera singer, when I thought I still had a shot at La Scala and the Met, auditions were what I feared most. The stage fright I always experienced before going on in an actual performance was nothing compared to the panic I endured when I had to sing for impresarios, directors and producers. My legs shook, my hands trembled, and usually I had to steady myself by gripping the open lid or a corner of the piano with one hand until after the first few phrases or until I was safely past the first high note. I exemplified what Richard Pearlman calls "the white-knuckle audition." During the winter and spring of 1950–1951, when I was living in Milan and trying to get jobs by singing for the impresarios who were then putting together seasons of opera in the provinces or organizing touring companies, I experienced one humiliating episode after another. Usually I was simply dismissed without any explanation, but once I was actually offered an Alfredo in three performances of a *Traviata,* to be put on in a small town somewhere in the south. The impresario was another in the ranks of the fat old men in dark suits who seemed to have a corner on this market. They all hung around a particular café across the piazza from La Scala. Of course, he informed me, I would be expected to pay him a retainer, which, it turned out, would eat up 80 percent of the fee I would be paid.

My only successful audition that year was for a big, splashy, old-fashioned musical revue called *Black and White,* in which I was hired to be the boy singer. I had two numbers of my own to perform, neither of them even faintly operatic, and in several scenes and both the finales I sang and danced with the chorus girls, an imported group of lovelies from England called Les Bluebell Follies. We played nine performances a week at the new Teatro Manzoni in Milan, with no days off. I had no understudy and caught a cold two weeks into the run, but went right on performing until I lost my voice completely and had to leave the show. It was eight months before I could sing again, and the experience effectively ended my professional career. The Teatro Manzoni was on the Via Manzoni, only several blocks away from Piazza della Scala but about as far away, figuratively, as it could have been from where I had hoped to be singing.

When I came back to New York and began to have a career as a journalist, with my operatic ambitions largely discarded except as an avocation, I no longer felt the same fear I'd experienced when I dreamed of becoming another Tito Schipa or Beniamino Gigli, the two Italian tenors I admired the most. Nervous before I had to go on, yes, always, but in a state of trembling panic, no. But now, in Chicago, as I followed day by day the challenges these young singers in the Opera Center had to face, I found myself almost overwhelmed by their courage and professionalism. And of all the challenges they faced, auditions were the toughest.

Not only were they being asked to sing in the Lyric rehearsal studios for the operatic eminences passing through during the season, but sometimes they had to show up at other venues. On November 11, two days after the audition for Michel and Such, they were asked to go the Chicago Music Mart downtown to sing for the Glimmerglass Opera, which puts on a well-regarded summer season in Cooperstown, New York, and whose artistic director, Paul Kellogg, also runs the New York City Opera. These outside auditions are doubly tough, because the artists are unfamiliar with the premises and may not be accompanied by anyone they've ever worked with before. Glimmerglass had scheduled the six LOCAA singers to show up between 4:10 P.M. and 5:00, allotting ten minutes for each of them to sing two arias. They ran them in and out of the room as if on an assembly line, but the procedure was nothing new to any of them. They all commented that at least the Glimmerglass people were nice to them, unlike at other auditions, in which the visiting big shots have been known to be curt, dismissive, even openly rude. Furthermore, the growing use of laptops is difficult for the singers to adjust to, since often the auditioners will hunch over their machines, typing in comments and rarely looking up at the artists.

Auditions, Pearlman feels, are a cumulative thing. Opera company representatives and managers looking for singers may hear them a number of times over a period of several years. Thus they can note how singers are developing or failing to develop. There are now so many would-be performers out there that the competition for jobs and representation can be intense, especially for lyric sopranos and baritones, the two most common voice categories. To make an immediate impression it helps to have an instrument in your throat that can clearly overwhelm an audience, as in the case of Quinn Kelsey, who already reportedly had four managers in hot pursuit of him. Every time he opened his mouth, whether in a studio or on the stage, I knew I was in the presence of a young artist with the potential for a grand career.

Most singers, however, don't have that advantage. Their voices may be beautiful and well trained, but they will have to compete very hard to make careers for themselves. "These are the ones we see year after year," Gianna Rolandi told me, or at least until Pearlman informs them politely that it will no longer be necessary for them to audition again. Both Wayne Tigges and Lauren McNeese had done themselves proud by stepping with very little onstage preparation into major parts in the *Figaro* and had been well received and reviewed, but neither had been immediately snatched up by an agent as a result. This was partly because there aren't that many good managers out there. The largest and most powerful is CAMI, and then there are a host of smaller agencies and independents, some of which are unscrupulous, if not outright crooked, and who demand retainers from singers in order to represent them. Normally agents earn 10 percent from an opera fee; 15 percent from a recital, usually held in a small hall; and 20 percent from a full-scale concert performance in a major venue or an outdoor facility. Out of what they earn, singers are expected to pay their accompanists and all relevant expenses. Then there are taxes withheld from their paychecks. The really crooked agents will also charge singers a fee for a so-called "evaluation."

Because he has to hear so many people every year, Pearlman uses a laptop; he's a touch typist and can do what he needs to do and still concentrate on the performer. He brings up on the screen all the information he has on the artist, then retrieves an audition form he's devised to evaluate him. The form lists the name of the singer and various estimates of his skills, such as voice classification, technique, intonation, musical expression, quality, range, projection and command of musical style. A separate category concerns diction in English, Italian, French and German. Expression of text is important, as are acting ability, poise and charisma. And, of course, there's a final line for general comments. Because his computer is what is called a docking laptop, Pearlman can plug it into the mainframe at LOCAA and ground himself on where he thinks the singer is as far as his progress is concerned. He can also generate appropriate form letters to notify singers of their status. "I try to make them as encouraging as possible," he said, "even the most negative ones."

As typical of the sort of thing that can happen, Pearlman cited the case of a young tenor who had a beautiful natural voice but wasn't far enough along to qualify for admission into the Opera Center program. "Unfortunately, he changed teachers, got worse and worse, and now he's a mess." Through the use of his laptop Pearlman can bring himself up-to-date on singers he's heard before and judge whether they're improving, spinning their wheels or deteriorating. "Then the ultimate rejection letter I send out," he said, "thanks the singer, but also makes it clear there is no need for him to be heard again."

Sometimes the outcome of Pearlman's persistence and meticulous record-keeping pays off, as in the case of Erica Strauss, a soprano with a big dramatic sound whom he first heard in 2001. In 2003 and 2004 she was a regional finalist in the Met auditions, but was admitted into the LOCAA ensemble for the 2004–2005 season. "She's a real New Yorker, in her mid-twenties, who still lives with her parents, in Queens," Pearlman told me. "She's worked like a dog and is obviously a person who knows how to work. Personally, she moves me very deeply. She has that extra intangible quality that makes an artist."

Pearlman also likes to point out that there are still people in the United States who are first-generation Americans, the children of immigrants, whose parents instill in them the importance of working hard and being grateful to be in the States, which is not typical of the younger American generation, which tends to take everything for granted. Still, wherever they may come from and whatever their backgrounds, every young singer deserves respect, Perlman feels. "I cannot leave my personal ethics at the door," he explained. "This is very personal, because it may affect a person's whole life. I give each one of them the same attention they would get if they were singing at La Scala. Even though sometimes, at certain auditions, I have to bite my lip."

With Roger Honeywell about to depart for Houston the Friday after his poor audition for Michel and Such, Pearlman asked for a session with him to help get him ready. David Gockley, the innovative and adventurous general director of the Houston Grand Opera, was looking for a Don José in *Carmen* and a Pinkerton in

Butterfly, so here was an opportunity for Honeywell to really launch his professional career. The audition would almost certainly be held on the main stage, which would work to Honeywell's advantage because of his imposing physical presence. Now, inside one of the smaller rooms on the fifth floor of Lyric, he planted himself beside the piano and launched into the *Macbeth* aria, with Pearlman and me seated across from him and Bill Billingham, one of Lyric's top accompanists, at the keyboard. The sound Honeywell made was huge, but sharp; he was pushing and was clearly aware of it.

"Separate the phrases; you might get off to a better start," Pearlman advised, while also declaring that Honeywell's presentation was "a hundred percent better" than at the Sunday audition. He gently pointed out that the tenor had a tendency to move his arms in a sort of swimming motion as he sang and he urged him to try to relax. He suggested that Honeywell sing the *Butterfly* before the *Carmen,* which is what he now did. "That was very good," Pearlman said after the Puccini, "the best I've ever heard you do it. They'll also probably give you a break between the arias, so you can get a drink of water, if you need it."

Honeywell's *Carmen* still sounded forced, with a quick cutoff on the first top note. "It's a little abrupt," Pearlman said. "I think you cheat yourself a bit. It sounds like you're pushing ahead so fast that you don't have time to get a breath." Again he stressed the need for the tenor to achieve a "Zen-like state." It would pay off on the climactic B-flat, that note not even Caruso could handle in his early days.

Honeywell was planning to show up in Houston prepared to sing any one of the five selections in his audition repertory, which included Tom Rakewell's aria from *The Rake's Progress,* Stravinsky at his most demanding, with cascades of words and leaps of tessitura. Twice Honeywell now attempted it, but couldn't manage to finish. "They'd better not ask for this one," he said.

"Cop an attitude," Pearlman advised him, after Honeywell sang the *Onegin* without strain, sounding at last just fine and in control of his technique. "If you make the most beautiful sound you can make, all that other stuff—being artistic . . . you're not going to have any trouble." At the end of the session, he added, "You're going to ace it."

Honeywell grinned. "If I don't get a cold on the airplane and it doesn't hit an oil well."

I found myself wondering about Honeywell, actually worrying about him. So much for him hinged on what would be happening in these auditions and during the rest of the season, in which he'd be singing Frederic, the tenor lead in *The Pirates of Penzance*. Born and raised in Toronto the youngest of five children, he came from a musical background. His father taught music and played in a touring Dixieland jazz band. His mother was a mezzo-soprano who sang professionally for years, including several appearances with Robert Goulet, the dashing baritone best known to American audiences for his starring role in the musical *Camelot*. Eventually, having to raise five children took her out of her career. Young Roger went right into the performing arts. "I loved role-playing," he told me. "I saw *Jesus Christ Superstar* and it blew me away. I had no interest in opera at that point. I just wanted to act."

He studied dramatic arts for three years, then at the age of twenty was taken on as an apprentice at the Stratford Festival of Canada, where he remained for four seasons and met his wife, actress Ann Baggley, during a production of Thornton Wilder's *Our Town*. After five more years playing all sorts of stage parts, he more or less chanced into being cast as the lead in a musical in which he had to sing a leading tenor part eight shows a week. "That was very successful for me," he recalled. "I won a lot of awards and now I also knew I wanted to sing. I wanted to sing opera but I had no idea how to do it." He looked up Joan Dornemann in New

York and flew down two or three times a week to work with her, while still doing theater and recording voiceovers to make a living. Then he was cast as Jonathan Harker in a musical version of *Dracula* at Stratford, "where they pay really well and I could save some money."

When he heard that Canadian Opera was auditioning for a young singers program, he worked up five arias, including such demanding ones as "Donna non vidi mai" from Puccini's *Manon Lescaut* and Verdi's "Celeste Aida," one of those arias not even most of the very best dramatic tenors can sing exactly as the composer wanted it to be sung. He'd gone to the audition totally on spec, having come across a flyer for it, so he went, sang and then began working with a highly regarded voice teacher named Marlena Malas. She steered him into the Chautauqua, New York, summer opera season of 2000, where Pearlman first came across him. "A bunch of us came out of that program—Quinn, Nicole, others." He auditioned for the Opera Center in 2001 and joined it a year later. What he lacked in experience as a singer of lyric drama was partly offset by his theatrical background, because he had worked with some very great stage directors—John Wood, Michael Langham, Robin Phillips, Neil Monro—and had performed onstage with some of the finest classical actors of the day. Nevertheless, the adjustment to the demands of the Opera Center program was daunting. "How much I didn't know was what hit me when I came in here," he told me. "But I'm very lucky. I was given this talent and I love just opening up and letting it fly, which, however, wouldn't get me far. With singing you can mess up your brain so much it can really screw you up. You forget sometimes about the joy and exaltation that comes of making the sound." He had a lot at stake, more than the other young singers in the program, not only because at thirty-six he was older than they, but also because he and his wife were raising two young children, two years and nine months old, whose pictures he kept posted on the wall of his bin in the LOCAA common room.

BEFORE LEAVING FOR HOUSTON, Honeywell had one more coaching session, this one with Gianna Rolandi in The Cell. Dressed in light green corduroy pants and a gray short-sleeved sweatshirt, he came bouncing into the room, evidently brimming with confidence and cheer. He told Rolandi he hadn't slept much the night before but had been awakened to an e-mail informing him that he'd been engaged by the Cincinnati Opera for the leading tenor role of Laca in a forthcoming production of Janáček's *Jenůfa,* one of those lyric dramas adored by the cognoscenti but still almost unknown to the general public. Still elated by the news, he now launched into the program he'd been preparing for Houston.

He sang the *Macbeth* with his usual verve, but without much subtlety, then attacked the *Carmen* and encountered his usual problems, beginning with the first high note, that troubling A-flat. Rolandi bounded to her feet to work him through the piece phrase by phrase. She told him to focus his voice more, made him hold the tip of his nose as he sang. "You're making it harder than it is," she said.

"I'm getting caught in the nasal," he told her.

"You never actually sing the French nasal sound," she explained. "It has to be more of an 'uh' sound than a true nasal."

The tenor was very quick to pick up on her suggestions and often appeared to be thinking ahead of what she told him. When he sang these phrases a second time, the vocal line sounded easier, purer, with no sign of strain. "That's beautiful, Roger," Rolandi said. "You hear the difference? You don't need to make everything that big. Sometimes, if you try for more of a *tenorino* sound, it will work for you."

When Honeywell tackled the *Butterfly,* however, his voice again sounded huge and he was belting every note. "It's got to be sweet, Roger," Rolandi declared, "a real Italian sound."

"Yeah, yeah, okay," Honeywell answered, a little impatiently, as if he'd been anticipating corrections. When he moved on to the *Onegin,* he experienced some language difficulties, which is not uncommon for Americans dealing with nasal and tongue-twisting Russian texts. Rolandi persistently coached him through them, her patter remaining resolutely supportive. At the end of the aria, she said, "That's beautiful, Roger. That's your voice. It's come so far in the last few weeks."

Before the end of the session, Honeywell sang a section of the second-act love duet from *Pirates,* in which Frederic delivers a soaring melodic line climaxing on a high G that demands a controlled mezza voce, a sweet and soft sound. He got it, but not easily, and at one point he seemed to be crooning on a falsetto rather than supporting the note with his diaphragm. When he tried it a second time, he was again pushing, and it was too loud.

When the session was over, I lingered in the room long enough to ask Rolandi what she thought. She indicated that she was troubled, but she was sure Roger would get there. He was too much of a worker and an artist to fail. As for me, I had reservations. I'd sung Frederic many times and I knew from experience how tough it was to sing that duet. And then I thought about all the other vocal problems Honeywell was having to deal with, as well as all the pressure he was probably under, both financial and professional, as he was attempting to launch a successful career. Maybe, however, he'd bear in mind what Pearlman always stressed in advising about auditions. "Don't audition," he liked to tell his singers. "Just perform."

That Friday, Honeywell flew to Houston to sing. I never found out exactly what happened there, but the report I received was that the audition had not been a success. I began to believe that Honeywell might not be able to handle *Pirates,* which was scheduled to open on February 2 and would soon be going into rehearsal.

12

Waiting in the Wings

*T*HE REHEARSALS for *Samson et Dalila,* which began in early November, seemed to drag on forever for the three young LOCAA singers involved in them. Scott Ramsay was cast as the Philistine Messenger, Patrick Miller and Christopher Dickerson as the First and Second Philistines, respectively. These were not roles that would catapult them to instant fame. Attired in the colorful and fanciful costumes designed by Carrie Robbins—originated for a production in San Francisco and last seen in 2002 at the Houston Grand Opera—they basically did little more than stand around to sing the few phrases the composer, Camille Saint-Saëns, had allotted to them. Nor was there much that stage director Sandra Bernhard could do to liven things up. *Samson* was originally intended to be an oratorio, and its first act is pretty much a tableau in which everyone just stands around and sings. By the time Samson pulls the temple down around his ears in the last scene, killing everyone onstage, matters have become a lot livelier, but the opera still comes across as static. What redeems it and keeps it in the international rep is some gorgeous choral music and the three stunningly beautiful arias Saint-Saëns composed for a world-class mezzo-soprano. The role of Samson requires a powerful dramatic tenor, but his one impressive aria, "Vois ma misère, hélas!" is sung while Samson is languishing blinded in a cell and, in this case, chained to an enormous millstone. It's the mezzo's opera.

What became onerous for the young singers involved in this production was the fact that neither of the principals, mezzo-soprano Olga Borodina and tenor José Cura, bothered to show up for rehearsals. They had sung the opera together a number of times and had also recently recorded it. Because they already knew their moves, had become familiar with each other's needs and had worked with Bernhard in San Francisco in this traditional staging of the piece, they saw no need to appear much before the dress rehearsal, scheduled two days in advance of the opening night, Saturday, December 13. The result was that the rest of the cast in the smaller parts would be compelled to repeat over and over moves they'd already mastered in the early going. The Opera Center kids had so much else occurring in their lives at that point, between auditions, coaching sessions and rehearsals for the rest of the season, that the itsy-bitsy doings of the Philistines became a chore.

The one young artist who did benefit enormously from the absence of the principals was Guang Yang, who was understudying the role of Dalila. Because of Borodina's absence, Yang was required to fill in for her in all the staging and musical rehearsals. I already knew she was a tremendous talent, but I hadn't quite realized, until I heard her in a run-through, what a powerhouse she could be onstage. This role of the Biblical temptress with the soul of a Mafia hit man fitted her talent like a wreath of roses around the neck of a Derby winner.

I first heard her sing in a sixth-floor rehearsal room, where she was running through Dalila's music for Gianna Rolandi, with Eric Weimer his usual assured and elegant self at the piano. Yang has the perfect physique for a dramatic singer. She's a solidly built woman with a broad, round face; white, even teeth; black hair and beautiful dark eyes. She was wearing a light tan sweater, corduroy pants and loafers and had on glasses to read the score, which was propped on a stand in front of her. Her feet planted firmly on the floor, she began by singing Dalila's opening aria,

"Printemps qui commence," in a flowing lyric line that was rock-solid from top to bottom. It was also amazingly full, warm and mellow, meltingly lovely. When she finished, we all just sat there. "I have almost nothing to say," Rolandi finally declared. "I haven't anything to say I haven't said before," Weimer added, then told Yang the first part of the aria was dragging a bit. To show what he meant, he sang through the line himself, bouncing it a bit more. When Yang sang it through a second time, she held one high note an extra beat. "Don't worry, you're going to be heard," Rolandi told her. "And don't put any extra pressure on the low notes. You have great chest tones."

Guang Yang's story is a remarkable one. She was born and raised in Beijing, China, and though she studied languages in school, she didn't begin speaking English until the late nineties. Her parents were both doctors who had survived the Cultural Revolution, when the Communist government cracked down on anything smacking of suspected bourgeois values, and no one in her family had ever had anything to do with music. But even as a baby, Guang was responding to music and was singing at the age of twenty months. "I think I picked up music by my ears," she recalled. "My mother must have heard something wonderful when she was pregnant." Yang heard her first Western opera when she was nineteen and fell in love with it. "I didn't know what that was about, how a human voice could be that beautiful."

After hearing a Joan Sutherland recording, she decided that was what she wanted to be. She found a teacher to vocalize with, then at the age of twenty entered the Conservatory of Music in Beijing. "It was a big shock," she remembered. "All the other students had had at least two or three years' experience. I was one of only two or three who were completely from another world." The school accepted an average of ten new students a year, but only a few were expected ultimately to have real careers. Yang's first teacher told her she had a very beautiful instrument, but that from the first day she would have to work very hard, to treat her time there like a full-time job. "Once you take it," her professor said, "there's no way for you to go back. It's going to be very hard, especially in your case."

She threw herself into the training, while living with the other students, as required, at the conservatory. "I became famous for hard work," she said. "Every time I was tired, an alarm bell would ring inside me: 'Hey, you can't stop, you have to catch up!' " She remained at the school for five years, sharing a room with four other students. Her teacher made her study a repertory that no one else was doing, and even on vacations Yang continued to work, because "it was not a good idea to take a two-month break. I was always the first one in the practice room and the last to leave."

She met her husband, Xiuzhi, there. He was a bass, but he immediately gave up singing to concentrate totally on her career, "which," she said, "made me a little bit scared." They were not allowed to get married while still in school, but did so as soon as she had graduated. "I'm lucky," she said. "I have this man with me everywhere." When she got permission to come to America, Yang was able to pick up a little foundation money, but it's her husband she credits for the help she received. "His support is not about money," she explained. "He cares about my singing." While they were in New York, Xiuzhi was summoned back to China and they were separated for some months, until he was able to convince the Chinese authorities that he was not a defector or a spy and was allowed to return. "Now he's studying traditional Chinese medicine and has found something of his own to be enthusiastic about," she said. "He loves it, and I'm so happy for him."

Guang Yang's first move in America was to enroll at Juilliard, but the experience proved to be pretty much a disaster. For one thing she couldn't yet speak English, which blocked her from studying acting with Frank Corsaro, who was teaching there that

year. He told her he couldn't take her on if she couldn't understand him. She had to use sign language to make herself understood, but was able to study with mezzo Cynthia Hoffmann, who
at least taught her how to use her body in the proper way.

By studying with her usual concentrated ferocity, Yang
learned not only to speak English but also to sing convincingly in
the other main operatic languages. She began to audition success-
fully for major roles in major opera houses and won two of the
most prestigious competitions in the world, the BBC Singer of the
World Competition, in Cardiff, Wales, in 1997, and Plácido
Domingo's Operalia, in Los Angeles, four years later. She sang for
Pearlman in the summer of 2001 in Santa Barbara, where she had
gone to work with Marilyn Horne, whom she now considered her
mentor and with whom she was in constant touch by e-mail. It
was Horne who steered her toward the Opera Center, to which
Yang, now a second-year member, soon felt totally committed.
The conservatory and Juilliard—that was student work. "They
say to you, 'No, no, you can't do that.' They want you to be good,
but they are too protective, they don't want you to take risks."

Guang Yang takes risks. In the middle of the Lyric season,
with all the rehearsals, auditions and coaching sessions in full
swing, she found time to fly overnight to Cardiff to audition for
the role of Princess Eboli in Verdi's *Don Carlo,* one of the big dramatic parts that demands the very best from the few mezzos
around who can do it justice, and was cast in it for the Welsh National Opera season of 2005. I asked her one day if she would ever
sing in China. She saw no reason why not, because Western opera
had become very popular there ever since the Three Tenors concert in Beijing. Despite the fact that tickets to it had cost the
equivalent of $1,200 apiece, it had sold out. One of Yang's friends
had told her parents that he'd bought a ticket, but hadn't been
able to see the stage clearly. "My daughter will come back," her
father told him, "and you'll be able to see her clearly."

OLGA BORODINA AND JOSÉ CURA did not arrive for the *Samson* rehearsals until the Friday and Saturday, respectively, before the premiere. I dropped in for their first rehearsal together to find the whole company onstage in full costume and makeup for act one, pretty much running through it for the umpteenth time under the supervision of Sandra Bernhard. Both Borodina and Cura were marking through their parts, but only the mezzo made any attempt at a characterization. When not singing, Cura seemed to be paying little attention to what anybody else was doing, but was indulging himself in little bits of stage business designed to call attention his way. Nobody seemed to mind, because, after all, Cura has become a sacred monster, at least in his own mind.

I first heard him in 1996, when he sang the role of Pollione in *Norma* opposite Jane Eaglen in Los Angeles. I was enormously impressed. Apart from an opening short aria that includes a sudden launch into the stratosphere on one note, a C, which Cura did not attempt—most tenors don't—the part calls for a big dramatic voice with a powerful middle range. Nor is it a very rewarding one, because the opera is a vehicle for a true diva, such as Eaglen or Callas or Caballé, and has an almost equally strong part for a strong mezzo-soprano. It's their music upon which the success of the piece depends, and dramatically Pollione comes across as a cheating churl who ignores his two young children and fails to realize until the very end of the drama what a great woman he has betrayed. Nevertheless, as an ex-tenor I found myself mesmerized by Cura, who, I'd been told, had been a protégé of Domingo's.

Born in Argentina in 1962, Cura began in music by studying classical guitar, became a choral director at fifteen, then studied composition and piano. He began singing in the chorus of the Teatro Colón in Buenos Aires and eventually moved to Italy in 1991 to study voice. Within two years he was singing major roles.

He first showed up in Chicago in November 1994, in Umberto Giordano's *Fedora,* a lush, romantic potboiler that includes perhaps the most lyrical of all this composer's melodies, the aria "Amor ti vieta," a piece absolutely guaranteed to bring down the house. By the time I heard him in *Norma,* Cura was already an established international star, a stature abetted by his brooding good looks, height and stalwart physique. He looked every inch the part of the romantic hero. As Pollione he was a dark, commanding presence, a portrait of the ruthless Roman soldier with the libido of a basketball star. Furthermore, though his voice was not particularly beautiful, it was powerful, with ringing top notes that caused jaws to drop.

Since then I'd become a little less enamored of him. I'd bought two of his operatic CDs and found them wanting, mainly because he sang the Puccini and verismo arias in them always fortissimo, without much grace or style. There is no denying, however, that on the operatic scene he's a force to be reckoned with and he knows it. Because he can sing the most demanding roles in the tenor repertory, especially Otello in Verdi's masterpiece, he gets to perform pretty much where he wants to. Five years before the *Samson* rehearsals, dissatisfied with the way his career was being handled, he fired his management team and formed another one answerable only to him. He does not see himself as the logical successor to the Three Tenors, but in a category all his own. "I couldn't walk in those shoes," he told a reporter for the *Chicago Sun-Times,* "so I removed them urgently." He also described himself to the reporter as "an eternal pain in the ass," because he didn't want to fit into what he saw as a preordained hierarchical world of opera ruled over by the demands and preconceptions of managers and general directors.

He also makes it clear that he has a limited tolerance for interviewers and photographers, which is perfectly understandable. In any case, he could pretty much do what he wanted, because he now had all the engagements he could handle and had developed a huge following of fans who could and did log on frequently to his adulatory Web site. Before he arrived in Chicago, someone in the tenor's entourage sent the Lyric management a memo informing everyone that the star should be addressed as Maestro Cura, in recognition of the fact that he is also a composer and a conductor. This aroused some mirth backstage, since all the Rehearsal Department schedules and dressing room assignments refer to cast members formally by their last names, but never as "maestro," a term always reserved for the conductor of the evening and for Sir Andrew Davis. To avoid confusion and controversy, one of the LOCAA singers suggested that everyone now be addressed as "maestro," so that no performer would feel demeaned by being categorized simply as a lowly troubadour. When Cura showed up, no one paid the slightest attention to his management's request, which at least indicated that he had not yet quite arrived at the status of sacred monster, one so exalted and powerful that he can bend management to his will.

Olga Borodina does not fancy herself anything but a singer, and she is a very great one, the possessor of a large, creamy sound many fans consider the most beautiful in all of opera. Offstage, she passes for a pleasant-looking middle-aged housewife, but onstage she is glamorous and dominant, in total control of her vocal resources. Not outstanding as an interpreter, she does admirably because of her command of what the critic for *Opera* called "her plushly sensuous vocalism." All during the few rehearsals she attended, she was thoroughly professional and unassuming, always the diva but never the monster.

On the opening night of *Samson,* however, she did cause the only crisis of the production. A couple of hours before curtain she informed the Rehearsal Department that she wasn't feeling well and wasn't sure she'd be able to go on. Guang Yang was told to get into full costume and makeup and be ready to sing. Borodina showed up backstage, still unsure, however, whether she'd risk performing. She refused to commit herself until it was almost curtain time. Jack Zimmerman, attired in his usual dark suit and conservative tie, hovered in the wings, ready to stride out onstage to deliver his message of gloom and doom. He'd already had one trial by fire this season when John Treleaven, suffering from a bad chest cold, had been forced to cancel his Siegfried over Thanksgiving weekend, allowing his cover, Mark Lundberg, to step in. At that same performance, Zimmerman had been forced to reappear before the curtain for the third act to announce that Eaglen also had a cold, which elicited a chorus of groans from the audience. "Nevertheless," Zimmerman had quickly added, much to the paying public's relief, Miss Eaglen would carry on and do her best. *Nevertheless,* Zimmerman had earlier confided to me, had become his favorite word, because at least it reassured the audience rather than dismayed it.

As Chicago's frigid winter weather sets in, people inevitably start getting sick. Not only principal singers come down with colds and the flu, but also chorus members and backstage crew. As for the orchestra members, if one of them gets sick, the bug is passed around the pit, as if they were sitting in an airplane with poor air circulation. The travails of sudden illnesses are most evident in the Rehearsal Department, where Josie Campbell, Marina Vecci and their staff have to cope hour by hour with the status of the performers. The only people who may benefit from sudden cancellations are the Opera Center artists, who can thus suddenly get a chance, as did McNeese and Tigges, to step into a major role.

Every night of the run of *Samson,* which was favorably reviewed and sold out its run of nine performances, Borodina declared herself doubtful about being able to sing, and Guang Yang suited up in full costume and makeup, just in case. She was emotionally poised to meet the challenge like a high diver ready to soar into the void. Dalila is one of those parts that can make a career overnight. Borodina, however, is the sort of artist who thrives on backstage drama and needs desperately to be needed. She arrived backstage every night wheezing and complaining, but never failed to go on, and sang with no trace of difficulty.

As for Cura, he proved to be a very believable Samson, though his voice struck me as lacking in that excitement I'd felt when I first heard him. True dramatic tenors who can handle the killer roles are a rarity, and even a merely competent one, especially with the physical stature and good looks of José Cura, will always be in demand all over the world. But the kind of stardom that has been achieved only by the very greatest of them—Domingo, Caruso, Vickers, Melchior, Pertile, Corelli, Del Monaco, Tamagno and maybe a couple dozen others; the list over a century of singing is relatively short—is an intangible. The public decides who deserves it, not the critics and certainly not the publicity agents.

13

Getting It All

"**O**PERA STARS ARE NOT ordinary people," a female executive at Decca Records, who has worked with many of them, told me in the early summer of 1980. "They are sacred monsters—overgrown, spoiled children who are indulged because they happen to have been born with gold in their throats." She was referring to Luciano Pavarotti, who was then in London recording a complete *La Gioconda* for Decca. "Luciano, at least, knows when he is misbehaving, and he is one of the few who even bothers to say thank you."

Not all great singers are sacred monsters. The category is strictly reserved by tradition for those artists who have the difficult, demanding personalities to inflict their needs and wants upon their colleagues and the hapless managements who hire them. A prime requisite for becoming one is an ability to sell out an opera performance or a concert venue, which makes it almost impossible for anyone to dispense with their talents, even when the caprices and often absurd demands made by them cause vast suffering and exasperation all around them.

Most sacred monsters are the great divas and tenors who throughout the history of opera have captured the fancy of a fanatical public. In Chicago, the first to qualify was Mary Garden, whose outspoken contempt for the philistines who dared to criticize her never failed to make headlines. Others, including Pavarotti himself, followed. Not all were sopranos and tenors, either. There have been great mezzos, baritones and basses who could also throw their weight around. Perhaps the most famous among the basses was Feodor Chaliapin, the magnetic Russian star who was especially celebrated for his tremendous interpretation of the title role in Mussorgsky's *Boris Godunov.* Life around him was one long turmoil, and he even clashed with Arturo Toscanini, one of a handful of great conductors who were also monsters in their own right. Once, when Chaliapin was supposed to be singing at an early-afternoon concert in America and failed to show up, he was tracked down to his hotel room, where he was still in bed. Informed that his public was awaiting him, he bellowed into the telephone receiver that "before three in the afternoon I cannot even spit" and hung up.

My first contact with Pavarotti came in the spring of 1980, when I found myself sitting in the New York office of Herbert Breslin, then the tenor's press agent, manager, promoter and number one fan. Breslin was sitting behind his desk, on the phone with someone in Chicago who was apparently ecstatic over the success the night before of Pavarotti's concert at the Civic Opera House. Tickets for the event had been put on sale two days earlier, at 10:00 A.M., and had all been snapped up by the middle of the afternoon. People had begun to line up at the box office before dawn. Finally, the management had consented to sell another hundred seats on the stage itself, behind the singer and his accompanist. These, too, had been quickly bought. During the concert itself someone in the audience had shouted, "Happy birthday!" and the whole great crowd had then burst into song in the tenor's honor, quite ignoring the fact that his birthday had taken place three days earlier. "It was a love fest," the caller told Breslin, "more like a sports event than a concert."

The notices in the Chicago papers had been equally ecstatic. "Pavarotti holds the stage like a master showman and sings like an anointed angel," wrote the reviewer for the *Tribune,* who also observed that "jubilant applause bordering on rapture followed every selection." "What lies behind this Pavarotti phenomenon?" the critic for the *Sun-Times* asked himself, while pointing out that the singer was admittedly "a tenor of superlative gifts." "It is something simple," the critic concluded. "He projects like a searchlight. And he is all heart. You listen to him and you love him, not because he's handsome (he isn't), or glamorous (no way) or even conventionally sexy, but because he comes before you as a big, open, warm human being and he sings to you, and you feel you must respond."

No one agreed with this assessment of Pavarotti's basic appeal more wholeheartedly than Herbert Breslin. "Luciano is fabulous," he informed me. "He has such an insatiable lust for life, he makes people feel great. He's a big fat guy who gives a lot of hope to people. And he's the only singer I've ever heard in my entire life who says to himself about his audience, 'I'm going to get you people to your feet.' You understand what I mean?"

Breslin was then considered by many to be the guiding genius behind Luciano Pavarotti's extraordinary success, especially in America, but that morning he downgraded his contribution. "I'm the best promotion person in the entire world," he said, "but I don't have to promote Pavarotti. He's the hottest thing I've ever seen. Who is Mister Opera today?"

When Breslin talked about the tenor's career, he could become positively lyrical. A hyperactive, self-styled workaholic, he was then a middle-aged man with thinning gray hair, dark eyebrows and a black Groucho Marx mustache. He had at the time about twenty-five other clients, mostly singers, and operated from a large room on the top floor of an office building directly across the street from Carnegie Hall. Neither the constant interruption of ringing telephones nor the babble of conversation from his three male associates could derail even momentarily his fierce partisanship.

He had other top clients—Bergonzi, Crespin, De Los Angeles, Freni, Rysanek, all opera stars—but none he cared so much about as his "friendly giant." "First we were friends, then I became his press agent, then his manager," he explained. "We didn't discard anything; we just added."

The adding had become an awesome exercise in the arithmetic of success. Although Breslin wouldn't reveal any of his clients' exact earnings, it was generally known that Pavarotti was then receiving fees of between eight and ten thousand dollars for an opera performance, while his recital fee of twenty thousand dollars two years earlier had at least doubled. When the Met season failed to open on time the previous fall, due to a labor dispute with the orchestra, the strike turned into a bonanza for the tenor. Breslin had no trouble at all booking concert dates for his client in Chicago, Buffalo, Norfolk, Virginia—any town able to guarantee the manager forty to fifty thousand dollars for exactly two hours of song. "Anybody who engages Mr. Pavarotti to sing for him is going to make money," Breslin insisted. "Nobody loses money on Luciano Pavarotti." The latest offer on Breslin's desk was for two hundred thousand dollars for a single performance, to be accompanied by a sixty-piece orchestra, in New York's Madison Square Garden, a sports arena that seats twenty thousand.

With almost touching sincerity, however, Breslin averred that commerce was not the bottom line, with him or with Pavarotti. "We are not commercial," he insisted, pointing out that he had recently refused an offer of $250,000 a week in a gaming casino in Atlantic City, New Jersey. "We've also been offered any amount of money for private concerts. You can't buy Luciano Pavarotti easily, unless it's something for the general public."

Breslin's main point seemed to be that Pavarotti, despite his huge popular acclaim, unmatched by any tenor since the era of Enrico Caruso, remained essentially a serious artist whose overriding concern in all he did was to bring people into the opera house. In this endeavor he had been an incredible success. He had replaced the great divas—Callas, Tebaldi, Price, Nilsson, Sutherland, Caballé—as the supreme box office attraction. When the

Metropolitan put on an open-air performance of Verdi's *Rigoletto* in June 1979, in New York's Central Park, the event was attended by a crowd estimated at well over two hundred thousand people. In 1978, Pavarotti's televised solo concert from the stage of the Met was seen by more people than Caruso performed for during his whole career, as was the joint recital Pavarotti gave the following year from Lincoln Center with soprano Joan Sutherland. His six half-hour broadcasts, *Pavarotti at Juilliard,* were among the most popular shows ever aired noncommercially. And wherever he appeared in public, he managed to upstage everyone else, including the president of the United States. During New York's Columbus Day celebration, the tenor, tastefully attired in a broad-brimmed hat, green jerkin and short cape of stars and stripes, descended from horseback at the head of the parade up Fifth Avenue to enfold Jimmy Carter in his arms and quite literally block him from view.

Pavarotti couldn't have accomplished what he has, Breslin and others have maintained, if he were not also a fine artist. "There are no careers in serious music that are made without great talent," Breslin said. "There are no ways to promote lousy talent. You know what I'm saying? Not every great artist has to have Luciano's approach to the public. You've got to get them first with what you can do."

Nevertheless, the phenomenon that became Luciano Pavarotti is worth examining from a sociological point of view, since clearly it transcends all questions of talent. Even Breslin wasn't ready to claim that his client was a greater singer than his chief rival, Plácido Domingo, who also happened to be much better looking and an incomparably finer actor. But what Pavarotti had that no one else could touch was a popular appeal that had broken through the fuzzy but quite real dividing line between mere stardom and the rarefied world of the super-celebrity, a domain usually reserved for movie stars and sports heroes. Every opera singer in the world, including Domingo, would have liked to break through that barrier, but no one else had. And what that break-through did, first and last, was keep the loot flowing in. "All right," Breslin said into the phone to the man in Chicago, "when are we going to get some of that beautiful money from you?" Being a super-celebrity and a sacred monster in America can be a lot of fun, if you can stand the pace and the constant glare of the spotlight on you day and night; it's also, in the immortal words of lyricist Ira Gershwin, "nice work, if you can get it."

I finally got to see Luciano Pavarotti up close that June in the Walthamstow Town Hall, in London, during a recording session of *La Gioconda*. This main assembly hall was much in demand for classical record producers because its acoustics are exceptionally fine. The room is very large, wood-panelled, with a lofty ceiling and a minimum of drapes; it is ideal to sing in. The tenor was dressed in a dark blue three-piece business suit and looked huge, much larger than his six-foot-one-inch height and his listed weight of three hundred pounds. Looking as immovable as Gibraltar, he seemed absolutely impervious to the impending chaos around him.

Before the session started, he remained silent, arms folded, perched on a high stool facing the orchestra, the conductor's podium and a row of tall microphones. On either side were other stools and music stands for the tenor's colleagues—soprano Montserrat Caballé, mezzo Agnes Baltsa, baritone Sherrill Milnes, bass Nicolai Ghiaurov—but only Pavarotti remained in place, placidly waiting. Behind and above him in the balcony sat the chorus. The orchestra members were tuning up and chatting with one another, while all around the room youthful assistants scurried like water bugs on various mysterious little errands. The record producer, the recording engineers and other company min-ions were already hidden from view in a back room, from where they would supervise the piecemeal immortalization on tape of Amilcare Ponchielli's fine old chestnut, always a showpiece for the great singers of any era.

I had arrived late that first day, only a few minutes before the recording got under way. Nevertheless, Pavarotti was the first person I noticed when I walked in, and he remained the focus of everyone's attention, no matter what he was up to. When he rose to sing, he seemed effortlessly to dominate the proceedings in a way none of the other artists did, with the possible exception of Madam Caballé, who was herself an electrifying presence. I thought at once of that now much abused word *charisma.* Some people exude it as naturally as the air they breathe, and it has almost nothing to do with talent, only with the force of personality that talent projects.

Between takes, Pavarotti, accompanied by personal coach and local pilot fish Maestro Antonio Tonini, a slight, gray-haired man in rimless spectacles, would rise and sail ponderously but gracefully into the engineers' quarters, where he and the other artists involved would listen to playbacks of the segments and make comments. Pavarotti was never satisfied. Primarily, he was unhappy with the volume of sound he was producing. "I can't hear myself," he would say. "Is not loud enough."

His objections were politely listened to by the harried producer, a painfully polite senior executive, and occasionally they necessitated another take, but the tenor seemed to know exactly when to back off before anyone's nerves became too frayed. This didn't always happen. "Luciano will ride over anyone who won't stand up to him," a record executive told me later. "But if you do, no matter what sort of tantrums he throws, no matter what sort of scene he creates—and he's created some beauties—he'll respect you. He's walked out of rehearsals and sessions that left blood on the walls, but he's always back the next day as if nothing had happened and always as charming and sweet as ever. The point about most of these people, really, is that they're Frankenstein's monsters. We've created them and now we have to live with them."

My very strong impression over the next few days was that no one had created Luciano Pavarotti but himself. The great Sicilian playwright Luigi Pirandello had a theory that we all to some extent construct ourselves, so as to present to the world that aspect of ourselves we wish the world to mistake for reality. The more time I spent with Pavarotti and the longer I observed him, the more firmly convinced I became that he is a prime example of Pirandello's thesis.

The surface of the man is what we all see: a jolly, amiable giant with an insatiable appetite for all the good things in life—food, drink, family, friends, hobbies, the company of beautiful women—and an absolute dedication to his art. His frequently avowed desire was to maintain the very highest standards of performance and to bring the benefits of good music to an ever wider public, while also helping to sponsor struggling young artists on their way up. That TV series *Pavarotti at Juilliard,* for example, was done for a relatively small fee, and during it he took great care with the young student singers he was coaching. Nathan Kroell, the producer of the program and no admirer of opera singers ("They are mostly stupid"), was impressed. "Luciano proved himself a musician of refinement, which is unusual for tenors," he recalled. "With their high notes they tend to aerate their brains."

The other Pavarotti, the one the public has glimpsed only occasionally beneath the confused uproar that has always constantly surrounded him on and offstage, is far more difficult, contradictory, insecure and, especially recently, hugely self-serving, a much more interesting and complex figure. It was never the one the American public had almost hysterically embraced, but then how could it have been? That public figure was a cardboard cutout, the exact image to Americans of what an Italian opera singer should be, and Pavarotti has played the part to the hilt. It enriched him beyond his fondest dreams of success.

He was born in 1935 and raised in Modena, a small industrial city on the flat, fertile land of the Po Valley. The entire area is noted for its partisan political involvements, first as a Fascist hotbed, then for its radical left-wing leanings; it's also known for its splendid cuisine and its devotion to opera. Luciano's father, Fernando, was a baker and an amateur tenor who sang in a local chorus. The upbringing the boy received was classically petit bourgeois, a weekly routine of school, church, family, friends and familiar traditional obligations. Despite growing up with the sound of opera in the house, from his father's extensive record collection, and with an early enthusiasm for the movies of Mario Lanza, the Hollywood Caruso, Luciano had an overriding passion for sports, especially soccer, the Italian national craze.

His father lured him into his local chorus when Luciano was in his teens. He discovered he had a voice, but took no lessons and studied instead to become an elementary school teacher. At the age of twenty, he went with his father to Llangollen, Wales, where their chorus won an international competition. The acclaim they received excited Luciano, and he returned home determined to become a professional singer. Encouraged by his fiancée, Adua, a strong-minded young woman he had met while training to become a teacher, he took a job selling insurance and began to study, first with a local maestro, then in nearby Mantua with the man who became his most important teacher, Ettore Campogalliani.

At the age of twenty-five he won a vocal competition in Reggio Emilia and, as a reward, was engaged to make his debut locally as Rodolfo in *La Bohème*. He celebrated the occasion by marrying Adua, and then launched himself into the gypsy life of a touring opera singer. He had at the time a sweet, well-focused lyric voice, perfectly suited to the lighter roles in the Italian repertory, but not to his size, which had begun to reflect a prodigious appetite for pasta and pastry.

In 1963, he understudied Giuseppe di Stefano, then in the twilight of his career, in a Covent Garden *La Bohème,* singing the role there several times. He impressed conductor Richard Bonynge, who engaged him to appear opposite his wife, Joan Sutherland, in a Miami production of *Lucia di Lammermoor,* then signed him up for a fourteen-week tour of Australia. The experience proved invaluable to Pavarotti. First of all, he was able to appear opposite the world's leading coloratura soprano and bask in her reflected light. Second, he learned how to breathe properly from her. "I was amazed," he recalled, "by the *line* of her voice, this way she had of producing endless sound." He would put his hands on her waist and feel the workings of her diaphragm muscles as she sang. Eventually, he mastered the technique himself, and almost immediately his voice became richer, stronger, "more projected." Third, unlike most young Italian singers, he had the experience of working closely with responsible musical artists whose first concern was for the music and drama itself, and not merely the vocal pyrotechnics. "Joan Sutherland is the original no-nonsense lady of all time," Sherrill Milnes told me in London. "It couldn't help but rub off on Luciano. When he came back from that tour, he was twice the singer he had been."

As a result, his career almost immediately took off, with engagements at La Scala, in Milan, and most of the world's other major opera houses. His debut at the Metropolitan in 1968, however, was aborted by a bout of Hong Kong flu that caused him to retire partway through his second *La Bohème* there. It wasn't until 1971, in Donizetti's *La Figlia del Reggimento,* again paired with Sutherland, that he exploded into prominence, mostly by hitting a flashy series of nine high Cs during a single aria. Tickets for these performances became very difficult to get and increasingly lucrative offers began pouring in from everywhere. In their wake came Herbert Breslin, a sound enough musician to appreciate the tenor's very real abilities, a shrewd businessman and above all a masterful manipulator of the burgeoning American hype machine.

Until the mid-seventies, Pavarotti was simply another opera star, one of a dozen or so top names in that world, but largely unknown outside it. Then Breslin maneuvered his client onto the

Tonight Show, hosted by Johnny Carson, himself a super-celebrity, and the great American television audience was suddenly introduced to the delightful spectacle of a very large, bearded, toothy Italian who could, first of all, really sing.

Pavarotti made an adventure of the *Tonight Show* appearance. He struck a stance beside the piano, a large white handkerchief clutched firmly in one hand, and hit all these obviously very difficult high notes. The audience knew they were difficult because the cameras moved in for a close-up of the worried features of this Italian as he hit them, sweat pouring down his face. When the song was over, the big man beamed with pleasure, as if surprised by his own achievements, and waddled over to sit beside Mr. Carson to exchange pleasantries and jokes with him and his other guests about his career, his weight and the main topics all Italians are supposed to know about—food, women, weather, clothes and children.

He also spoke in heavily accented, charmingly broken English, obviously had a terrific sense of humor and was properly flirtatious without being dangerous. He was clearly a dedicated family man—he chatted about his wife and three daughters back in his hometown in Italy—despite a twinkly roving eye. (When a handsome woman interviewer once asked him between the acts of a televised opera performance whether it was true that he believed God had kissed his vocal cords at birth, Pavarotti replied that she was luckier than he because obviously God had kissed her all over.) "The only thing he didn't do," one critic commented, "was come out with a hand organ and a monkey on a leash. How could he miss?"

WHAT HAS HAPPENED to Pavarotti since those early glory years and the construction of this overwhelming public personality can be cited today as an object lesson in what can happen to even the most talented young artists who, as they age, begin to slide into sloth and self-indulgence. At first, as a form of flight from the tyranny of constant public exposure and the bone-wearying schedule that kept him on the road for eleven months of the year, Pavarotti cultivated hobbies such as painting, tennis and horseback riding. "Until you are forty," he said, "you fight for yourself. Then you realize that you are a prisoner of the public. It is a pleasurable prison, but there are other things in life."

Those "other things" couldn't supply the heady satisfactions his status conferred, even during his infrequent visits back home, where he moved surrounded always by a retinue of thirty or more people. His mealtimes became as uproarious and confused as sessions of a Latin American parliament. "A month in the country with Luciano Pavarotti is not too different from life backstage at the opera house," an American visitor remarked. "I imagine it's a great relief to everyone when he finally goes back on the road."

Whatever the distractions, Pavarotti for a long time was disciplined at least about his singing. "If you don't practice one day, *you* know it," he said. "If you don't practice two days, the public knows it." To protect his voice he took pills to counteract jet lag and to help him sleep eight to ten hours a day. Like most singers, he was terrified of colds, and traveled with enough vitamin C pills to fill a suitcase. His luggage accommodated changes of clothes for every season as well as his costumes, and his progress through airports has always resembled that of an Arab oil sheik. Everything he did became geared to his personal comfort, which, of course, contributed to keeping him in good voice. He always stayed in the same hotels, where he could be assured of being given a suite not exposed to dangerous drafts. He always insisted on a hard mattress with a board under it, and required management to provide him with a piano.

He used to be fussy about what he sang, even though, unlike Domingo, he was never adventurous in his choice of repertory. He understood his limitations and avoided roles that might shorten his career by straining his resources. His avowed main concern as an artist was to maintain what he called *la linea del bel canto,* a smooth flow of well-focused tone, in the tradition of such past greats as Gigli and di Stefano. He shunned the dramatic parts, such as Manrico in *Il Trovatore* and the one not even Caruso tackled, Verdi's Otello. "I am not Del Monaco or Corelli," Pavarotti declared. "I admire them, but it is not my style."

He has always been accused, however, of being lazy. Again unlike Domingo, he's never been interested in tackling new pieces, probably because he doesn't read music and had to have his notes pounded into him by a small retinue of coaching maestri he kept on tap wherever he was in residence. Apart from purely vocal histrionics, he devoted little attention to dramatic interpretation and strolled amiably through his parts in loose-fitting costumes designed primarily to disguise his bulk. Once, when he appeared onstage at Covent Garden in Verdi's *Luisa Miller* attired in some sort of floor-length poncho and opened his arms to embrace the soprano, someone in the theater shouted, "And God bless all who sail in her!" But the incident didn't mar the performance, since no one expected credibility from him, only beautiful singing, a commodity Pavarotti could then supply in abundance.

Behind this affable, loving front was also a tough, tight-fisted businessman, with a peasant's cunning about money. Like many very rich men, he treated himself always to the best in life but was reluctant to spend lavishly on associates. He traveled almost everywhere accompanied by an entourage of flunkies, as well as by a series of young women who did more than simply wait on him. At the time I met him he was involved with a good-looking young brunette named Madelyn Renee, whom he billed as his protégée and who occasionally sang duets with him in public. He also managed to get her hired to sing a leading role or two late in the run of his appearances for companies so eager to have him commit to them that they would grant him a favor or two. Renee's main visible function in London that year, however, was to be his traveling secretary, dietician and cook.

Despite having become almost indispensable to him, Renee did not board the Concorde or share first-class cabin accommodations with her benefactor, but trailed after him, often as a standby passenger in economy class.

The one area in his life that even in his great years Pavarotti was never able to control was eating. Even with Renee in attendance to watch over him, he managed to snatch bites from passing pastry trays or would suddenly gobble up whatever had been left behind by some less ravenous fellow diner. At Joan Sutherland's fifty-fourth birthday party he was observed wolfing down eighteen pieces of cake. Only Adua could control him—witnesses had actually seen her slap his hand to keep him from raising it to his mouth—but she was increasingly rarely with him. "She's the only one who tells him what he may not want to hear," a recording executive once told me. "When he complains about anything, she can always stop him, even at his loudest. I think he needs her now more than he realizes. He's getting everything he wants, far too much and too easily, in fact."

The remark was prescient. The more famous and in demand Pavarotti became, the more difficult he was to deal with. Internationally, he seemed to be at his peak during the years of the Three Tenors extravaganzas, but his career was already in decline, and demands for his services in the opera house became fraught with peril. He canceled performances left and right, causing havoc nearly everywhere, then also began to sing exactly the roles he had always said he wouldn't tackle—the big dramatic parts only heroic tenors can do justice to. He tried a Manrico and it flopped; his Radames in *Aida* proved barely tolerable; his recorded Otello was salvaged by sound engineering. Then he deluded himself that he could return to the roles with which he had established his reputation, such as the Donizetti *La Figlia,* in which he could no longer hit either the high Cs or the high notes transposed down a full tone to suit his dwindling vocal resources. It became a hazard to hire him, and on August 30, 1989, Ardis Krainik an-

All for one and one for all: Twelve rising stars with the whole season before them. From left to right, top row first: Lauren Curnow, Wayne Tigges, Erin Wall, Roger Honeywell, Patrick Miller, Levi Hernandez, Quinn Kelsey; Chris Dickerson, Lauren McNeese, Scott Ramsay, Nicole Cabell, Guang Yang. *(Photo by Dan Rest)*

Diva Jane Eaglen, who doesn't believe in master classes, even her own, nevertheless wants Quinn Kelsey to focus a top note a bit more forward. *(Photo by Cheri Eisenberg)*

Diva Catherine Malfitano, always in character, lets Quinn Kelsey do his stuff. *(Photo by Cheri Eisenberg)*

Nicole Cabell soars aloft on a phrase obviously just the way Malfitano would have done it. *(Photo by Cheri Eisenberg)*

Patrick Miller airs it out for mezzo-soprano great Marilyn Horne during one of her master classes. *(Photo by Cheri Eisenberg)*

Bass Samuel Ramey, in his signature role of Mephistopheles in *Faust*, explains the way the world really works to Lauren McNeese, as the clueless Siébel, and Quinn Kelsey, as Wagner (the hapless soldier, not the composer). *(Photo by Dan Rest)*

Erin Wall as Marguerite about to be seduced by tenor Marcus Haddock as Dr. Faust, who has already sold his soul to win her. *(Photo by Dan Rest)*

The horny teenager Cherubino (Lauren McNeese) confides his hopes to an astonished Susanna (Isabel Barakday-rian) in *Nozze di Figaro*. *(Photo by Dan Rest)*

Wayne Tigges comforting his Susanna (Isabel Barakdayrian) during the *Figaro* dress rehearsal, before having to step into the part cold halfway through the second performance of Mozart's masterpiece.
(Photo by Dan Rest)

Scott Ramsay as the ill-fated Lord Arturo Bucklaw being conned into a disastrous wedding night by baritone Ashley Holland as Lucia's unscrupulous brother. *(Photo by Dan Rest)*

Lauren Curnow as Alisa, the least rewarding role she'll ever have to sing, tries in vain to dissuade Lucia (the incomparable Natalie Dessay) not to pursue a doomed love affair. *(Photo by Dan Rest)*

Chris Dickerson makes the most of his few bars as the Imperial Commissioner in *Madama Butterfly*, while tenor Roberto Aronica, as the feckless Pinkerton, looks on. *(Photo by Dan Rest)*

Guang Yang creating perhaps the only Suzuki ever to steal the opera away from Madama Butterfly, interpreted by soprano Sylvie Valayre. *(Photo by Dan Rest)*

Roger Honeywell and soprano Elizabeth Futral find love in *The Pirates of Penzance*, he as the humorless pirate apprentice and she as Major General Stanley's favorite daughter, while Nicole Cabell and the rest of the brood chatter about the weather in the background. *(Photo by Dan Rest)*

The author with Richard Pearlman, Gianna Rolandi and Dan Novak at the celebration after the Rising Stars concert. *(Photo by Dan Rest)*

nounced in a press release that Lyric would no longer engage Pavarotti. This was after he had canceled a *Tosca* scheduled for the company's thirty-fifth anniversary season. From 1981 to 1989, Krainik pointed out, the tenor had opted out of twenty-six of the forty-one performances he was supposed to appear in. Even his biggest Chicago fans had urged her to dump him permanently.

Pavarotti's personal life was also in disarray. His eating continued to be out of control and he began to have difficulty even waddling around the stage, much less acting a role. His philandering continued and then the inevitable occurred: he fell in love with a young woman, Nicoletta Mantovani, who was thirty-four years his junior. Adua was outraged and unforgiving and filed for divorce. The settlement must have cost him a small fortune. The Italian tax authorities came after him, too, dunning him for additional millions of lire. Now not only did he find himself emotionally unable to retire gracefully on his laurels, but he had to go on singing to support his lavish lifestyle. Nicoletta, the new love of his life, has been steering him into pop music, for which he is singularly unsuited.

Apart from practicalities, the tragedy of many of the great sacred monsters is that they cannot give up the intoxication of performing for the fans whose waves of adulation wash over them at every performance. Even before Nicoletta, it would have been hard to imagine Pavarotti doing without this and retiring to live the good life of a patriarch in the peaceful Italian countryside. Caruso, whom he much resembles in temperament and who received the same sort of hero worship, perpetuated his legend by dying early, at the age of forty-eight, before his talents began to decline. Some singers do manage to go on performing well into advancing age, mainly by adapting their diminishing vocal resources to the kind of parts they can still do well. The great Spanish tenor Alfredo Kraus sang leads well into his seventies, practically up to the day he died, and Domingo now sings roles that put less strain on his top range, which was never his strength anyway. But then there are the Callases, the di Stefanos, the Renata Scottos, who linger on too long, leaving behind them memories of cracked high notes and big wobbles.

The precipitous decline of Luciano Pavarotti was sad to see and hear; he had become almost a parody of himself. Sadder still to read were not only the reviews of his later performances but also a memoir by Herbert Breslin that, under the guise of praising Pavarotti as a great artist, sets out to trash him as a human being, documenting all his eccentricities in searing detail. Breslin, with whom Pavarotti has had a parting of the ways, is a classic example of a man who spits in the plate he has been eating from for thirty years. Still, nothing he or anybody else can say will take away from those of us who love opera the memories of Pavarotti at his best, when he sang like a god and brought us up out of our seats to shout, "Bravo!" A sacred monster indeed.

14

Joining the Program

ON NOVEMBER 18, Gianna Rolandi held one of her regular classes for the LOCAA singers, in Room 550, a studio large enough to accommodate comfortably at least twenty-five people. The artists sat in a row of chairs facing the piano, where Bill Billingham waited, ready to accompany them. Like it is at most of these sessions, the atmosphere was informal, with no one being compelled to perform who didn't want to. The idea was simply to give anyone who had a need to subject himself to coaching and criticism a chance to get it.

Quinn Kelsey was the first to rise to the occasion. He struck his usual calm, confident stance in front of his peers and launched himself into the big dramatic aria "Cortigiani, vil razza dannata," from Verdi's *Rigoletto.* His voice seemed to explode into the room, so big and powerful and dark that it froze me to my seat. I glanced to my left and caught Pearlman's eye. He gave me a little conspiratorial grin, then told me later, "You can say you were there." With Kelsey's last high note still ringing in my ears, Rolandi finally simply suggested that Kelsey might want to focus his voice more forward. I thought if he did that in a smaller studio he might shatter the glass windows looking out onto the street five stories down and kill somebody. No one else uttered a word, because there wasn't much to say, really.

Roger Honeywell, always eager to perform, now bounced to his feet. "I ain't afraid of the big Samoan," he said and promptly launched into a cabaletta, the bouncy final section of the aria from *La Traviata*. He sounded constricted, and Rolandi got up quickly before he finished to cut him off and ask for comments from the group. "Let go the air so it travels through your body," Guang Yang advised, after which Rolandi asked for someone to fetch the big yellow ball from the room next door. When Patrick Miller returned with it, Lauren Curnow looked puzzled. "I've never seen this," she said. "What do you do?" Honeywell now sat on the ball, bouncing on it as he sang, with Rolandi standing closely behind him. He sounded better, more relaxed, but broke off and said he couldn't concentrate. When he stood up again to give it a third try, he improved, but still couldn't handle the climactic high note, a C. For his fourth attempt, Guang Yang got up and put both hands on his back to help him support the tone, but he still had trouble. "Roger, don't worry too much about it," Rolandi said. "Nobody can sing a high C on an O vowel." I again found myself wondering about Honeywell; the voice was there, but his technique to control it seemed to be lacking.

When Lauren McNeese got up to sing an aria from *La Cenerentola*, Rolandi asked for volunteers to play Cinderella's two nasty sisters. To much laughter, Levi Hernandez and Honeywell rushed up to flank her and everybody in the room became subject to what my wife calls a case of the simples: helpless giggles. It broke the tension that had surrounded Honeywell's efforts. McNeese now did some thrilling singing, with clean coloratura runs and dead-on top notes. Rolandi's comments were directed not so much at the technical aspects of her singing as at her need to convey the meaning of the piece. She suggested that McNeese focus intently on what she's doing. "What does that trill mean?" Rolandi asked. "It has to be there for a reason." Line by line she took the mezzo through the aria, breaking it down one section at a time, then added mischievously, "Of course, when in doubt, smile!"

The session that day was clearly intended to help the young singers improve what they had to accomplish at all the auditions they'd be going through, so crucial to their being hired for roles elsewhere. Singing technically well is only part of what they had to master. "This is where you have to use your brain," Rolandi told them. "You have to sit down and figure out what you're doing. You have to really know the character, you have to know what's happening before and after. It's called acting." She cited Marilyn Horne as an example of the complete artist. "You have to be your own director," Pearlman told McNeese.

One by one the singers got up to perform, including bass Chris Dickerson, whom I hadn't really heard before. He was covering the role of Raimondo in the forthcoming *Lucia,* and he now sang that character's one important aria smoothly and beautifully, looking imposing and regally calm in his delivery. "That's good, Chris," Rolandi said. "You've got to get used to hearing yourself." Apart from that one comment, she didn't have much to say to him, and I had the impression that for some reason she wasn't as involved with his progress or lack of it as she was with that of most of the other people in the program.

Nicole Cabell was the last to sing. She chose "Caro nome," the introspective coloratura showpiece from *Rigoletto* that every self-respecting light soprano has to have in her audition repertory. It's the one Verdi aria I usually cannot abide, as it's almost always sung utterly without feeling and simply to show off clusters of high chirping sounds equivalent to those made by a deranged songbird. But Rolandi led Cabell through the aria phrase by phrase, giving her a dramatic reason for all the musical leaps Verdi had written. She made her move physically to illustrate dramatic points, then persuaded her to sink toward the floor on her closing phrases and actually to lie down on her back to sing the very difficult final high notes. Rolandi recalled that Frank Corsaro had once directed her to sing the aria exactly that way, but then he "was always getting everybody to lie down."

I was all the more impressed by what Rolandi had just accomplished with Cabell because it had finally succeeded in

making me appreciate subtleties in the piece I had never appreci-
ated before. Of course, performing the aria that way is not something most singers can do, since the need to support the tone
comes from the diaphragm and only a technically highly skilled
artist can sing lying on her back. Nicole Cabell, only in her second year in the program, was just the kind of performer someone
like Rolandi could coach into a big career. She had a very clear,
firm concept of her talents and goals and an unfailingly positive
attitude toward everything she did, and would not be pressured
into singing music she didn't think was right for her. "Richard
says that if you can't find it in your soul to sing that part," she
told me, "then you shouldn't do it."

Gianna Rolandi's only previous teaching experience came in
the late 1980s, when a friend at the University of Michigan persuaded her to fly in there to try her hand. It was not a success.
"That convinced me I never wanted to teach in a college,"
Rolandi recalled. Like her mother, who had been a coloratura soprano singing abroad under the Italian stage name of Giovanna
Frazieri (for Frazier), Rolandi launched herself very quickly into
a professional career. No sooner had she graduated from the Curtis Institute of Music in Philadelphia in 1975 than she was engaged by the New York City Opera to sing the very demanding
roles of Olympia, the clockwork maiden in Offenbach's *The Tales
of Hoffmann,* and Zerbinetta, in Richard Strauss's odd but com-
pelling *Ariadne auf Naxos.* She was an immediate hit—a beautiful woman with a rich middle voice and soaring top notes, a
talent perfectly suited to all the major coloratura soprano parts.
She moved on to the Met, then sang all over Europe, not only in
the more important opera centers but also as a soloist with various symphony orchestras. She was still at the height of her career
when she married Andrew Davis and somewhat reluctantly decided to retire, a decision she didn't regret, although she admitted to me that there were still some operas she had once starred in
that it pained her to hear again. As in most of the professions that

require great skill and total commitment, it's never easy to step onto the sidelines.

When she moved to Chicago with her husband in 2000, her ex-manager Matthew Epstein, newly installed as the company's full-time artistic director, suggested she begin to teach. Until then no voice teacher had ever been formally connected to the Opera Center. "Matthew thought I'd be good at it," she told Roger Pines in a program interview. In the spring of the following year, she began working with Stacey Tappan, after which more of the LOCAA members started coming to her. "Suddenly I had all of them!" she recalled. The young singers began to urge her to join the program officially, so she and Pearlman got together to talk about it. She agreed to do it only if she could be totally involved, which Pearlman readily acceded to; he had grasped at once how beneficial her involvement had been from the first day. One of the important intangibles she brought to the program was her experience in the profession. There was nothing any of these young people had to confront that she hadn't already gone through in her own early career.

Based on what she knew technically about the art, she quickly began to develop her own ways of working with the singers. "The way I look at it," she said, "they also have to listen to each other and trust each other. You know, originally I didn't want to do this, because I felt it was such a large responsibility. But now I find it great fun. There's nothing like hearing these voices develop."

No one in the program is forced to study with Rolandi, and the one danger she has to confront is that what she teaches may be in direct contradiction to what some young artist may have been taught by his own maestro. The danger is slim, because a correct vocal technique calls for pretty much the same criteria at every level. You have to breathe correctly, you have to support the tone from the diaphragm muscles, you have to open your mouth properly, articulate vowel sounds appropriately and keep the voice focused forward into *la maschera* (the mask). Still, the process is never easy. "You know where you're going," Rolandi said, "but you also have to kind of make it up as you go along. First you have to build a technique, which comes in when you're not in good voice, and you have to rely on it to get you through."

Another of Rolandi's innovations was to create what is now being called an in-house performance by the LOCAA artists, with only piano accompaniment, but in full costume and on a set. "One of the ways you learn," she pointed out, "is to perform. I was very determined. I had the idea that we could do a *Figaro,* and I got Andrew involved to find a way to do this for no money." A way was found, for minimum money, and in the spring of 2004 the Opera Center put on a full production of *Le Nozze di Figaro* in Room 200 for an audience of about a hundred invited guests. It was a smash, because until then the young singers had only prepared scenes from various operas and performed them informally. The innovation quickly paid off when Wayne Tigges, the Figaro, and McNeese, the Cherubino, had to step in that fall into the Lyric main stage production. "I was twenty-two when I made my debut as Olympia in New York, with Sam Ramey in the cast," Rolandi said. "That was a little intimidating. What the kids got here was needed experience. You sing in a big house like that or in this one, you have to be able to produce on the spot. All these singers know the basics, but it's not enough."

BEFORE ROLANDI'S NEXT open class, on December 3, there was an audition on Saturday, November 29, in Room 200 for Christopher Hahn, the artistic director of the Pittsburgh Opera, and David Di Chiera, the general director of the Michigan Opera Theatre in Detroit. These smaller opera companies can't compete for the sacred monsters and international stars and are always looking for talented young singers whose engagements they can afford and whom they can launch into major careers. Hahn is a tall, elegant, youthful-looking man with a charming smile who exudes positive vibes, as does Di Chiera, who is middle-aged, short and gray-haired, with a mustache and the look in his eyes of someone who has heard a lot of good singing in his lifetime. Di Chiera expressed interest in what I was doing there and asked me to be sure to send him a copy of whatever I wrote about Lyric and its young artists. Naturally, I took an immediate liking to him.

We sat together behind a long table facing the room, which had been set for the third act of *Lucia,* with a tall, curved stairway stage left, several large pillars, two banquet tables set to celebrate Lucia's wedding to her unwanted suitor, Arturo, and chairs and other furnishings. A rehearsal of the opera had been scheduled to begin at 3:00 P.M.; Lauren Curnow and Scott Ramsay would be participating in the comprimario parts of Alisa and Arturo. Neither Rolandi nor Pearlman was present, which perhaps contributed to a certain coldness I sensed in the room, as if we were about to participate in some of sort of tiring but futile exercise. I had attended several of these auditions by now and I had begun to feel that perhaps in earlier days it had been easier on the singers; at least we had been singing to be hired on the spot, not simply stored away in somebody's computer to be recalled another day.

Another factor I had soon become aware of was that the singers all seemed to feel it was obligatory to dress for these affairs as if they were being asked to perform before a paying public. The men wore dark suits or slacks and conservative blazers, the women mostly gowns, cocktail dresses or pantsuits and high heels. Why? I asked myself. What did it matter what they wore, if they could really sing? Dressing up for a real audience I could understand, although if the idea was to bring opera to a wider public, a little less formality might be fruitful. I'm not talking gangsta pants, piercings and tattoos, just a little friendly informality. When I asked Pearlman what he thought about this aspect of the audition process, his answer was, "I don't care what they wear, if they have a voice."

At this particular audition the process was unvarying. Each artist came in with a list of five or six audition pieces, picked the first one he wanted to sing, then allowed Hahn and Di Chiera to put their heads together to choose the second one. Both men made notes on lined yellow pads and were courteous with every singer, some of whom they'd heard before or even worked with. They seemed to be favorably impressed by what they heard, but basically dismissed each singer with a friendly "Thank you" or "Thank you very much," and that was it. It was obvious, however, that they were most enthusiastic about Quinn Kelsey and Guang Yang. After the baritone had knocked off the drinking song from Thomas's *Hamlet,* with that easy top and a plethora of what the Italians call *slancio,* which means a sort of reckless impetuosity, they called him over to quiz him about what he was doing and who was managing him. It was becoming clear that Kelsey's problem at this early stage of his career was not going to be getting work but making sure he wasn't rushed into the big dramatic parts too early. The history of opera is littered with the broken larynxes of once-promising singers who tackled certain parts too early or for which they were unsuited.

As for Guang Yang, who showed up in a long black skirt and dark purple blouse and concluded her audition with that beast of an aria from *Don Carlo,* Hahn and Di Chiera called her over to congratulate her on what they'd been hearing about the progress of her career. When Hahn mentioned that he knew she had been covering Borodina in *Samson et Dalila,* Yang smiled and revealed that she had been rehearsing in the part since ten o'clock that morning. It left us speechless, because her voice had sounded as fresh and strong as if she had just warmed up to sing a few minutes earlier.

Patrick Miller auditioned with Lenski's aria, singing the first verse while sitting down on the steps of the *Lucia* set, the way Corsaro had gotten him to sing it in his master class. He sang with great feeling and well-thought-out interpretation, but neither Hahn nor Di Chiera seemed much impressed with this approach, a departure from the usual stolid manner that singers habitually are expected to adopt in these auditions. In formal attire, singers are mostly expected to just stand there and sing. Opera, it occurred to me, has a tendency to worship tradition to such an extent that it stifles any attempt at innovation or creativity.

The last to sing that day was Honeywell, who strode into the room with his customary bravado and said, "I think Patrick sang the Lenski, so all right, I won't. I'll start with Macduff's aria." He performed it stylishly, singing softly in the first verse, then blasting away in the second. Hahn and Di Chiera now asked for "Salut! demeure," from *Faust*. Like the Flower Song from *Carmen*, this is a signature aria for a strong lyric or dramatic tenor, with that big climactic high C. So few tenors these days can cope with that note that the piece is often lowered a half or a full tone. Whatever it may have been at this audition, it was all too evident that Honeywell was not going to be able to handle it. He barely touched on the note and then quickly got off it. Nevertheless, he was obviously a tenor of such potential that Hahn and Di Chiera called him over afterward to ask what he would be doing after the end of the season. Honeywell told them he'd already been engaged for a *Traviata* in Vancouver and for the tenor lead in Puccini's rarely performed *La Fanciulla del West* later that summer at Glimmerglass. "It was great to hear you again," Hahn told him. "You sang very well."

What had Hahn and Di Chiera heard that I hadn't? In the operatic hotbeds of Italy, for instance, not being able to sit on the high note a bit would have brought an outpouring of discontent from the audience, but then American and English ones are generally less critical and more tolerant of an artist's shortcomings. Maybe Honeywell would be able to tackle the Puccini, which calls for a big tenor voice on the order of a Corelli or a Del

Monaco. Nothing I had heard just now, however, had reassured me about Honeywell's progress, especially with the challenge of *Pirates* now confronting him.

AT ROLANDI'S NEXT open coaching class, in Room 550 on December 3, with ten of the singers present, she began by asking the class how things had been going for them, especially at the various auditions they'd been attending. Not surprisingly there were complaints, especially from the young artists involved in the *Samson,* who were exhausted and bored by having had to attend so many rehearsals during the prolonged absence of the principals. Hours had been spent just sitting around waiting to go up and sing their few lines.

Rolandi is such a positive force and so relentlessly cheerful that she soon had everybody relaxed and eager to sing for her. She shouted encouragement, lavished praise and bounced around the room correcting posture, pronunciation, breathing, focus—every aspect of the singer's art. Again the only major concern seemed to be with Honeywell, who this time struggled with the Lenski aria, singing unmusically without an even flow of sound, as if it were being cut off somewhere. "You know, Roger," Rolandi pointed out, "the last few phrases you're gasping for breath." When he tackled the piece again, she urged him to stay calm. After his third rendition, which showed considerable improvement, she said, "It was really good, Roger, but make yourself breathe. It's a question of air." Despite the improvement she'd urged out of him, I had just about decided that the tenor would never have a serious career in opera. His auditions, as well as his coachings, had been shaky at best and he seemed not to have found his confidence. Without that, in such a difficult and demanding profession, no one could succeed, something I had long ago learned for myself.

The class concluded that day with Miller singing "Parmi veder le lagrime," one of the three beautiful arias for the tenor that Verdi composed for *Rigoletto.* Miller delivered with his beautiful, lyric, open flow of sound, which reminded me of a young di Stefano or Carreras. Rolandi spent some time trying to get him to focus his voice more forward, but I wasn't sure he ought to take that advice; there are some voices that sound best when the performer just lets go, allowing the air to carry the sound along like a stream. You may sacrifice some top notes doing that, but with proper support such an approach can be thrilling in a way a tighter control will not.

After the class, when the talk returned to the subject of auditions, Rolandi gave the singers some very practical advice. She pointed out that Quinn Kelsey had the correct approach. She imitated what Kelsey did, walking, arms slightly apart, toward the table where the audition people sat and then taking the trouble to shake their hands. "Then, after singing," she said, "don't just sneak out with a nod and a grin." The singers should go up to the table, make their presence felt, shake hands again and depart exactly as they came, forcefully, confident in their own abilities. She also warned them not to bring a water bottle, something many singers will do. She performed a hilarious imitation of a soprano setting a bottle down on the floor before singing, then leaning over to pick it up with her butt turned toward the audience or standing sideways, legs stretched out to look like a huge wading bird. One of the things about opera singing to remember is that performing it is often one small step removed from low comedy.

15

Survival

S O MANY THINGS can go wrong during the production and performance of any opera that it's something of a miracle when nothing does happen. Usually, the public remains unaware of what's been going on backstage, mostly because the situation is salvaged or covered up by the heroic machinations of the talented people connected with the enterprise. Nevertheless, books have been written and stories abound about all the disasters and mishaps that have taken place. The now-legendary tales of matters gone wrong survive either in the memories of those who have witnessed them or because they occurred in full view of the paying patrons. In my own experience the two lyric dramas most likely to descend into farce, apart from the Wagnerian ones that lend themselves so readily to satire, are *Tosca* and *Il Trovatore*. They are both highly melodramatic pieces, so drenched in blood-curdling events that any misstep will inevitably provoke laughter.

No sooner had I arrived in Rome in the spring of 1948, for instance, than I went to see a performance of *Tosca* in the open-air amphitheater at the ancient Baths of Caracalla. The role of Floria Tosca was being sung by one of my favorite sopranos, Maria Caniglia, then in the twilight of her career but still an electrifying performer onstage. Before she had a chance to make her first entrance, however, the audience was already in a tumult. Early in act one, Tosca's lover, the painter Mario Cavaradossi, has to sing an aria to a picture he has been working on, comparing the portrait to the features of his beloved Floria. Before launching into the aria, the tenor mounted the scaffolding to pull aside the curtain covering the canvas. Unfortunately, when he tugged at the drawstring nothing happened, so he very sensibly decided to ignore the problem and turned to sing straight out to the audience. As he did so, we were treated to the spectacle of a large hairy arm, apparently belonging to a stagehand, emerging from under the platform to tear at the offending curtain. Once again nothing happened, but the laughter of the audience disturbed the tenor in mid-flight, who perhaps thought his fly might be open. He stepped backward and fell off the platform, necessitating a blackout and a short delay.

A couple of years later, while I was studying for the summer at the Accademia Musicale Chigiana, in Siena, a touring company starring a once-great but aging baritone named Benvenuto Franci as the evil Baron Scarpia put on a *Tosca* outdoors on the edge of town. During the second act a brisk wind came up that threatened to topple the sets. Franci, who was then supposed to be chasing a terrified Floria Tosca around the room, was forced to remain in place, one arm holding up a wall of the Castel Sant'Angelo. The third act was canceled.

And then there was the famous performance of *Tosca* in Capetown, South Africa, when Rita Hunter, the portly soprano singing Floria, complained to the backstage crew that the mattress provided to receive her when she jumped to her death from the battlements of the *castello* at the end of the opera was too hard. At the next performance Floria Tosca sang her great closing scream of defiance and leapt into the void, only to bounce immediately back into view from the trampoline the crew had thoughtfully provided.

But of all the operas in the rep, surely none has been the scene of more mishaps than *Il Trovatore,* one of the most difficult of all operas to stage, both dramatically and musically. Its plot is obscure and not easily understood. Much of it occurs offstage, and the background is explained in an opening aria by the bass that no one, before the era of supertitles, ever understood or paid much attention to. The plot convolutions of Salvatore Cammarano's libretto, adapted from a romantic Spanish play, may strike modern audiences as absurd, though the conflicting human passions on display are not. The opera survives all over the world mainly because of Verdi's exquisitely beautiful melodies, which, however, are very difficult to sing well and require four major artists in the lead roles—soprano, mezzo-soprano, tenor and baritone. With a first-rate cast, the singing will carry the day, but there are never that many great singers around, even for the major companies who can afford to pay their fees.

Some years ago the San Diego Opera's brave and talented general director, Ian Campbell, allowed me to hang around backstage and follow a production of *Il Trovatore* from start to finish. General directors as a group are not comfy about having a reporter constantly on the scene, but Campbell, like Bill Mason, trusted me and gave me full access to everything going on. That trust is invaluable, because most of the work in an opera production takes place over a tight rehearsal period of a couple of weeks, about the time a Broadway-bound musical allots just for going over the book and score and blocking out a few dance steps. Not even a disaster at sea is as conducive to panic and desperate improvisation as a grand opera headed for a premiere, once things start to go wrong.

Everything seemed to be going along reasonably well when I dropped in at the first stage rehearsal of the opera at the San Diego Civic Theatre one evening in mid-February, only ten days before opening night. The male chorus was massed onstage inside set designer Ming Cho Lee's idea of a medieval bastion, a narrow courtyard flanked by two enormous gray battlements pierced by narrow windows and containing broken columns and scattered chunks of stone. The men were being positioned in groups about the stage by director Richard Gregson, while the conductor, Thomas Fulton, watched the proceedings from his podium above the pit, where the accompanist sat waiting to provide the music to which the scene would eventually unfold. The atmosphere was informal, with a lot of bantering going on among the choristers, most of whom were working for the first time with their cumbersome props—swords, halberds, crossbows.

Gregson was British, a regular at Covent Garden, and his directorial style was affable and understated. He was a pleasant-looking man, dressed in rumpled slacks and a baggy sports jacket. He calmly guided his charges through their movements. "Gentlemen of the chorus," he instructed them at one point, "every time a prop comes through and you are singing, it would help if you expressed some excitement: 'Oh, good, things are hotting up,' that sort of thing." It became immediately clear that the company was not dealing here with a martinet for detail or a radical visionary. Gregson had been handed a cast and a physical production about which he had had no say, and it was his job simply to make as much sense of the goings-on as he could. "I'd very much like to have a go at a truly realistic staging of this opera," Gregson would tell me on dress rehearsal night. "Not this storybook approach one always sees." But his hands had, in effect, been tied, because in order to save money it had been decided to use a set the company owned, one that had been built for an earlier production.

Money and singers are the two prime movers in the opera house. The total cost of this *Trovatore* would come to almost a half-million dollars, of which about a quarter would go to the principal singers and chorus, with the box office recouping about 60 percent of the total sum. The rest would have to be raised from the company's annual fund-raising drives. Still, "Lots of people get employment through the opera," Campbell pointed out. "You take the arts out of a city like this and you leave a hole worth millions of dollars." The money is poured back into the community, not only in the form of salaries and taxes, but into services such as hotel rooms and restaurants. "We take the money from one sector," the company's technical director said, "and put it back into another one. All except for the singers, of course."

And there's the rub. The singers sell the tickets, and because top artists are in short supply, opera companies have to plan their seasons and sign up their major singers several years in advance. The role of Manrico in *Il Trovatore* calls for a top dramatic tenor, the scarcest of all operatic commodities. So four years earlier Campbell had begun going after Giuseppe Giacomini, a hefty singer with one of those big, brawny sounds that can shatter marble. Three years later the tenor's agent notified Campbell that his client would not honor his contract, mainly because the weakness of the dollar abroad had reduced the exchange value of what he would be paid.

There wasn't much Campbell could do about the situation. The top foreign artists cancel engagements all the time, often at the drop of an arpeggio. A doctor can always be found to confirm the sudden onslaught of a bad cold or strep throat. In this case, Giacomini could hardly claim illness, since he was busy singing everywhere else at the time and had not canceled his other engagements before coming to San Diego. Campbell, like other general directors, was reluctant to sue. The American Guild of Musical Artists is never helpful, because the union's basic attitude is that American artists should have been hired in the first place. In any case, the basic problem had become finding a new Manrico, quickly and at a price the company could afford to pay.

San Diego's top fee was then $8,000 a performance, but only a Pavarotti or a Domingo could command that, and neither of these gentlemen was available. Most artists received between $3,000 and $5,000 a performance, but Campbell could go higher for a dramatic tenor. The trouble was that Giacomini, who was not by any means among the immortals of song, could command up to $20,000 every time he cleared his throat on a European stage. Faced with such demands, Campbell would have preferred not to schedule an opera such as *Il Trovatore,* but a more modest rep of Mozart or Donizetti and other bel canto works in which ensemble values are paramount and for which there is a cornucopia of good young American singers. "But the public demands these operas," Campbell explained, "and they should be done. So you have to count on singers to honor their contracts. I always try to sign Americans because they are, on the whole, very reliable."

With limited time and resources available to him, Campbell now found himself with not much of a choice. It soon boiled down to a journeyman Venezuelan artist named Ruben Dominguez and an unknown Hungarian, Janos B. Nagy (pronounced Natch), whom Campbell had heard sing a "very acceptable *Tosca*" in Düsseldorf eighteen months earlier. Nagy was the leading tenor of the Hungarian State Opera, in Budapest, where he had sung many of the big tenor roles. The clincher was that he was available for most of the two-week rehearsal period, whereas the other candidates, even the uncelebrated Dominguez, were reluctant to rehearse at all. Campbell opted for Nagy and hoped for the best.

"THIS IS THE MOST EARTHY of the early Verdi operas," Thomas Fulton explained to Jeffrey Wells, the young bass singing the small but important role of Ferrando. "You can refine for weeks, make sure all the sixteenth notes are right, but if you don't punch it, you've got nothing. You have to let it out, especially with this one, go with it."

The company was running through the opera's opening scene, in which Ferrando has to sing the musically tricky aria that explains and sets up the entire plot. Wells was tall, with macho good looks and a Louisiana back-country accent you could fry.

His Italian was better than his English and he could sing birds out of trees. "Tom's right, you've got to forget about technique and let it go," he told me later. "I've only had five voice lessons in my life, so I don't have to worry about that shit." The only thing he did worry about all week was the Santa Ana, a hot desert wind that had been blowing for a couple of days and could dry out a larynx. He kept a bottle of mineral water handy, just to keep the right juices flowing.

This was the first time that the entire cast of principals had been assembled to work through the whole opera from start to finish, under the guidance of Gregson and Fulton. The rehearsal was taking place in a big windowless space below the main stage with a low ceiling and mirrored walls. Various members of the backstage crew were also present, including Chris Mahan, a tall, elegant-looking man who presided over the props and generally made himself useful. After having worked many years at the Met in a variety of responsible posts before moving to San Diego, Mahan struck me at once as nearly indispensable. He always seemed to know more about what was going on than anyone else and it was he who had dubbed the claustrophobic rehearsal hall Nibelheim, the underground home of the cunning dwarfs in Wagner's *Ring* cycle. Every opera company needs its Chris Mahan, because what these people, the lifelong addicts of great singing, don't know about opera is generally not worth knowing.

As the rehearsal progressed, I had a chance to assess the talents of the leads. Jonathan Summers, the Australian baritone portraying the Count di Luna, had a pleasant lyric voice, but not one I thought would be quite up to the tremendous outpouring of sound required in one of the toughest roles in the Verdi rep. Soprano Susan Dunn and mezzo Dolora Zajick appeared to be two young American singers on the edge of brilliant careers, especially Zajick, who occasionally would cut loose with a phrase or two that revealed a voice of enormous beauty and power. Wells caught my look of amazement at one point, grinned and winked at me, as if to indicate that I hadn't heard anything yet. He'd sung with Zajick before and he *knew*!

The big problem was Nagy. He had a dark, dry, metallic voice that sounded secure enough on the top notes, but he seemed to be unable to shade it or to spin out a long melodic phrase. Also, he spoke and understood only Hungarian, so he had to be walked through every gesture or bit of business, an exhausting, time-consuming process. No one but I seemed to be worried about his appearance. He was short and nearly bald, with a fringe of gray hair and a small but pronounced paunch. Dressed in sneakers, scuffed jeans, a shirt and a sleeveless sweater, he was several inches shorter than his inamorata, the statuesque Susan Dunn, and looked about as heroic as a bus conductor. The wig and makeup department would have to perform prodigies of creativity on him—but then dramatic tenors are never hired for their good looks if they can sing.

At the conclusion of the rehearsal, Fulton seemed preoccupied. A youthful-looking man with a shock of red hair that he combed forward and that gave him a boyishly mischievous look, he was clearly an accomplished musician and a stickler for details. He had not been impressed by the somewhat cavalier way the tenor had attacked his music. As a result of this rehearsal, it was decided over the weekend that a prompter's box would be used for Nagy, with Karen Keltner, the company's music administrator and associate conductor, hidden within it to flash the tenor his cues. No one was happy about the move, because the box sits downstage center and cuts off part of the action from people sitting in the front rows of the orchestra section. Campbell regards the device as an anachronism, a throwback to the bad old days of opera when many of the singers, even great ones like Caruso, couldn't read music. The idea, however, was to make it as easy as possible on Nagy, who had sung mainly in central Europe, where the prompter's box was still an ugly fixture.

ONE OF THE BUSIEST PEOPLE in any opera company is the wig master and makeup designer. In San Diego, Paul Best and his associate, Donna Couchman, had to make everyone onstage look believable, while trying to reconcile the director's view of the show with the personal demands of the singers. "If someone says, 'I will not wear that,' you have a problem," Best explained to me when I dropped in one afternoon at his headquarters, a long narrow dressing room near those of the leads. "PR is a big factor in this department. You have to take responsibility for the show and also keep the singers happy. We're the last people to see them before they go onstage and you want them in a good frame of mind." The women, he added, were usually harder to please than the men, often because their ages and looks were not those called for by their roles. "We really can only do so much. I have a brush, not a wand. I can't make a fat woman thin."

Best was a plump and cheerful young man who obviously didn't rattle easily. "To survive in this business you learn to do a lot of different things," he said, fluffing out one of the dozens of wigs mounted on shelves along one wall. He was enjoying working with Gregson, who was easy to deal with, knew what he wanted and said so. "He doesn't want a cookie-cutter look, which is refreshing to us," he explained. "He wants a variety of ages and looks. In the past we've had, 'Okay, this is a blond show; we want everybody blond.' He wants these people to look like real people and he's giving us some leeway, so we can enjoy what we do. Some directors can't describe what they want nor can the singers. They know only what they *don't* want."

His main problem in *Trovatore* was making Nagy look sixteen, an impossible task. Gregson also wanted him dark. "I tried everything on him and of course he picked out a blond wig," Best said. He went to Gregson, whose reaction was, "Oh, dear. Well, we'll try it. But if that's what he wants, that's what he wants." In an opera as demanding as *Il Trovatore* the singers usually have the ultimate muscle. Susan Dunn, for instance, was convinced she looked younger with her hair long and down, even though the director wanted it up, because the style was more correct for the period and for her social status as a lady-in-waiting. Best was trying to design a compromise hairdo, which would also affect how all the other women in the cast would have to look to match it.

Despite what amounted to a lot of extra work, imposed upon them for reasons that had little to do with art, Best and his staff seemed resolutely cheerful. Their cozy headquarters, brilliantly illuminated by rows of mirror lights, also functioned as a backstage social center; people periodically popped in and out to chat and gossip. "This is an easy show," Best observed. "You don't have body makeup, as in *Aida,* or lots of kids, like in *Carmen,* or many changes, like in *Hoffmann. Nabucco* was tough, because of the sheer numbers and fast changes. People went from being Babylonians to Jews and back." He laughed. "Asking for the impossible is the rule in opera," he said.

MY FAVORITE REHEARSAL in any opera house is the *Sitzprobe,* the "sitting rehearsal," during which the singers go through all of their music with the full orchestra for the first time. (In Italy it's called *la prova all'italiana,* "the rehearsal Italian-style.") They don't have to worry about costumes, props, makeup, wigs or acting, just being up there onstage, letting it all out vocally and riding that great cushion of sound the composer has provided. It's an exhilarating feeling, after all the hours of stop-and-go rehearsals with only piano accompaniment. A row of chairs and music stands, one for each artist, faces the empty auditorium from in front of a drop cloth. The singers stroll in and out, as they are needed, and can either remain seated as they sing or stand up, depending usually on whether or not they are marking. Most of the time they sing out, because it's their only chance to do so unhindered and to get a feel for the acoustics in the hall.

This *Sitzprobe* was a revelation, because for the first time I became fully aware of each singer's strengths and weaknesses. Susan Dunn had a smooth and musical vocal line and was clearly a favorite with the orchestra, but her highest top notes sounded shrill. Dolora Zajick was impressive. She sang effortlessly up and down her whole range, bellowing out huge dark chest tones and, in her opening duet with Manrico, popping off an interpolated high C that rocked me in my seat.

Of the men, only Wells seemed secure, providing a fresh, youthful bass that seemed likely to improve with maturity. Summers sang lyrically, securely and with taste, but his voice was small for di Luna and he was swallowed up in the climactic moments. As for Nagy, he seemed no more than adequate at best. His singing sounded dry and hard, though solid enough on top. "He sings as if he has no teeth," Bernard Fitch, the character tenor in the small part of Ruiz, said to me later. He was right; the voice seemed old and worn. And Fulton clearly did not like what he was hearing.

After the rehearsal I went backstage, where the crew had been working steadily on lights and props, and found John David Peters, the production carpenter, looking up toward the first-act moon, which had revealed a tendency to sway rather than sit quietly in place. I asked him how he thought things were going. "What's everybody worried about?" he answered with a grin. "We've got their money." Peters clumps about the stage in workman's boots, shorts and a belt filled with tools. He peers out at the world from under a full head of long blond hair flecked with gray, and over a bushy beard, looking like an amiable Visigoth. I had also become aware that he headed one of the best crews I had ever seen in operation—hardworking, cheerful and innovative. He presided over his fiefdom from a desk offstage right that was shielded by a plywood partition. Resting on the desk facing out was a large piece of wood on which a half circle had been painted in various colored sections to indicate how Peters and his squad thought the production was going from their point of view. A movable arrow provided the answers, ranging from DAY OFF at extreme left to TOTAL BULLSHIT at extreme right. In between there were sections painted green (PIECE OF CAKE, NO SWEAT, LIKE A WALK IN THE PARK); yellow (IT'S AN EASY SHOW, JUST A MINUTE); and red (MAY I MAKE A LOCAL PHONE CALL, ANY STAGE MANAGEMENT SUGGESTION). This was the "Bullshitometer," also designed by Peters and still in operation. It provides an excellent indication of the way things are going from day to day. When I glanced at it that day, after the *Sitzprobe,* the arrow pointed straight to a yellow square: IT'S AN EASY SHOW.

He was wrong. The dress rehearsal two days later, before a small invited audience composed mainly of schoolchildren, was a disaster. The set looked bare and dull and the costumes foolish, like the illustrations in a second-rate children's book. The men were uncomfortable in their thick woolen tunics and leggings, with ill-fitting helmets on their heads and holding weapons that looked as phony as they were. Dolora Zajick's outfit, topped by a Medusa wig, reminded me of Harpo Marx in *A Night at the Opera,* and Dunn looked uncomfortably constrained in a dress that, she said, made her feel "like a sausage stuffed into a casing." Poor Nagy fared worst of all. He wouldn't wear a mustache or eye makeup, so that, barefaced in his wig and costume, he looked like a middle-aged man in drag.

So much depends in opera on the precise fusion of all the disparate elements in a production, so that every bit of action, every dramatic effect makes its point within the configuration of the composer's creation. The score is like the steel framework of a building; a great one makes the opera nearly indestructible, but it can be marred and mocked by poor construction, missing bits and pieces, decorative and directorial obscenities and just plain bad singing. At this dress, the lighting effects were often out of sync with what was going on onstage and contradicted by the supertitle projections explaining to the audience in English what the characters were saying. There were laughs galore, especially when Dunn was supposed to mistake the baritone villain for her lover in a scene intended to be played in darkness, but which on this occasion took place in broad daylight. Not even a great score like Verdi's can survive buffoonery, and Campbell was clearly not amused.

Even more disastrous, however, was Nagy's singing. He began the performance strongly enough, on pitch and loud, but by the second act his voice had begun to deteriorate alarmingly and by the third he seemed unable to sustain any sort of vocal line. Even his top notes, normally secure, were barked, and it was painful to listen to them. Fulton summoned Campbell to his dressing room during the last intermission and informed him that he would refuse to conduct with Nagy in the role.

Conductors are more expendable than dramatic tenors, but Campbell couldn't risk a fiasco. By seven the next morning he was on the phone, hunting all over the globe for a new Manrico. (Unlike Lyric and the Met, smaller companies like San Diego's cannot afford to keep a paid understudy on hand for these big parts.) Campbell was hoping against hope that somebody somewhere in his international network of connections might be able to come up with some exciting new prospect who would prove to be a revelation in the part, but it was not to be. Only Ruben Dominguez was available on such short notice for all four performances and by that afternoon the deal had been made to fly him in. He would have about forty minutes onstage with Gregson and an hour with Fulton to go over his part before opening night. But he'd sung the role before and was reportedly secure in it.

The tough part was telling Nagy. Campbell and Marianne Flettner, the company's artistic administrator, who speaks fluent

German, went to see the tenor at his hotel. Campbell spoke English and Flettner translated into German for the tenor's son, who then passed the word on to his father in Hungarian. "Nagy was a perfect gentleman," Campbell recalled later. "I said it was clear that his vocal health was deteriorating and that it was not in his interest to face the critics at this time." Nagy asked for specifics on his singing and Campbell delivered them while also assuring him that at least a portion of his contract would be honored. The tenor was clearly distraught, but on parting there were hugs all around. He left the next day for Germany, leaving behind a gift he had brought for Campbell—a recording, just about to be released, of Verdi's *Attila,* with himself in the leading tenor role.

At the end of that opening night in San Diego, I wandered out onto the empty stage, illuminated now by a single work light, and looked out into the auditorium. It looked huge, with rows of empty seats soaring up into the dim light. How, I wondered, had Ruben Dominguez found the courage to go on cold that night, to confront that great beast that is the public? He had shown up earlier in the evening, a tall, good-looking man with a head of thick, black, curly hair, and sequestered himself in his dressing room to warm up. One by one, the other singers had stopped to introduce themselves or to say hello (several of them had sung with him before) and Fulton had dropped in to tidy up one or two musical points, but most of the time Dominguez had been alone. The official announcement to the company had been made over the intercom at 7:30 P.M., and the audience had been informed when Campbell went out before the curtain at 8:05 to tell them that Nagy had had to withdraw because he "had become indisposed during the week." Dominguez had had plenty of time to muse on the possibility of total catastrophe.

It hadn't happened. The tenor's voice was not pretty—it was a dark, throaty sound that became pinched and white on top—but it was secure and could be heard. It even improved a bit as the evening wore on and its owner became surer of himself and of his colleagues. He would be savaged later by the critics, but as far as I was concerned, he deserved a medal for bravery.

The incident served to prove once again how indestructible a great opera like *Il Trovatore* can be, no matter what goes wrong. Verdi's sublime melodies will almost always carry the day, and everyone had rallied to the emergency. The costumes had been improved, the wigs spruced up, the cues checked. Nobody panicked, nobody threw a tantrum, everyone went about his business as if the whole company had been together for months, united in this single arduous enterprise. The arrow on the Bullshitometer had never strayed into the red, some of the singing had been excellent and the audience had mostly enjoyed itself, so it wouldn't matter in the least what the critics said.

This wouldn't have happened in Italy. In the spring of 1949, when I was studying in Rome, one of my fellow students, a young baritone named Vittorio, was signed to sing a di Luna at some small town south of Rome. I was working as a stringer for the Rome bureau of *Time* then and I was sent to Sicily on a story, so couldn't attend what amounted to Vittorio's debut. I worried about him, because he was a good friend and I knew how tough the part was. He had a well-trained baritone, but the voice was small. Still, he was singing in a modest provincial theater and maybe he would get away with it.

The minute I got back from Sicily, I called him to ask how the performance had gone. Just fine, he told me, except for the Manrico, an aging Roman who sang in the chorus of the Teatro dell'Opera. He apparently fancied himself a dramatic tenor and had somehow wangled himself into the production. In those days you could sometimes buy yourself a leading part in the touring companies assembled by independent impresarios. In any case, no sooner had this Manrico opened his mouth than whistles and boos and shouts filled the air. Vittorio sang his music solidly, well under the radar of the public outrage with Manrico. Finally, in the third act, when Manrico cracked his first high note in the cabaletta "Di quella pira!" one furious citizen leaped onto his seat to shout imprecations at him. "Beast! Goat!" he screamed. "How is it possible to sing like this? Criminal! Murderer!" At which point the tenor, sword in hand, advanced furiously downstage to confront his accuser. "All right, shithead," he shouted, "you come up here and sing the high note!" The outraged audience rose bellowing to its feet and the curtain had to be quickly drawn. "We never did the last act," Vittorio said, "but they liked me, at least."

16

Attitudes

THE PROBLEM of what had been happening to Roger Honeywell had obviously begun to preoccupy both Rolandi and Pearlman. During still another audition, this one on December 1 in Room 550 for John Baril and Bill Lewis of Central City Opera, the tenor had found himself in difficulty. He began by singing the Lenski aria very nicely, then asked for a break to leave the studio long enough to get some water. During his absence, Pearlman told Baril and Lewis, "Roger's doing *Fanciulla* at Glimmerglass," which impressed them. Baril is Central City's resident conductor and Lewis is the company's assistant conductor, who works often with young singers. They came on as chatty, informal, agreeable guys, not the sort who would put any undue pressure on a young artist, and they had worked with several of the LOCAA members in the past, including Ramsay and McNeese. Their season consisted of three operas a year, and the company also had an apprentice program. They were unfailingly courteous and upbeat in their spoken and written comments and lavished praise on several of the singers they heard. Honeywell, too, had begun well and there had been every reason to think that he'd do equal justice to his second selection.

When he returned, however, to sing Pinkerton's short but demanding aria from *Madama Butterfly*, he suddenly had to break off in mid-phrase. He said he was suffering from phlegm, though

I hadn't heard a trace of it in his singing, just the usual forcing of the tone and constriction in his high notes. Nevertheless, both Baril and Lewis seemed interested in him and quizzed him about his future plans. There was no question in their minds that this was a potentially major talent, with a big sound and the tall good looks to go with it.

After the proceedings were over and the young singers had gone, Pearlman asked if there were any questions. "So Roger is still in the program?" Baril asked. Pearlman told him he was in his last year and would be singing Frederic in *Pirates* as his farewell to it.

The morning after this audition, Honeywell stopped by Pearlman's office to talk about what had happened to him. He told Pearlman that he had been very tense and that when he got that way it brought up phlegm, which would make him even tighter. He recalled a recent session he'd had with John Treleaven that had really helped him. Treleaven had told him first of all never to start singing until he was absolutely ready. "Make them wait, don't rush into it," he'd advised. Nevertheless, Honeywell said that matters kept getting out of hand; he would tighten up and his vocal technique would desert him.

Pearlman listened quietly and sympathetically, then gave him some tips on how to achieve "inner calm," so that his technique would essentially take care of itself. "You've somehow lost touch with your inner metronome," he said, "so that you rush and forget to breathe properly." He backed up Treleaven's advice by telling Honeywell not only to take all the time he needed but also to be sure to breathe correctly. It would help him to achieve the technical control he'd need to sing well.

I went one afternoon to talk to Eric Weimer, who had accompanied the Central City audition and who had been working frequently with most of the young singers. I'd seen and heard enough of Weimer by this time to have arrived at the conclusion that he was something truly special, not only a musician of great refinement and impeccable taste but also an opera coach of the kind who could help a young singer build a repertory that could launch a career. In every session I heard him work, he never allowed a single musical misstep or misuse of language to pass unnoticed. He had been associated with the Opera Center since 1992 and functioned as the main link between LOCAA and Lyric, but his situation was also, as he put it, "a bit more complicated than one might think." This was because he was also involved with the young artist program at the Met, where he would be in residence mostly in the spring. And he had also worked with the Washington Opera—in fact almost anywhere his expert services might be required. A tall, elegant, resolutely cheerful man with a droll sense of humor, he exuded an aura of professionalism and artistic integrity that exactly suited the needs of his charges.

Weimer saw the situation of the LOCAA singers as threefold. First, of course, they'd have to prepare for their assignments during the regular season in the comprimario parts and as covers for major ones. Second, they would need to work on their audition packages, the five or six arias they'd need to master so totally that they could pull them out at a moment's notice. Third, there were the summer assignments, the operas they'd be performing around Chicago after the formal end of the season. There would be a *Die Fledermaus,* Johann Strauss's sappy but charming operetta, scheduled for a go in late May; an in-house *Don Giovanni* in the last week in June; and, finally, Puccini's riotously funny one-acter, *Gianni Schicchi,* to be sung outdoors along the lakefront in early August.

"For some people it's almost too much," Weimer said. "Everyone has a different configuration of obligations. Everyone has a different set of resources as to technique, language facility, musical training. People who come here in most cases have spent four years in undergraduate programs, and their language skills are basically nonexistent." The problem in dealing with all these needs is finding not only the right people to teach but also the time for it.

Nevertheless, Weimer clearly felt that there had been an enormous improvement in the past couple of years. "The average quality of the singing is far higher than it was," he said, going on to point out that relatively few people who had gone through the program before had managed to have careers. He knew of two ex-LOCAA singers who were currently driving taxis around town. "Now, however, we're hiring people out of LOCAA, giving them more and better covers and chances to sing major roles." He cited Tigges getting to do his Figaro; Guang Yang covering Dalila and about to sing Suzuki in the forthcoming *Butterfly*, then already preparing to cover Amneris in next season's *Aida*, another of those ferocious Verdi roles only a top dramatic mezzo can deliver; Lauren McNeese stepping into Cherubino, then singing a delightful Siébel in *Faust*. "A lot of that has to do with Gianna," Weimer pointed out. "She's a key part of the singers' experience. Before her, nobody worked vocally full-time with them."

I commented that I had been impressed from my first day with the company by the feeling of cooperation I sensed inside the Opera Center. No sniping, no sly digs, no put-downs of the other artists by anyone involved. I knew that Pearlman would not have tolerated it, but still it was unusual. Singers can be really hateful with one another. Beniamino Gigli, for instance, had so detested his great rival, Giacomo Lauri-Volpi, that when he found himself one night in Milan eating at the same restaurant as him, he asked for a screen to be placed around his table so he wouldn't have to look at him. "Yes, usually, when you have singers together, they all have different teachers and it causes competitiveness," Weimer said. "Here, as far as technique is concerned, they all help each other. They can talk about their issues. It's easy to discuss vocal problems with each other. It's healthier here than elsewhere or here before Gianna came. This atmosphere also gives them the strength to resist bad advice from others. One of the things singers have to be aware of is guarding this precious commodity they have. Gianna has given them the capacity to do that."

Still, he pointed out, there are difficulties. Singers come into a major company like Lyric lacking in experience and find themselves thrown in with very experienced people. "Nationwide there are limited opportunities, which is another confidence-shaking factor they have to deal with," Weimer continued. "They need to develop self-confidence so they can resist pressure that could damage them. Most opera singers have an attitude. If they don't, they need to develop one."

One of those pressures could come from a hands-on artistic director intent on imposing his vision on the artist by insisting, for example, that the singer use a particular aria to open an audition package. If the singer feels strongly that the piece is not for him, being forced to use it can shake his confidence. It's very hard to resist pressure from someone in the opera world who can have a tremendous effect on the progress of a career. Singers need not only to be receptive to suggestions but also to abstract themselves from the potential politics of any such conflict. What worked best, according to Weimer, was what Wayne Tigges, Guang Yang and Quinn Kelsey exemplified—a relationship with a coach that would help them flourish. They had to have incredible drive, incredible talent and an intangible—call it charisma—to go with that drive and talent. They had to realize that the person they were working with was someone who could help them. They wouldn't have to accept everything the coach told them, but they'd have to be open to it. Weimer recalled working on a daily basis with Guang Yang on an aria from Handel's *Partenope,* one of those incredibly convoluted, florid pieces typical of this composer, with seemingly endless variations on a melodic line that I find stupefying but that some worshippers of elaborate vocalizing adore. "She had a very good attitude," Weimer recalled, "took notes, taped herself. She doesn't feel negative about accepting help. Her self-confidence was totally unaffected by very grueling, intensely detailed, line-by-line work." Weimer felt that it takes time, at least several weeks, to establish a rapport between the singer and the coach, and having the coaches on hand for long periods of time helps to form that bond.

A FEW DAYS AFTER the Central City Opera audition, Honeywell returned to his native Canada to take part in the annual Opéra de Montréal Gala, a tremendous bash put on primarily to raise money and featuring singers from not only Canada but also the United States. "Too much, too many and too long," was the opening comment of the *Montreal Gazette* music critic. "And too bad there was no more." The affair, he continued, "remains one of the great tributes to excess in a city not known for its moderation." The gala lasted four and a half hours, during which a seemingly endless parade of singers in all categories were trotted out, including an American male soprano named Michael Maniaci, who sang "Voi che sapete," one of Cherubino's arias from *Le Nozze di Figaro.* Cherubino is a male part, but it is always sung by a youthful mezzo. "It was lyrically phrased, fresh in tone, creatively ornamented and, of course, a little strange," the critic commented.

There were lots of good moments, apparently, with the singers concentrating mainly on the more familiar arias, which delighted "the big crowd of vocal fanatics" who packed the concert hall. The hit of the evening, however, was Roger Honeywell, cited by the Montreal critic as "the big discovery" among a group of already established artists. Honeywell sang Lenski's aria "with clarity, pathos and an agreeable ping." The critic looked forward to hearing him again soon in forthcoming performances of Handel's *Messiah.*

Word of Honeywell's success in Montreal excited everyone in Chicago. What exactly had happened to him to turn it around? No sooner was he back at the Opera Center than he told everyone that there was no mystery to it. "I just opened my mouth and it was the best I've ever sung," he said.

At one o'clock on December 12, I dropped in on still another audition, this one for the English National Opera and the Florentine Opera of Milwaukee. Once again, it was in Room 550 and the singers came filing in, one after the other, to present their wares. Quinn Kelsey made his usual dynamic impression and was asked by the man from ENO whether he might be available to sing Melot, a major part in the *Tristan und Isolde* they were planning to produce the following season—if the baritone now under contract couldn't do it, an odd request. Maybe they wanted to get rid of their baritone, but wanted to make sure Kelsey would be available first. The world of opera teems with schemes and intrigue, and paranoia often rules.

Except for Kelsey, who sang with his customary brio, the audition did not show off most of the other young singers at their best. They were tired from putting in long rehearsal hours and coaching sessions and having to audition over and over again. The holidays were approaching, and the pressure on everyone connected to Lyric was high. I, too, was looking forward to getting home for ten days or so, before coming back for the last three operas of the season.

As I sat there waiting for the audition to end, Honeywell came bouncing in with his usual flair and an aura of masculine bravado that had been missing from his previous efforts. He immediately took his stand by the piano and launched into the Lenski aria, singing with great power and freedom, his voice flowing out of him, by far the best I'd ever heard him sing. It was thrilling. I was sitting to the right of the audition table, with Gianna Rolandi on my left. I looked at her just as she turned toward me, obviously near tears. "I've lost it," she whispered. "I've just lost it."

Honeywell followed up the Lenski aria with Macduff's impassioned call to arms from *Macbeth*. He sang the first verse plaintively, with great feeling, then launched into the second one like a trumpet call, the top notes solid and ringing, a rendition Verdi himself would have delighted in, every word clear and meaningfully rendered. I was stunned, because nothing, not even the news of Honeywell's success in Montreal, had prepared me for such a dramatic turnaround. I was listening to a potentially fine singer, not just another struggling apprentice.

No sooner had Honeywell left the room, a big confident grin on his face, than Rolandi bolted out the door after him. I rose to follow her and noticed Epstein sitting toward the rear of the room, his legs crossed, and leaning back in his chair, looking more relaxed than I'd ever seen him. When I emerged into the corridor, I found Rolandi weeping in Honeywell's arms, both of them grinning at each other. I waited and then congratulated him, after which he left. When the elevator doors closed behind him, Rolandi turned to look at me. "He's worked so hard," she said. "Two years ago, when he came here, we had to start from scratch."

There is no one sure way to guarantee a successful career in the demanding world of opera or in the arts in general. Intense dedication, hard work, consistency, courage and a bit of luck all play their part, assuming you have the talent to begin with. It's important to have a good teacher, you need expert coaching, you have to master foreign languages, eventually you'll need to have a good manager and you'll need the patient and unfailing support of friends and family. "How all this finally plays out depends on you," Pearlman declared at the National Opera Association meeting in the winter of 2004. "The task is large, and the time grows shorter. Success is going to involve continually reinventing yourselves and the circumstances of your professional lives."

All of the above is true, I realized that afternoon, after hearing Honeywell sing, but there is also an intangible. There comes a moment when all the hard work and the seemingly never-ending concentration on technique have to be forgotten. You just have to step out one day and sing, glory in the music and the sound of your own voice and let it fly. What must have happened in Montreal, and what I had witnessed that afternoon in Room 550 of Lyric, was the birth of an opera singer.

17

Everybody Wants to Get into the Act

NO SOONER HAD I walked into Susan Mathieson Mayer's office one morning shortly after my arrival in Chicago than I became aware that I was in the presence of a beautiful, supremely elegant woman who was not exactly enchanted by my presence. "What can I help you with?" she asked me as I sat down across the desk from her. She wasn't exactly hostile to my being there, but it was clear that, as the head of Lyric's marketing and communications department, she had a lot more on her mind that day than wasting a lot of time on a bumbling reporter. She knew who I was and why I was in town, but her primary job was to sell tickets, and she had been at it long enough to know that what she had to do was a hell of a lot more important than feeding statistics to someone who would probably get them wrong anyway.

It wasn't so much the statistics that interested me, I assured her, as wanting to know what it was that made the Lyric operation so successful. Why was it the only major opera company in America that could balance its books year after year at a time when the arts in general were in big trouble everywhere? I cited some stats of my own: the Metropolitan Opera facing the withdrawal of funding for its Saturday-afternoon broadcasts; the crisis in the classical recording business; the failure of symphony orchestras all over the country; the lack of funding for educational arts programs. As Richard Pearlman put it, "Obviously all of this has to be related to general trends in American society—the relentless lowering of the bar in marketing everything." In other words, another aspect of the general dumbing-down of America. Perhaps opera, too, would have to go along in order to survive. How about Andrea Bocelli as Siegfried and Sheryl Crow as Brünnhilde? I didn't suggest that solution to Susan Mathieson Mayer, but I hoped she'd share some of her secrets with me.

There are no secrets, it turned out; the only requirements are imagination, dedication and very hard work. Fund-raising—mostly from the rich folks and the corporate types who get a bang as well as a tax deduction out of supporting the arts—accounts for only about 30 percent of the yearly budget; the rest has to be raised from ticket sales. No one in the world of American opera today is better at that than Susan Mathieson Mayer, who believes that when singers look out at the house from the stage they should not be able to spot a single empty seat. She considers it sort of an insult to the artists who are out there singing their guts out and may be giving the performance of their lives. Opera is a great art form, but it's also entertainment and for today's audience it has to be sold as such. The superbly illustrated hard-sell brochures Mathieson Mayer and her staff mail out to their potential subscribers bristle with hyperbole and innuendo, portraying each opera in the season as an occasion not to be missed by even the most jaded voluptuary or action-movie fan. After all, the real opera buffs will always renew their subscriptions; it's the innocents, the young and the unworldly, who have to be convinced that there's a lot more to opera than just a bunch of overweight people standing around in funny costumes bellowing their lungs out. Today, about a quarter of the Lyric subscription audience is under the age of forty-five, and you don't lure those people into the theater unless there's some sort of exciting action going on. A coterie of young, mostly German stage directors working mainly abroad have been luring the younger audiences by trashing the masterpieces of Verdi, Wagner and Mozart with modern interpretations featuring rape, mutilation, group sex and orgiastic violence, but so far the trend has failed to establish a foothold in America and certainly not at Lyric. Mathieson Mayer's brochures may hint at some pretty tasty goings-on, but they do not misrepresent what is being offered onstage, and their only intent is to pique the potential ticket buyer's curiosity. They are small masterpieces of their genre. "He slays the dragon who guards the Rhine gold!" reads the opening paragraph on *Siegfried*. "He destroys the power of the mighty god Wotan! He bursts through a ring of fire and rescues Brünnhilde, who returns his love with wild abandon. He is Siegfried, hero supreme, and Wagner's inspiration for his monumental testament to the human spirit, the *Ring* cycle." Cool! Awesome! Sign me up!

Mathieson Mayer first became aware of opera as a child taking piano lessons in her native Canada, but was far more interested in horses than in music. In college she took advertising and journalism courses, and her first job was writing advertising copy for a radio station in Vancouver. She found her true calling when she became marketing director for the Vancouver Symphony, where in eight years she built a subscription base of forty-two thousand subscribers, then the largest for any orchestra in the world. Unfortunately, after the orchestra went on strike, she told me, "the whole thing fell apart after that." So she struck out on her own and became director of marketing for the arts at Expo '86, the World's Fair in Montreal, where she helped sell out 102 of the 106 events. "It was a fantastic experience," she recalled, "because every country in the world was contributing to it. There was something going on every night."

Her toughest assignment was what to do with La Scala. "La Scala, La Scala, everybody wanted La Scala and they would come but only with Verdi's *I Lombardi*." It was her job to sell out a handful of performances of this early Verdi gem nobody had heard of and that was going to be produced in an ice rink. *I Lombardi* has some nice tunes and some rousing choruses, but its story line is a confused mishmash involving fratricide, patricide, mistaken identity and frustrated love, all set against the background of the First Crusade, in which the good Christians are bent on recapturing Jerusalem from the naughty Arabs. "It was a huge undertaking," Mathieson Mayer said, "and I figured I was either going to come out of this as a hero or a bum." She succeeded in selling every ticket, and figures that over the course of those five performances more people saw *I Lombardi* than had seen it since Verdi composed it.

After the failure of her first marriage, Mathieson Mayer found herself living in San Jose, California, when she was recruited in 1988 by Ardis Krainik to come to Lyric. Lyric hadn't been doing too badly before she arrived, selling out about 90 percent of capacity, but Mathieson Mayer soon helped to boost that figure to well over 100 percent, a figure arrived at by reselling seats turned in by ticket buyers who for some reason couldn't show up. In sixteen years on the job she set a standard that no one else has been able to match.

At the time I met Mathieson Mayer, I had no idea how she had managed every year to sell about three hundred thousand seats, a huge number even in a city as big as Chicago. It's one thing to mail out peppy, colorful brochures, build up your mailing lists and lure buyers into the fold; it's quite another to be able to keep doing that year after year after year, even when the national economy slumps. Did it mean having to compromise on what kind of a season you put together? Yes and no. "Every couple of weeks we sit down with the business department," she said, "and we try to figure out where we are in relation to where the company is. It's a fascinating job because it's a combination of art and business. We evaluate the season in terms of costs and ticket prices and consider the effect of sales on the repertory. You balance what you want to do artistically with the demands of the marketplace. In opera you have to plunk down at least a hundred dollars for a good seat, much more than for a theater ticket. In good times you don't care. In bad ones, and when customers get more choosy, you have to work that much harder." She leaned back in her chair and smiled. "I don't do this alone, you know." She suggested I talk to Danny Newman, who, she said, first thought up the whole subscription process a long time ago.

I found Danny Newman occupying a cubbyhole of an office on the eighth floor, not far from Mathieson Mayer's. He turned out to be a delightful character, an eighty-five-year-old elf, short, plump and bald, with a round cherubic face featuring an upraised black eyebrow that gave him a quizzical look, as if he wasn't quite sure you clearly understood what he was all about. He was wearing gray slacks and a black shirt, and when I sat down he began to regale me with tales of his many accomplishments. He wasn't boasting, even though he obviously had a lot to boast about, but he wanted to make sure I got it all and got it right. It was he, he immediately pointed out, who had written the book *Subscribe Now!*, which has become the Bible in this country for marketing the arts. His basic idea? Force people to subscribe if they want to be assured of good seats. Reward the loyalty of your subscribers by giving them the choice seats and allowing them to upgrade every year. Bombard this audience with missives and propaganda and enticements and ensure their loyalty by granting them little perks. Don't let the people who want to go to just the best or the most popular offerings shoulder aside the faithful who come to everything. You would imagine that in a country built on entrepreneurship, publicity and advertising, this technique would have been adopted from the very beginning, but it wasn't until Danny Newman dreamed it up a half-century ago and trumpeted it to the country at large that anybody thought of it.

Newman retired years ago, but was still coming into the office once a day for a couple of hours or so to sit behind his desk, make phone calls and bask in his triumphs. "I'm the only survivor of the founding staff of Lyric," he pointed out, having come on board in 1954, when Carol Fox, then only twenty-six, and Nicola Rescigno launched their first season. And as he talked, all I had to do to understand who he was to gaze at the walls, which were plastered with photographs of the great singers and people he had known. When, after an hour and a half, I finally managed to shut the front door of his office behind me, my ears still ringing, I noticed that it, too, was covered with photos and clippings, the latter going back as far as World War II, in which he had served as an infantryman. Quite a career, if he did say so himself, and Lyric owes much of its success over the years to him.

IT ISN'T ONLY TODAY'S fans that Lyric concerns itself with. There is an Education Department, whose sole purpose is to open up the world of opera to younger audiences, ranging from the primary grades to college students. Combined financially with the goings-on at the Opera Center, the Education Department operates out of a total budget of approximately three million dollars. Its activities are multitudinous, offering a newly commissioned children's opera put on by the kids themselves called *Stone Soup,* based on a classic story, *A Noteworthy Tale,* and fifteen other programs of lecture tours, backstage visits, student matinees, teacher education and workshops, discussion groups and access to Lyric's media library, which includes more than three thousand historic opera LPs, CDs and videotapes. The Education Department also sponsors Opera-in-the-Neighborhoods, abridged English-language productions using young professional singers performing under an AGMA contract in full costume with sets and props in the local and suburban elementary schools over a period of about five weeks, from mid-October to mid-November. Accompanied by cheery printed student guides and coloring books and timed so that the kids can attend in harmony with the demands of their schoolwork, the performances are free, though donations are accepted. When I was informed that this year's production was Rossini's *La Cenerentola,* being put on in English as *Cinderella,* I decided to attend what I was told would be the season's last performance.

I was driven to the site by Jean Keister Kellogg, the head of the department, a tall, attractive woman with long, curly brown hair, a gleaming smile and a ready laugh. Her father was a professor at the University of Florida in Gainesville, where she grew up, studied piano and also took singing lessons. A lyric soprano, she told me she still sang as an avocation. She was hired by Lyric in 1999 and arrived on New Year's Day to find twenty-four inches of snow on the ground and a temperature, with the wind-chill factor, hovering at twenty-five below zero, where it lingered for weeks. Her car immediately died. Having been born and raised in Florida, she found herself not quite prepared for this kind of meteorological reception, but did manage to show up for work by eight-thirty her first morning. "Oh, you're here!" the first person to spot her said to her. "I thought you might have turned around and gone home."

Getting to North Central College, where the performance was to be held, took nearly an hour—a long, boring drive through a succession of mostly dismal neighborhoods of run-down housing, empty lots, abandoned factory buildings, grim-looking churches and trash-strewn avenues that reminded me of Liebling's descriptions of Chicago in *The Second City.* Not much has changed in these parts of town where the poor still live, though the college itself, while not draped in ivy, is a respectable-looking institution in a neighborhood of fairly friendly-looking tree-lined streets. Several big yellow school buses were parked outside.

Inside the spacious, austere auditorium the front rows of seats were full of excited, jabbering little kids all dressed in dark pants or skirts and white shirts. The middle-aged red-haired woman who ushered us in told me that this year they had had one group of fifty-one children who had been regarded as hopelessly wild and uncontrollable, but that once the opera started "you couldn't have heard a sound." When I asked her how they had managed to get a college auditorium to perform in, she answered, "We go around begging from everyone."

We sat down behind the kids, about halfway back in the theater, just as a sturdy-looking woman began to speak to them from the front of the stage. This was Mary Kurz, a retired high school English teacher now employed by Lyric and considered one of the best at what she did, which was to get the children's attention and get them interested in what they were about to experience. Behind her onstage the curtains were open to reveal a simple but lively and colorful set depicting Cinderella's home, with a grand piano for the accompanist downstage left. It didn't take very long for Kurz to prepare the kids for the action. They listened to her attentively, after which the small cast of seven launched itself into the heart of Rossini's minor little masterpiece.

La Cenerentola usually takes about two and a half hours to perform, but this *Cinderella* had been cut down to a fifty-minute version. It had all the good stuff, including the major arias and ensembles, and the young singers performed with vigor, with no cheapening of the music or artistic compromises. The acting and dancing featured exaggerated gestures, prancing and posturing that delighted the audience and had me laughing along with them. Michael Mayes, in the part of Dandini, the Prince's manservant, effectively stole the show, not only with his silken baritone but also with a hilarious imitation of Elvis Presley that brought shrieks of delight from the front rows. Also vocally and physically impressive for his tall good looks in the role of Alidoro was bass-baritone Brandon Mayberry, who had been accepted into the Opera Center program for 2004–2005.

After the performance, the cast, still in full costume, lined up onstage to introduce themselves to the children and to explain to them what sort of voices they had, where they were from and where they had studied. Then they asked for questions and a forest of hands shot up: "Do you have to work really hard?" "Where do you get the clothes?" "Are the dresses comfortable?" "How long did it take to learn the opera?" "What was the hardest part about working?" "Are you scared?" After the question-and-answer session, the singers left the stage to mingle with the kids, who crowded excitedly around them to ask more questions and comment on their looks, characters and interpretations. This was the first opera experience any of these mostly poor children had ever had, and it was moving to see them so involved. "If you give kids top quality," Jean Keister Kellogg said to me as we rose to leave, "you turn them on immediately."

"The students see this *Cinderella* and then they get a chance to put it on themselves, if they want to, through our Opera in the Classroom program," she said on the drive back to Lyric. "In this version of the story, there's no magic; the magic comes from the heart." What Kellogg and her staff were focusing on was the process of breaking down barriers, providing the kids with the experience of having gone to an opera and recalling that experience. For the older young people, Lyric offered tickets to college students at 50 percent off, so it would be possible for them to go to all of the operas in a whole season for a total of less than a hundred dollars. There are some twenty-five colleges in the immediate Chicago area, so it was hoped that many of the young people who experienced opera in any of these ways might later become subscribers. "We reach about sixty thousand kids in five hundred to six hundred schools and about twenty thousand adults every year," Kellogg said. "These programs are not aimed at people who can afford regular ticket prices."

No major opera company these days can afford to waste money—every dollar counts—but the long-range view Lyric has adopted seemed to me to be the very best way to ensure that opera remains a vital art and entertainment form in the United States.

After every performance of the *Cinderella,* Jean Keister Kellogg told me, the company receives showers of mail from the children. A typical one read: "Dear Cinderella, The best play I ever saw was *Cinderella.* I wish I could see the play over and over. Also, I wish you performed in our school because we wouldn't have to ride in a smelly old bus. I have to go now and dream about me being you, Cinderella." What we have here is possibly a future diva or, at the very least, a subscriber. Not, we have to hope, another Paris Hilton wannabe.

AS THE 2003–2004 SEASON progressed in Chicago, the company became increasingly cagey about releasing any figures concerning ticket sales and finances, which made me believe its tactics were succeeding. It wouldn't have made a lot of sense to trumpet abroad too early the existence of a surplus, if only because everybody involved might relax and the pressure on contributors might slack off. I stopped worrying about it and went home for Thanksgiving and the Christmas holidays, just as Chicago's bitter winter weather began to grip the city. It wasn't until after the season was over that I found out exactly how well Lyric had succeeded. A little paragraph in the July issue of *Opera* revealed that, after having faced a shortfall of $1.1 million in 2002–2003, Lyric had ended the year with a tidy little surplus of $700,000, a nice cushion with which to launch its fiftieth anniversary season.

18

A Night to Remember

AT THE FIRST REHEARSAL of *Lucia* that I attended, I found the director, John Copley, busy staging the big scene in act two that celebrates the wedding of the heroine to the man she is being forced to marry, the unlucky Arturo, a comprimario tenor role being sung by Scott Ramsay. The rehearsal took place in Room 200, where the backstage crew had mounted the set portraying the great hall of the Ashton castle. None of the principals—Natalie Dessay in the title role, Marcelo Alvarez as Edgardo, Ashley Holland as Lucia's brother, Enrico—was present, only Ramsay, Lauren Curnow in the very small role of Alisa, and Chris Dickerson, who was covering the part of Raimondo. Copley, a stocky Brit with a round, cheerful face, was energetically flitting about the room positioning the chorus and moving clumps of them around here and there to achieve the effect he wanted. As he did so, he chattered away, spouting a stream of witty observations and jokes that had the chorus periodically in stitches. In between his sorties, the cast sang away. I noticed that Donald Palumbo, the chorus master, did not seem overly amused by the director's monologues; he was much more preoccupied with the sounds his singers were making. They sounded just fine to me, but Palumbo, who is considered in the opera world to be one of the two or three best at what he does, suffers visibly at the mangling of a syllable. Between Copley's jokes and witticisms, however, I noticed that not only the chorus

but also the three young LOCAA singers involved were singing well.

During a break in the proceedings I strolled over to where
Copley was again holding forth, this time to a small group of en-
thralled listeners. He is a famous raconteur and a fearless gossip.
On this occasion he was recalling having had to direct a *Norma*
the year before in which the title role was sung for the first time by
a Russian soprano entirely incapable of coping with the difficult
bel canto demands of the part. Copley proceeded to do a hilarious
imitation of her "Casta diva," choking his way through it like a
strangled chicken, then informed us that the famous duet with the
mezzo, "Mira, o Norma," had been lowered "by a full third, my
dears. The Adalgisa was singing bass. It was so dreadful I should
have refused my fee. Of course, I took it. I'm such a whore!"

I asked him about today's young singers coming up and this
set him off on a rant about the absence of great talent on the
operatic scene. "Where are the Aidas, the Amnerises?" he asked.
"In the old days there were plenty of them." And he rattled off a
list of big names from the past. "Today there are no big voices,
no divas. Where are the divas?" This is a common complaint of
the older operatic generation. The fact is, there never was an
overabundance of great talent, which is why we remember the
big ones.

Copley directed his first *Lucia* for Lyric in 1975 and has staged
it all over the world. Like Frank Corsaro, he has directed in most
of the major opera houses in the United States and abroad, and he
also teaches at London's Royal Academy and Royal College of
Music, Britain's National Opera Studio and in several young
artist programs. Nor is he shy about appearing onstage himself.
At the final dress rehearsal for a *Lucia* being produced by the
Scottish Opera's Newcastle Festival some years earlier, the soprano felt she was losing her voice and left the premises before
the Mad Scene. "The act had already started," Copley likes to recall, "so with no understudy available, there was no alternative

but to sing the role myself! Raimondo was not the only one *amazed* at just how crazy Lucia seemed to have become. Conductor, orchestra and chorus all continued completely professionally, and I sang one or two quite good notes."

Copley began his operatic life as a countertenor, and he recalls having once hit "a perfect B-flat onstage at Covent Garden and realizing in that moment the thrill that a singer must experience when that happens to him during a performance." That B-flat, Richard Pearlman informed me later, dated back to sometime in the 1960s, when Copley was working as an assistant to Franco Zeffirelli and they were rehearsing a *Tosca* starring Maria Callas. When Callas failed for some reason to show up, Copley suddenly appeared onstage and sang her entrance music. The problem was that no one had informed the Italian maestro Cillario, who promptly stopped conducting, his baton frozen in midair.

Now once again, when the *Lucia* rehearsal resumed in Room 200, Copley stepped in for the heroine, making his grand entrance down the long flight of stairs toward the wedding reception. No one giggled or laughed, however, because Copley himself had become intensely serious. It was necessary for everyone present to nail this scene, so that by the time the principals showed up precious minutes would not be wasted. Hemmed in by union rules and outrageous costs, no opera company can afford to fool around for too long. What can be done in the movies over a period of months and in the theater over a period of weeks has to be accomplished in the opera house in days.

I wanted to spend more time with Copley but was unable to then because he was rushing out of town for another commitment and would not be back for several weeks, until well into the final *Lucia* rehearsals. I did catch up with him by chance, however, in the main hallway of the Presidential Towers, where we were both staying. I asked him again about his take on young singers, and this set him off on another rant about how unprepared most of them were and how they paid so little attention to the meaning of the words. His vehemence surprised me, because I thought Ramsay, Curnow and Dickerson had sung well. Ramsay had been battling a cold, however, and had sounded a bit hoarse, while Curnow had had literally almost nothing to sing. But Dickerson? He had made a majestic presence and sung with great dignity and force. "Ah, that one," Copley answered. "Yes, I think there's hope for him." I gathered that this passed for high praise from him in his present state of mind.

ON FRIDAY AFTERNOON, January 23, the day before the opening of *Lucia,* I dropped into Room 550 for a complete run-through of the opera for the understudies. The floor had been set with stools, chairs and other bits of furniture to substitute for the set, and the cast was wearing capes, hats and a few other items of clothing, and was carrying swords and other necessary props. The singers were told this would be a nonstop run-through unless the director, the conductor or some other dignitary felt there was a real need to go over something. Copley was not in attendance, but his assistant director, Thor Steingraber, a Lyric staff member, was present. Also missing was Matthew Epstein, who was represented by the company's artistic administrator, Andy Melinat, a cheerful young man whose administrative duties apparently included keeping Epstein informed of goings-on he could not or would not attend himself. The indispensable Eric Weimer faced the cast, baton in hand, to guide them through the opera.

From the artists' point of view the most important people in the room, sitting quietly off to one side, were Sir Andrew Davis and Jesús López Cobos, an eminent Spanish conductor who had made his American debut with this opera in San Francisco back in 1972. Their presence guaranteed that the singers would do their very best and sing out full voice. You don't get jobs or make an impression by marking through every rehearsal. Taking it easy during the rehearsal period is for the leads, the people who have already established themselves; everybody else is in a constant state of auditioning. The only singer in this group I hadn't heard before was the baritone Christopher Feigum, who was covering Enrico. An LOCAA graduate from the group of 2001–2002, Feigum began his career as a chorister. "I never intended to become a singer," he informed me cheerfully before the start of the rehearsal. He proved to have a big, solid voice and projected a manly stage presence.

I was familiar with everybody else in the cast from having listened to them through so many coaching sessions and auditions, but nevertheless I was impressed by what I heard that afternoon. Stacey Tappan sang with power and precision as Lucia, her trills, high notes and extended lyric passages all beautifully rendered. Patrick Miller as Arturo looked dashing and made much of his one small aria, Curnow's voice as Alisa sounded sweet and strong and Dickerson sang nobly as Raimondo, his Italian diction as clear as if he'd been born to the language. Ramsay worried me a bit. His Edgardo was adequate, but he sounded a bit hoarse again and it turned out that he was once more suffering from a cold. It had been brutally frigid for weeks, with Chicago's typical icy winter winds whistling down the avenues and around the corners of buildings, and not only the singers were suffering from the weather. Gianna Rolandi was sick, and I'd been told that sniffles and coughs were afflicting dozens of members of the company. Ramsay began to mark in act two, though everybody else continued to sing out. It would be their last chance to do so and they took advantage of it, even though both Davis and López Cobos left long before the last scene, apparently satisfied with what they'd seen and heard.

What was particularly interesting to me about this forthcoming *Lucia* was that it included almost all of the music in the original Donizetti score. Over the years since they were first performed, many famous opera scores have been whittled down, sometimes with entire scenes omitted to speed the audiences home faster, or musical sections altered to suit the caprices and talents of various stars. "The only music that will not be heard," López Cobos declared in his program notes for this production, "will be a couple of repeats in the big ensembles at the end of act two that are tiring for the voice. We are not cutting the big duet between Enrico and Edgardo, which is fantastic musically and dramatically. It also clarifies why Edgardo would be expecting Enrico to appear in the last scene." López Cobos had made a study of the composer's autograph score and concluded that the role of Lucia had not been written for a coloratura soprano but for a more lyric voice. The role, since Donizetti's time, had been taken over by piping little nightingales like Adelina Patti and Lily Pons, anyone able to chirp away high up above the staff to a flute accompaniment Donizetti had also never composed. The famous Mad Scene had thus become, like Verdi's "Caro nome," an opportunity for vocal acrobatics that had little or nothing to do with the dramatic sentiments supposedly being expressed. In the autograph score Lucia's music had been written in higher keys because there had been no need for the acrobatics performed in the later versions. For this production, López Cobos was asking the Lucia, Natalie Dessay, to sing the original tessitura, without the squeaky top notes or the flute obbligato. It was going to be interesting, because audiences since Donizetti's time had become so accustomed to Lucia's going mad while standing stock still to squeeze out an improbable E-flat that they might find themselves wondering if she were really going nuts after all.

It is always dangerous in the opera house to mess about too much with tradition. I recall a *Tales of Hoffmann* at the Los Angeles Opera years ago when the company decided to put on a version of the work that restored great chunks of music to the prologue and cut one of the most famous arias in the score, "Scintille diamant," because the academic type who had ferreted out Offenbach's original pages had concluded that the composer had not written it. The result was a disaster. The prologue lasted more than an hour, longer than any of the actual acts, and the missing aria, one of the most thrilling in the bass-baritone canon, screamed in vain to be heard. Most of the L.A. audience, in its ignorance, applauded in puzzled politeness, but there were well-merited boos from the cognoscenti. It's okay, especially in Germany today, to cut women's nipples off in Mozart's *Abduction from the Seraglio* or dress up the Priests of Babylon as bumblebees in Verdi's *Nabucco,* but you leave the score alone. Still, as I reflected on what I was about to hear, I reminded myself that *Lucia* was the fifty-second of this composer's prolific offerings and that Donizetti himself probably would not have minded the liberties being taken with his work, so intent was he on whatever commission he had in hand. There is a famous story that when he was informed that Rossini had composed the overture to his *Barber of Seville* in a single night, Donizetti observed, "I always said he was lazy."

WHEN I SETTLED into my seat at Lyric the following evening for the opening of Donizetti's fine old chestnut, I was entirely unprepared for what transpired onstage. I hadn't been attending any of the late rehearsals, so I was unaware that I was about to experience one of those evenings in the opera house that all of us who love the form dream about and will remember for the rest of our lives. A truly great performance in a major role can lift you, as a lover of great singing and acting, into a realm bordering on ecstasy. It exalts and enriches your life in the way all great art can.

From the moment Natalie Dessay appeared in the second scene of act one to sing her opening aria, "Regnava nel silenzio," I knew instantly that I was in the presence of not only a fine singer but also a superb actress. Neurotic, distressed, but also determined and willful, she moved about the stage like a cornered cat, her voice soaring strongly and beautifully over the orchestra and matching her lover Edgardo's ardor note for note in the ensuing duet, "Verranno a te." Dessay is a small, pretty woman, delicate-looking, who moves with the grace of a trained dancer, her every gesture a meaningful one. As the evening progressed, she continued to fill out a portrayal of this tragic heroine that brought home to the audience the full measure of her tragedy and that of her lover. She played her Mad Scene not as a pathetic victim standing stock still to chirp away and show how high she could sing, but as a woman used and betrayed, forced to commit a murder in order to defend her honor and brought to despair and madness by the machinations of the men in her life. As she sang, her nightdress drenched in the blood of her hapless victim, she moved about the castle hall, darting here and there to pull the settings off the wedding tables, then retreating pitifully into her delusions and the ultimate madness powered by her grief and rage.

The reviewers were unanimous in their praise. This little French soprano, everyone agreed, had become a great star, a true diva. There was no end to what she would be able to accomplish in the future, and it was pointed out not only that this was her first performance of *Lucia* in Italian—she had already sung and recorded it in a French version—but that the fact she was able to perform at this level of excellence in anything was in itself a kind of miracle. In 2001, Dessay had had to stop singing entirely to have nodes surgically removed from her vocal cords, a not unusual ailment that afflicts singers but one that can end a career. It had taken her two years of hard work to be able to return to the stage. Married to the French baritone Laurent Naouri and the mother of two small children, Dessay has said that she intends to limit her yearly performances in order to balance her professional and family life. "Opera is only a job," she told an interviewer. But at her level it's a great art.

She wasn't alone onstage in this performance, of course, and the other cast members mostly did well enough to support her. The English baritone Ashley Holland proved to have a well-balanced lyric voice and acted convincingly as Lucia's bullying, alcoholic brother, Enrico; and Tomas Tomasson, with his big, hollow-sounding voice, got by as Raimondo, though with far less style and conviction than I'd heard in rehearsal from his understudy, Dickerson. Lauren Curnow sang sweetly and clearly as Alisa. But David Cangelosi, clearly a bit over the top from his triumph as Mime, hammed it up as Normanno, Enrico's chief gunsel, and Ramsay sounded and looked insecure as Arturo. I found myself worrying about him, because he didn't seem comfortable in the part. His voice sounded a bit thin on top and his fluttery cavalier's costume was not flattering to his stocky frame. For me, however, the only real disappointment of the evening was Marcelo Alvarez, the swashbuckling Argentine tenor who is regarded by many as a forthcoming superstar. He sang adequately, but his voice sounded a bit dry, and as an actor he gave a splendid imitation of an Italian prosciutto, going through the motions as if pushing his way through a subway turnstile. Dump this guy, I found myself wanting to shout up at Lucia. He's just another poodle!

Over the next several weeks I went to three more performances of *Lucia* just to hear and watch Dessay. Every night, I stood in the wings stage left and watched her make her entrances and exits and listened to her sing. Every performance was a triumph, every one a bit different from the one before, full of tiny nuances, little gestures, bits of vocal artistry I hadn't noticed before. And every night, at the end of the Mad Scene, those of us who had come backstage to listen to her—stagehands, administrators, front-of-the-house employees, chorus members, supers—applauded her when she came running off, waving and smiling to us with self-deprecating little gestures of her hands as she scurried for her dressing room.

In opera, as in sports, you remember the great ones, the artists who awed you with their talents and whom you were lucky enough to have been on hand to hear: Birgit Nilsson in her first Isolde at the old Met, when that clarion soprano blasted magnificently over the orchestra; the debuts also at the old Met of tenors Ferruccio Tagliavini and Giuseppe di Stefano, caressing my ears with those mellifluous open Italian voices; the aging Beniamino Gigli singing gloriously in concert at the open-air Basilica di Massenzio in Rome, that golden sound soaring into the cool Roman night; that *Sonnambula* at La Scala when Maria Callas had the audience on its feet roaring its approval at the joyous skill of her closing rondo. And then, for me, the greatest experience I've ever had in any opera house, when, in the fall of 1972, I was allowed by the late Paolo Grassi, then the general director of La Scala, to sit through an orchestral run-through of the first act of *Norma* in which my favorite soprano, the incomparable Montserrat Caballé, would be rehearsing for her first performance in Milan of Bellini's Druid priestess. I had already acquired a number of her recordings, some of them pirated, but had never heard her in person. Out she came, demurely dressed in a black skirt and sweater with a double strand of pearls around her neck, her black locks swept up into a beehive hairdo. She was the picture of a jolly Barcelona housewife, but the instant she began to sing I was looking and listening to the character the composer had created, her warm liquid soprano soaring effortlessly toward the upper reaches of the empty cream-and-gold boxes of this great house—a "Casta diva" that left me in tears and that I would never forget. When it was over, the Scala orchestra stopped playing in order to applaud.

These are the performances we opera fanatics remember and cherish. And now, with her amazing Lucia, Natalie Dessay had left me with another one.

I HAD GONE HOME to San Diego in late February, after the first nights of *The Pirates of Penzance* and *Madama Butterfly,* to begin organizing my notes prior to coming back to Chicago for the end of the season when Magda Krance called. "You better get back here," she said. "Scott's going on as Edgardo."

I was astounded. "What? When?"

"For the last performance, on the twenty-eighth," she said.

I asked her what had happened and she told me that Alvarez had said that he needed to get home for personal reasons. "And so he just left?" I asked. "What about his contract?"

Krance just sighed. "All I know," she said, "is that Scott is going to sing the last performance."

I was stunned, mainly because I was absolutely convinced that Ramsay would not be able to sing Edgardo in a house as big as the Civic. He had a sweet and true lyric tenor, but even as Arturo his voice had sounded a bit thin and reedy in that cavernous space. Edgardo? Well, maybe he could get away with the opening duet, but that big dramatic scene with the baritone and then the final one with all those demanding top notes? No way, and I said as much over the phone. I figured that Alvarez, another tenor with a huge ego, had probably had just about enough of having to play second fiddle night after night to Dessay and languish in her shadow, so he had chosen this way to remind everyone of his vocal splendor. Or maybe I was just being unfair to him and he did have to get home for some reason. Contracts are made to be broken by tenors and divas, especially foreign ones. Toward the later stages of her career, Caballé missed so many performances that the joke in the opera world was "this year Madam Caballé is accepting only a limited number of cancellations."

I had seen and heard a lot of Ramsay over the weeks of coaching sessions and auditions and I'd been favorably impressed by him, also because of his attitude. He was kind and polite and persistently cheerful, seemingly able to cope with everything thrown at him. He showed up for every audition, always smiled and greeted everyone pleasantly, never sang less than his best. Ramsay was from Green Bay, Wisconsin, the youngest of four children from an upper-middle-class family (his father had been a TV news anchor for ABC and his mother an interior designer), and one of his earliest memories was of singing when he was in kindergarten. While he was in high school, the local opera company put on a performance of Lehar's *The Merry Widow* and Ramsay "just fell in love with the whole Viennese thing." The next year, the company put on Donizetti's *The Daughter of the Regiment* and "that cemented it." He sang all through college, at the University of Wisconsin at Milwaukee, then studied with the well-known soprano Diana Soviero, who also gave him his first tickets to the Met, for a *Lucia* and a *Magic Flute*. He was then twenty-four.

In 1998, he was hired by the Florida Grand Opera, in Miami, to sing in the chorus and in comprimario roles, one of ten young artists under contract. The chorus work he remembers as "a pain," but in those two years he learned twenty-six roles. "It was kind of sink or swim," he told me. "Vocally you learned how to get through things. I'm not an academic. I don't sit down and study, so this was all about learning how to study. And I also learned a lot about acting onstage." He'd also never had to deal with languages, but spent two seasons at the Berkshire Summer Festival, in Massachusetts, where instructors from Mannes and Juilliard taught courses in French, Italian, German and Russian. Now he'd put in his three years at LOCAA and he was ready to move on, even though nothing special or spectacular had broken for him in all this time. He had no agent or manager, but he was sure he'd be getting enough work to have a career. He was clearly one of those people for whom the glass was always half full, not a bad trait to have in any kind of show business.

At eleven-thirty on the morning of February 26, my first day back from San Diego, I was sitting once again in Room 550 for still another audition of the Opera Center singers. This one was for Eric Mitchko, one of CAMI's numerous vice presidents and therefore an important agent. He was young, with a pleasant demeanor and a positive attitude toward the young artists who paraded before him to sing their two or three arias. What made the audition unusual for me was the presence at it of Scott Ramsay, who was scheduled to begin rehearsing forty minutes later with Natalie Dessay in Room 200, the only chance he'd have to work with her before going on as Edgardo two nights later. It didn't seem to faze him in the least. He opened his audition with a sweetly rendered "Una furtiva lagrima," then, at Mitchko's request, tackled two more arias, a very ornate and difficult one from Handel's *Semele* and one of his best audition pieces, "Le Rêve," from *Manon.* After which he bounced out of the premises, cheery as always, to head for Room 200, with me trailing in his wake.

I found out later that when Dessay heard that Alvarez was leaving early and Ramsay would step in, she went straight to López Cobos to make sure there would be at least one music rehearsal for the two of them, this despite the fact that she'd already sung ten performances of the role and had begun to work every day on a *Manon* that she would be doing for the first time later in the year. Marina Vecci, who has seen them all come and go, said of Dessay, "No one works harder on a role." But then this is what the great ones do.

The rehearsal in Room 200 began just after Ramsay got there, with Dessay strolling about as she sang, mostly marking her solo passages and concentrating on the music. Dressed in black slacks and an open-necked jersey, her long brown hair pulled back into a ponytail, she looked even tinier than she did onstage. Phil Morehead accompanied the singers, while Eric Weimer conducted, with López Cobos seated next to him. From time to time, particularly toward the end of the duet, which is musically complex, Dessay and Ramsay would stop to reprise phrases, but on the whole Ramsay held his own and it was clear that Dessay was happy and comfortable with him. At the end of the act they proceeded to the famous sextet, with only one quick minor fix on the phrase *"t'amo ancor,"* which was a half beat off. After it was over,

Dessay waved a quick farewell to everyone and left; it was all she had to sing with the tenor in the whole opera, which led Ramsay to observe, "For an opera about two lovers, they don't spend a lot of time together." "And it's not even quality time," Weimer said with a smile.

The rest of the rehearsal was spent going over all of Edgardo's music, with Weimer bravely singing in a quavery light tenor all the other parts from memory as he conducted. Ramsay seemed totally comfortable having to work alone in front of all these operatic heavyweights, and when he got to the Tomb Scene he stopped marking and let it fly. His voice sounded lovely, but then this was in a room, not in the auditorium. Nevertheless, we all applauded when he finished, and López Cobos said, "Bravo!" I looked with admiration at Ramsay. He had sung three arias at an audition, then changed out of his formal clothes into a rehearsal outfit of brown corduroy pants and a brown open-necked shirt to work through an entire difficult part all by himself, with the notable exception of the incredible Dessay. I began to believe that he might just get away with singing Edgardo, and I was rooting hard for him. "Anything else?" Ramsay asked after he'd stopped singing. "Just a couple of little details," Weimer answered, proceeding to correct him on the pronunciation of a few key words and to warn him that toward the end of the opening aria in the Tomb Scene he was a shade under pitch. Then even Weimer ran out of things to say, except to add, as Ramsay gathered up his things, "Try not to do more than three auditions on Saturday."

I arrived early backstage on the night of Ramsay's Edgardo to find the Lyric brass already present. Mason, Davis and Epstein were clustered together in Room 102, chatting about something. The fact that they were there for the eleventh and last performance of one of the operas in the rep was significant. Whatever their feelings about what would happen onstage, they were committed to Ramsay and would have to live with it if the evening turned out to be a disappointment, not to say a fiasco. Comprimario tenors do not move into major roles in first-rate opera houses, and the reaction of the audience would tell Mason et al. if they had erred.

In the Rehearsal Department, Marina Vecci was presiding behind her desk, looking calm and very pleased with herself, like a happy cherub. She clearly felt absolutely confident that the evening would go well, which reassured me. Vecci is a small, perky, energetic woman who is capable of maintaining a kind of majestic calm in the midst of the chaos that is the Rehearsal Department on performance nights, and also at any other time when there is a crisis of one sort or another. A native Italian, she has been at Lyric since 1975, when hardly anyone in the company spoke English and she was recruited from her job at the Northwestern University library to be an interpreter and translator. She remembers everyone and everything and has become as much of a fan of the singers as anyone in the company. Now, when Patrick Miller suddenly appeared in the hallway dressed in his costume for his first performance as Arturo, looking very dashing in a great plumed hat, she commented that perhaps Lucia should think twice about rejecting him as a suitor, even though it would change the plot of the opera. Miller looked happier than I'd ever seen him. He, too, was at last getting a chance to sing a real part with a little aria of his own. I went over to him to tell him *in bocca al lupo,* which means "into the mouth of the wolf," the traditional Italian way to wish a singer good luck.

I spent the first act sitting out front and I was immediately struck by how well Ramsay was doing. Whereas as Arturo he had seemed tentative and awkward, as Edgardo he moved about the stage with assurance and verve, his voice clear and clean and sweet all through the difficult duet. How he would do the rest of the night was another question, but I found myself feeling very reassured, and the public applauded vigorously. I went backstage at the intermission and remained there for the rest of the evening. Once again a small audience gathered in the wings to listen to

Dessay's Mad Scene, including both Marina Vecci and Josie Campbell. Again we all clapped when the soprano came skipping past us, smiling and waving on her way to her dressing room. Phil Morehead, who is much given to understatement, looked at me with a sly grin on his face. "Not bad," he said.

Ramsay continued to sing well all through the confrontation scene in act two, which includes the sextet and an outburst of furious denunciation by Edgardo of Lucia's supposed treachery, but he still seemed to be pacing himself. The first real test of his dramatic vocal resources came in the next act, during the so-called Wolf's Crag Scene, in which the tenor and baritone confront each other in the ruins of Edgardo's castle and agree to fight a duel to the death the following morning at dawn. Suddenly, Ramsay began to display vocal resources I didn't know he had, matching Holland's solid outpouring with some big sounds of his own. Then, in the final scene, he not only sang beautifully and affectingly but actually managed to convince the audience that he was truly distressed and then mortally wounded. At no point in his performances had Alvarez ever achieved that basic essential, the display of a convincing emotion. The critic for the *Sun-Times* noted as much in her review two days later, when she commented that Ramsay proved to be "a much better actor than Alvarez" and that he had "brought a passionate intensity to the role to match the fire of Dessay's riveting Lucia. The opera's tragic tale took flight as it had not with Alvarez."

Backstage afterward, Mason, Davis and Weimer gathered around Ramsay to congratulate him, as did the rest of the cast. Ramsay, sweating profusely in his heavy costume and long wig, beamed with pleasure. I noticed Epstein standing there slightly apart with his arms crossed but looking satisfied, if not ecstatic. I waited until I could catch up to Ramsay on the way back to his dressing room. "I wasn't nervous," he said, "but I don't think I really hit my stride until the Wolf's Crag Scene. Then I realized, 'Hey, I can do this!' I stopped worrying about the singing and just thought about the moment. By the time I got to the aria, I didn't have to worry about it."

Weeks later I talked to Ramsay again and he said, "It was so much fun for me, and I had such great colleagues, so many people behind me." He had since auditioned for the New York City Opera and he'd received some nice letters from people who had attended the performance that night expecting to hear Alvarez and had been agreeably surprised. Then he'd also bumped into people who had been there and said to him admiringly, "Oh, you're the guy who stepped into the *Lucia.*" It was his big break, and now he was waiting and hoping for something to happen. "You can go back to being Arturo again, which I'll be doing in San Diego, or a Parpignol in *Bohème*," he said. "But now I know what craziness is like, the big role, the big responsibility. It's a lot of sweat, a lot of tears. But, as Bill Mason says, 'Hey, it's only opera.'"

Whatever might happen to him in his future career, Ramsay will always be able to recall the success of that night, his first and maybe only Edgardo ever. And there is one other memory he can cherish. As he was coming offstage at the end of the first act, Natalie Dessay grabbed his hand and said to him, "You looked at me!" "What?" he answered. She told him she had sung the role with two other tenors, Roberto Alagna, another big star, and Alvarez. Neither of them had ever looked at her even once during their entire love scene. Tenors—their love affairs with themselves are among the great ones of history.

19

Careers

MATTHEW EPSTEIN DIDN'T GIVE interviews anymore. At least that's what I had been told from my first day in Chicago, but at the same time I knew I couldn't really give a complete picture of what the Opera Center's young singers were going through without talking to him. His presence as the company's artistic director, with enormous influence over all aspects of Lyric's operations, made it imperative for me to see him.

Everywhere I went inside the building, from the rehearsal rooms to the offices and the auditorium itself, day after day I kept running into him. Some of the time he'd ignore me; at best he'd nod quickly to me and immediately look away. I'm sure that if it had been up to him, I never would have been given free access to just wander around and get an idea of what can happen inside an opera company and to its young singers during the course of a season. I didn't blame him. After all, who wants some reporter, however well-intentioned, hanging around asking dumb questions and making notes? Nevertheless, I quietly pressed my case with Bill Mason and Susan Mathieson Mayer about the importance of getting an interview with Epstein, and they graciously agreed to intercede for me.

Matthew Epstein probably knew more about singers and today's opera world in general than anybody I'd ever get to meet, and I'd already heard all sorts of stories, both pro and con, about him. He is not an immensely popular figure like Domingo, but popularity has little to do with ability. So I waited to be summoned, while continuing to talk to everybody else and just wandering around—into and out of coaching sessions, auditions and rehearsals. Even if he decided not to talk to me, I figured that eventually I'd be able to sniff out, just by observing, exactly what the extent of his power was and how he operated. Then, early one afternoon, I walked into Room 550 because I had heard that Quinn Kelsey would be auditioning for an agent named Andrea Anson, another in the large cluster of important managers and agents operating under the CAMI banner, and that Epstein would almost certainly be present. Whatever the circumstances, anytime Quinn Kelsey was going to sing, I wanted to be there.

The first thing that had struck me about Kelsey when I met him, apart from his voice, were his unique good looks, not conventional by any standards. He's a very big man with a light complexion and broad Polynesian features—strong cheekbones and a well-defined jawline. A shock of black hair is combed straight back off his broad forehead. I'd been following Kelsey now long enough also to become aware that nothing seemed to bother him. He had the calm, cool demeanor of a great quarterback, the sort of person who performs best under pressure. This might have been because he'd been exposed to performing at a very early age. His Hawaiian-born mother had studied piano and sung in a church choir. His father, who was born in Carmel, California, had been a singer in a high school rock band and had also performed in choruses and an a cappella group specializing in native Hawaiian music. "In the Pacific Rim the cultures are very oral," Kelsey had explained to me, "heavy on song and music. I went to public schools, where music was all around me." Growing up, he'd sung in his mother's choir and in groups that supplied children's chorus singers for the Hawaii Opera. With his father he appeared in a 1991 production of *Aida,* the first time he'd ever been on a stage, and he loved it. He was then in the seventh grade and singing first tenor, but as he got older it became harder for him to sing high. "So I just dropped down," he recalled. "It was fine. I didn't worry about it." Basically, he didn't worry about much of anything.

He credits his mother—who had a good voice but never pursued a career of her own and continued to teach school—for pushing him in the right direction. "At the time, she was at the top of her game, and a lot of what she did rubbed off on me," Kelsey said. "My mother was like Gianna: really nitpicky." By the time he entered the University of Hawaii and started studying with John Mount, a local bass-baritone, he was ready to go. "It was another situation where a lot of things got taken care of. Music was such a no-brainer for me."

By his second year in college, after years of singing in choirs and choruses, he'd begun to perform as a soloist, at first in Handel's *Messiah* and then in small opera parts. "I was making all kinds of money," he remembered. Pearlman heard him in Hawaii and came out three years in a row to follow his progress, then suggested he go for seven weeks to Chautauqua, New York, to study with Marlena Malas. Kelsey had always lived at home and had never been out of Hawaii before, but the time he spent with Malas gave him the polish he needed. His next major step was getting into the Opera Center program. He was only twenty-five years old and looking forward to going all over the world. "I've never traveled," he said. "When I went to New York it was the first time away for me."

So now here he was in Room 550 preparing to sing for a man with the power to speed him to every corner of the globe. Anson was big news in the world of opera and concert management, and he'd clearly been brought to Chicago by Epstein to hear Kelsey. This was unusual, if only because Kelsey was the only one of the young singers being asked to strut his stuff on this particular afternoon. It indicated, to me at least, that Epstein had a very strong personal interest in the occasion. I slipped into the room just before Kelsey was ready to sing and sat down off to one side, well away from Anson and Epstein, who glanced once in my direction with what I took to be disapproval, but let me be.

Kelsey led off with the *Puritani* aria, which he delivered cleanly and effortlessly, as usual, with a smooth lyric sound, clear diction and firm top notes. When he finished, Epstein barked, "How's your *Rake* coming along?" Kelsey told him he was working on it, as well as on some other arias. "So those are cooking? Good! Right!" Epstein said, rocking back and forth in his chair, a pudgy black-clad bundle of energy, as if plugged into a wall socket. Kelsey stood quietly in place, waiting for Epstein's energy to subside, then launched into his second selection, the "Song to the Evening Star" from *Tannhäuser,* which he sang gorgeously. This was succeeded by an intimate tête-à-tête, with Epstein and Anson huddled closely together, conferring sotto voce. They looked like plotters in an early Verdi melodrama.

When they finished, Kelsey launched into "Vision fugitive," the great baritone aria from Massenet's *Hérodiade,* in which Hérod sings of his obsession for Salomé. It's a tremendous piece, calling for great breath control and ringing top notes. I'd already heard Kelsey sing it splendidly several times, but he seemed more and more comfortable with it at each rendition. He delivered it as well and as easily as any of the great baritones I'd ever heard do it. Epstein must have felt the same way, because he seemed almost to bounce out of his chair. "That's a very strong aria for auditions," he said. "Forget the others for now!" It was a command, not a suggestion. When he and Anson again put their heads together, with Kelsey standing placidly before them, I quietly let myself out of the room.

WE WERE WELL INTO the Lyric season before I was finally able to get the interview I wanted with Epstein, and then only after I'd caught up with him outside the Rehearsal Department one day and told him how essential I thought being able to talk to him was to the book I was planning to write. He nodded, gave me a couple of possible dates and asked me to check with his office to confirm one. He was off to New York again for a few days, but would be around after that for much of the rest of the season. I thanked him, made a note about the possible dates and waited.

Meanwhile, however, I'd been able to do a little research on him. Earlier in his career, it turned out, he had been not only available for interviews but also a veritable chatterbox about himself. In his early days he was brash and fearless to the point of being rude, but his ruthless honesty in expressing his opinions, backed up by an encyclopedic knowledge of everything operatic, launched him swiftly to the top of his profession. By 1973, when he was only twenty-five, he was already an important figure at CAMI, with a roster of top singers in his charge. And he developed a reputation not only for discovering artists who would become stars, but also for nurturing, guiding, coaxing and pushing them into making the right decisions about their careers. He is credited with being largely responsible for the meteoric rise to stardom of Renée Fleming, whose success has elevated the soprano with the golden good looks and the creamy tone to supercelebrity status. Nevertheless, people have always been put off by him. Some are appalled by his outspokenness, some infuriated by his rudeness, but no one has ever said he didn't know what he was talking about.

One of the best articles I read about him, written by Tim Page, appeared in the February 2, 1992, issue of *Fanfare,* a British magazine, shortly after Epstein was appointed general director of Welsh National Opera, a job he held for three years. WNO is one of the world's most adventurous companies. It performs mainly on the road, in all sorts of venues, from movie theaters, rental halls and sports stadiums to conventional auditoriums. "I have no doubt that some people over here don't quite know what to make of me," Epstein told Page. "After all, I'm an American. I'm a New

Yorker. I'm Jewish. I'm fat. I'm gay. And I have AIDS." This was an astonishing admission to make at the time, and a courageous one. He proceeded to tell Page that he had probably contracted the virus sometime in the early 1980s, and that ever since then he'd been on the new medications, which he hoped would prolong his life. By the time of the interview, he had become asymptomatic, but he told Page that he carried around with him, "as a reminder of the odds facing him," a list of more than seventy-five friends and acquaintances who had died.

Like so many opera aficionados, Epstein, who grew up in New York City, began attending performances at the Met while still in high school. He often managed to wangle himself backstage, where he'd pigeonhole the singers to tell them what he thought they'd done wrong as well as right. He was so brash that he made enemies everywhere, but he also impressed many artists with his honesty. By the time he became an agent, with one of the best client lists in the business, he was almost as well known in the world of opera as the artists he represented. He remained at CAMI for twenty-six years, while also working as an artistic consultant, not only to Lyric but also the San Francisco Opera, the Santa Fe Opera, Carnegie Hall (for its concert-opera programs) and several recording companies. He has been influential and deeply involved with young singers studying at various top conservatories, and he shows up every spring at the Music Academy of the West, where Marilyn Horne, one of his earliest supporters, coaches young artists. He's here, there, everywhere, as fiercely opinionated as ever, indifferent to whether he is revered or hated, a man powerful enough to launch and nurture a career and perhaps also to break one. I did find myself wondering how Epstein could continue to balance all these possibly conflicting interests, now that he had officially relinquished his connection to CAMI, but then no one inside Lyric seemed bothered by it. Conflict of interest is apparently not something people in the opera world worry too much about; what matters above all else is the right singer in the right role in the best possible production.

When Epstein and I finally did get together it was in the small ground-floor office near the Rehearsal Department. He was dressed as usual in one of his Darth Vader outfits—black pants, black shirt, no tie, black leather jacket. Short, stocky and bearded, with dark curly hair, a bald spot and fierce eyes staring out at the world through thick eyeglasses, he projects an aura of tremendous self-confidence. His manner is always very brisk, on the verge of explosiveness, as if he is gripped by some inner dynamic force that keeps him in constant motion. Even when he is seated, one of his legs is usually jerking up and down, which makes talking to him an exercise in restraint. I felt I was definitely imposing on him and hoped I could say something that would keep him either from bolting out of the room or levitating straight up out of his chair like the child in *The Exorcist*. Sometime before I met him, one of his acquaintances—definitely not a fan—described him to me as a "hyperkinetic three-year-old." And I wasn't exactly put at ease by Epstein's opening statement that he never, *never* gave interviews, but was doing so now only because I "seemed like a good guy."

When we did at last begin to talk, however, information poured out of him in a torrent of observations unmarred by hesitation or doubt. He knew exactly what was going on and exactly what had to be done, and he was not prepared to compromise in areas that he felt were crucial to the opera company as a whole and to the young singers under contract to it. He began by tracing the development of young singers programs back to the regime of John Crosby in Santa Fe, who had launched the first of them; then to Carol Fox at Lyric; to the Merola program in San Francisco; to the Met under Levine and to Houston back in the seventies. "These programs can be ones for cheap labor, which affects whom you take and why," Epstein said, "the premise being that they can be useful to you in the chorus or in tiny comprimario parts. Or there's the opposite idea that you take these young people, touch them with a wand and they become stars. No program is foolproof, because people can be completely overlooked. Sometimes because the singer will develop in an unexpected way." He cited the example of a promising heldentenor who in his early days had been singing the light Rossini parts. He mentioned that soprano Elizabeth Futral, now a star and about to sing the lead in *Pirates,* had begun at the very bottom, in the chorus.

One of the features Epstein takes credit for is the so-called buddy system, in which a young singer is put together with an established artist. To explain the concept he recalled how the great American bass-baritone George London would prepare a new role: "First he'd learn it with a coach, then he'd always seek out a famous singer in the part, whether he was working on Mephistopheles or Boris or Wotan. That's an example of how the buddy system operates." He pointed out that Kelsey had been working with Sherrill Milnes, Guang Yang with Marilyn Horne, Wayne Tigges with Samuel Ramey, Erin Wall with Renée Fleming, Maria Kanyova with Renata Scotto and Catherine Malfitano, Nicole Cabell and Stacey Tappan with Natalie Dessay. Then, almost as an afterthought, he added, "I sometimes wonder if they get too much help."

But he quickly brushed that negative thought aside to declare that he himself spent a great deal of time with the young singers, especially in getting them to prepare for auditions. "They have a real opportunity here, because a lot of people come through to listen to our singers," he said. "One of the reasons we ask singers to stay on for a third year is because we have something to give them. I always feel their careers should be in roles they can become identified with and helping them to find those roles is crucial to launching them." He cited the example of getting Guang Yang to develop several of her most important future parts in *Aida, Samson* and *Don Carlo.*

"With young singers," he continued, "it's important for them to understand the importance of the opening few phrases of a role, which can help them define it." He referred to Erin Wall and her first Marguerite. "The challenge there is in the words, where you put the commas. Words have to be perfectly pronounced. We kept her doing it over and over. You also talk to them about the inner world of the part, the imagination. You can talk about it to them, but they do have to find it on their own. We want them to be distinctive, that's what we want from these guys. I say to them, 'I think you should do this, but remember I said it. It's up to you to find it.'"

When I commented on the stress that the progress of the season was putting on the young artists, Epstein replied that few people understood what going into an opera career entailed. "Fleming, Pavarotti—it doesn't matter how big the name; all will have a bad day," he said, "after which your emotional state will depend on how you handle it." He reminded me that Fleming had recently been booed at La Scala. "Your job as a manager is to tell them the truth. My job with the young singers here is to advise them, to prepare them. A lot of tough singers thrive on challenges. With young singers in general, if you don't push them a little and stretch them, they won't grow." He mentioned Kelsey. "We've completely revamped his audition rep to be more lyric. His voice is flowering, and eventually he will go on to the big repertory. We have to challenge and push and also stay conservative."

I had heard that Ian Campbell had recently come through Chicago to audition the young singers and been so impressed with Kelsey that he had offered him the leading baritone parts, both highly dramatic ones, in the double bill of *Cavalleria Rusticana* and *I Pagliacci,* scheduled for the 2008 San Diego season. This is the kind of proposal you make only to an established star. When Epstein got wind of it, he made sure that Kelsey turned down the offer. As Epstein kept insisting, the idea with the young singers was to "expand and contract, expand and contract." I had this sudden image of a young singer in the grip of a giant rubber band and about to be propelled into space, but this was not exactly what Epstein was getting at.

I needed to see Epstein in action with one of the young singers, so I persuaded him to allow me to sit in on his first meeting with Erica Strauss, the young dramatic soprano Pearlman had felt so positive about and who would be joining the Opera Center in the spring of 2004. Epstein meets one-on-one with all of the incoming young artists, and it is apparently he who sets the tone and establishes the ground rules, though by all rights it would seem to me to be an area that Pearlman himself ought to be most concerned with. I didn't ask Epstein about overlapping responsibilities, because obviously he and Pearlman had established some sort of modus vivendi between the two of them. My take on it was that Pearlman and Rolandi would be working with the singers day to day, with Epstein holding some sort of ultimate veto power over everything. Was this the right way to run an opera program? Well, it seemed to be working.

The meeting with Strauss took place early one afternoon, in Room 550, with Epstein sitting directly across a table from her. Strauss looked like the conventional idea of an opera singer. She was a large young woman in her late twenties with long brown hair, a pleasing round face and the usual strong singer's jaw. She seemed sweet and eager to please, but also self-confident— always a good sign. She had been pursuing her career while living at home with her family in Queens and commuting into Manhattan to work with her singing teacher, the soprano Dodi Protero. Without any time-wasting minor civilities, Epstein, his usual bundle of suppressed energy, immediately asked Strauss what she'd been working on. Rosalinda in *Die Fledermaus* and Donna Anna in *Don Giovanni,* Strauss told him, also that Rossini tongue-twister, "Bel raggio lusinghier."

Her answer ignited Epstein, who proceeded to warn her in no uncertain terms about trying to add too much to her repertory her first year in the program; there would be many audition opportunities for her, so many that by early August she should be "up" on her audition pieces. "People will be coming to hear you here two or three times and you might get a job out of it," he said. She would have to learn to master every language, every style, but he advised her strongly to concentrate on Donna Anna, as she might be singing the part in the in-house *Don Giovanni,* scheduled to be put on in Room 200 in late June. "Leave the Countess alone for now, and 'Bel raggio' is not so important for you. Start learning 'Ernani, involami,'" he added, citing one of those big Verdi gutbusters that only a top dramatic soprano can handle. When she mentioned her desire to add a French aria to her rep, perhaps from *Robert le Diable,* another of those now-ignored Meyerbeer operas in which the grotesque and the improbable blend into a mishmash of wildly contrasting styles, Epstein quickly shot her down. "We'll worry about adding a French aria later," he said, "but for now stick with everything we have." In addition to the *Ernani* aria, he pushed her toward another Verdi monster, *Il Trovatore.* "It will give you an entrée into a repertory that's indicated for you." They discussed what she'd be covering and singing during the coming Lyric season, but Epstein stressed again, "Basically, Donna Anna is your key part for the whole of this year."

"Am I going to work with Gianna?" Strauss now asked.

"Nobody has to work with Gianna," Epstein replied, "but it's important for you to work with her to find out if you like it. I don't want you to feel pressure from me or from Bill. Even if you do want to work with Gianna, you can stay with your voice teacher."

This seemed to reassure Strauss, who told Epstein that she'd been studying with Protero for six years and credited her with developing her potential. "I went to college without even a G and my first teacher was a man who just couldn't cut it," Strauss said.

"I'll support you with any decision you make," Epstein answered. Strauss told him she had scheduled a session with Rolandi the following Thursday. "Come back to me and tell me how it's going," he urged her. "I just don't want you to feel any pressure."

Epstein now began to talk to her about her weight, which could threaten to become a problem for her, and told her he didn't want her to put on any. She told him she had been as much as thirty pounds heavier. "I know what works for me," she said. "I never ate that much, but the wrong foods."

Epstein warned her not to lose control and cited the recent episode of Deborah Voigt, then a large woman, who is one of the best dramatic sopranos in the world, being released from her contract to sing *Ariadne* at Covent Garden because the director had insisted on a modern-dress production in which she would have had to wear a skimpy cocktail dress and not the conventional flowing robes of a tragic Grecian heroine. Epstein went on to indicate that there were several young singers in the current program he was concerned about. He cited Scott Ramsay, who had been repeatedly talked to about his weight and ignored it before finally getting the message and doing something about it. (I had noticed that, in the *Lucia,* Ramsay, though not exactly a dashing cavalier, had managed to cut a more graceful figure than when I met him a couple of months earlier.) "It's also even more important to be fit," Epstein continued, and revealed that he himself worked out regularly at a nearby gym and that Strauss should look into it. "Use your years here, feel good about you," he urged her. "You've got the goods, the vocal goods, and I feel good about you. You have more voice than Renée Fleming had at your age, when I heard her sing in this theater." He wanted Strauss to buddy up with Malfitano. "She was really fat in her early twenties and her weight went up and down, up and down," he said. "Now she's fifty-six and knows what to do. You're going to have to do it. You're going to have to do it all your life. If you're feeling tormented or unhappy, talk to me."

Before their meeting ended, Epstein again returned to the repertory that he insisted was appropriate for her. He touched again on the arias and roles that were not for her, either because they were too lyric or were from the bel canto rep. She wouldn't get hired to sing any of those parts, he told her, so why bother with them? Verdi, Donna Anna—her career lay securely in those heavier roles. Could he be wrong? Well, he had once reportedly counseled Fleming to stick to Richard Strauss and Mozart and to ignore most of the bel canto rep, as well as Verdi and Puccini. Fleming, as all opera lovers now know, can sing almost anything. But Fleming remained his client, so he must have been doing something right.

20

That's Entertainment

T HE FIRST TIME I watched Donald Palumbo work with the Lyric chorus was early in December, about two months before the opening night of *The Pirates of Penzance*. I thought it was important that I do so because in a house the size of the Civic, it is absolutely crucial that the English text of Gilbert's brilliant libretto and lyrics be clearly understood all the way to the back rows. The Gilbert and Sullivan operettas bounce along at much too rapid a clip for the audience to have to rely on supertitles, and what the chorus is singing in these works is as important as what the principals have to say.

When I showed up in Room 550 that afternoon I found three parallel rows of chairs facing a music stand and a high stool, with Bill Billingham already seated at the piano, waiting. The chorus, an informally dressed motley group of cheerful citizens, was busy seeking their assigned seats and chatting with one another until, at three-thirty sharp, Palumbo walked briskly in, set his score down on the stand in front of him, opened it, raised his right hand and said, "Pirates, let's start where we left off." He was wearing gray slacks, a white shirt and a gray sleeveless sweater, his full head of gray hair parted on the left. (He reminded me of a math teacher I had once had who had flunked me in trigonometry. He'd expected the best from me and I had let him down.) "How sad, an orphan boy," the chorus now sang, with Palumbo delivering the Major General's lines. But he soon stopped them. " 'See, at our feet they kneel,' " he said. "Not clear."

No one got away with anything. "He's telling a terrible story," Palumbo sang out. "Te-ell! Make sure you get it. And don't sit on the quarters." Then later: "Now, once more. Don't breathe too late . . . Some people are sitting on 'story.' You're late." Up went his right arm, down came the beat and the chorus sang. "Very good," Palumbo said, "but we never seem to get it the first time."

One of the prettiest moments in *Pirates* is the a cappella chorus "Hail, Poetry!," which Palumbo precisely and meticulously conducted with both hands, calling out, "Every syllable here, not just one!" He went over the whole thing with them phrase by phrase, urging them on as they sang: "More! More!" He was a bundle of energy, throwing himself into it, often walking away from them while still beating time, turning his head away to concentrate on listening. "This should be a parody," he told them, "a parody of *Meistersinger,* almost. It doesn't work if you just sing it straight."

Palumbo is the kind of choral master who reminds me of a jockey urging a tiring front-running horse toward the finish line, his whip flailing, his body flattened against the animal's back, every fiber of his being concentrated on bringing his animal in first. Not for him the relaxed moment or the pause to allow his charge to regroup; there was too much at stake. You win or you lose; you get it right or you fail.

On and on it went. "To get married with impunity," the chorus sang. *"Impunity* falls apart, guys!" Palumbo shouted. The chorus repeated the phrase. "Go, go!" Palumbo yelled. "A doctor of divinity is located in this vicinity," the chorus sang. "Men, can you be more men!" Palumbo urged. "Women, can you be more . . ." and he flounced about the room in an exaggerated feminine manner. No, maybe not a jockey, I suddenly realized; he was more like Bobby Knight, the super-hyper men's basketball coach for whom losing was a major catastrophe.

I hung around the rehearsal for another hour, listening and watching Palumbo tirelessly at work. When the men delivered what he thought was an inadequate rendition of the famous Policemen's Chorus—"When the foeman bares his steel"—all Palumbo could find to say was, "Boring! Boring! If we can't sing this like *Trovatore,* we're in trouble!" Every time he said "boring," he pointed thumbs down, like a Roman emperor condemning a losing gladiator to death. The chorus came back at him with a much more rousing version and Palumbo merely said, "Okay? Better? Yes? Memorized? Want to do the whole thing without scores?" It was not a question, but an order. Back to the beginning now, but without the music in front of them.

In *The Mountebanks* (later revised as *The Chieftain*), one of his operettas written without Sullivan, W. S. Gilbert wrote a number for the chorus in which everyone onstage pantomimes gestures while bellowing away on the syllable "la." This was because, as one of the characters explains, "No single word is ever heard when singers sing in chorus." If Donald Palumbo had been around at the time to prepare Gilbert's erring choristers, that number might never have been written. I realized, when the rehearsal ended, that I had understood every single word the Lyric chorus sang as precisely as if they had been spelled out for me on a title board. Nor did I sense any resentment or unhappiness from the singers in the room. Excellence is its own reward. After the rehearsal, I ran into one of the chorus members in the corridor outside an elevator and congratulated her. "Yes," she said cheerfully, "he didn't scream this time, probably because you were there." Oh, well, I thought; whatever it takes.

FOR THE NEXT FEW WEEKS, right up to the opening night, I kept dropping in on the *Pirates* rehearsals, partly because I had such a personal connection to the opera. Frederic, the obtuse slave of duty apprenticed as a baby to an incompetent band of sentimental pirates, had been one of my favorite parts, and I had sung it several times. My next to last professional performance anywhere had been as the Major General—the comic lead and an even better part—in a production by the San Diego Comic Opera some years ago, and I've never tired of the piece. Unlike many of Lyric's subscribers, I had been delighted by the canceling of Berlioz's cumbersome melodrama *Benvenuto Cellini,* and the substitution for it of this comic masterpiece. Berlioz may be a genius, and he is undoubtedly a very fascinating composer, but his lyric dramas rival Meyerbeer's and Wagner's for sheer long-windedness. The argument against *Pirates* had come from that large segment of the opera-going public that believes no major opera house should become home to operettas or, God forbid, musical comedies. This despite the fact that the dividing line between opera and the musical is by no means a wall, but more of a disputed demilitarized zone.

I had talked to Matthew Epstein not only about the choice of *Pirates,* but also about the whole question of putting together an effective season. He explained the need these days to balance the repertory, "because I believe that today the old audience is dying out." With that in mind and working as a team, he and Mason and the various department heads consult with one another to come up with the right mixture every year. Not the least of their considerations is where the young singers will fit in in terms of the smaller roles and the covers. Ultimately, however, according to Epstein, "Bill Mason is the boss. He takes the responsibility for what we do, right or wrong."

There seemed to be an alternative audience coming along that was younger and more adventurous, Epstein maintained, while also reminding me that "in this country the arts have to be run as a business." The public funding of the arts abroad poses its own challenges, mainly because of the bureaucracy involved and shifts in political power, but in the United States, where private financing is essential to meet deficits, the need, above all, is to be practical. Epstein envisions trying to strike a balance between the so-called heavy stuff and the lighter pieces, at a ratio of about two to one, especially by including among the latter popular successes from Broadway and the world of operetta. Major opera companies everywhere were now doing just that, or at least being forced to contemplate it, even at the Met, where the winds of change always blow less briskly. "Obviously," Epstein hastened to add, "shows like *Thoroughly Modern Millie* and *The Sound of Music* are wrong; but *Carousel* and *Candide* are right for the rep." He cited *Pirates* as a good example of the sort of adjustment to reality that opera companies now need to make. "You want a little bland, a little sweet, a little spicy," he said. "It is show business, after all."

About this particular production of *Pirates,* Epstein felt the company was doing it exactly right, with the same number of chorus members and the same size orchestra of the operetta's first English production, at the Opera Comique in London, on April 3, 1880. The production team had carefully listened to the various D'Oyly Carte recordings and had come up with a concept that Epstein defined as "a Victorian Valentine." He also revealed that he'd known every singer in the cast from the very beginning of their careers, including Gillian Knight, who had sung the comic mezzo leads for years with the D'Oyly Carte Opera Company, and Peter Rose, the British bass, whose cockney interpretation of the Sergeant of Police was his first venture into G & S. Sometimes I got the feeling, just from being around Matthew Epstein, that if opera were suddenly to disappear as an art form, he would vanish in a puff of brimstone, much like the resident Djinn at number seventy, Simmery Axe, in Gilbert and Sullivan's *The Sorcerer.*

At the rehearsal of *Pirates,* on January 23 in the auditorium, I paid particular attention to Roger Honeywell. He had finally recovered from a bad cold, which he had contracted over the Christmas holidays when he and his wife and kids had gone back to Toronto to sell their house. Small children, as everyone who has ever had any knows, are ambulating germ factories, but maybe

Honeywell had been felled by the Canadian winter or by stress. He had bought a house in Stratford, sight unseen, over the Internet, though he had sent a friend to check it out. Meanwhile back in Toronto, he and his kids had gotten sick and the pipes in their home had burst, delaying the sale. Nevertheless, he seemed totally at ease and confident, singing Frederic with no sign of strain and knocking off the difficult second-act duet with ease. And not only was he singing well, but his experience as a classically trained actor was serving him brilliantly. His befuddled, idealistic and pompous Frederic was a delight. During a break in the rehearsal he told me that since his breakthrough concert in Montreal he had been offered all kinds of jobs. Right after *Pirates* he'd be going to Vancouver to do an Alfredo in *La Traviata,* and he had signed a contract to sing seven performances over the summer of Puccini's *La Fanciulla del West,* at Glimmerglass. He had also been offered a chance, by Montreal, to tackle the Calaf in *Turandot,* but had wisely turned it down. The part of the lovelorn suitor determined to shatter the ice encasing Puccini's frozen princess, mostly by belting wall-cracking top notes at her, is one of those roles that can break a career as well as launch one. "Too much to do now; too many new roles," Honeywell explained. Whatever the reason, he had chosen wisely.

When the curtain rose on the opening night of *Pirates,* on February 2, the concept of the Victorian Valentine was immediately evident in the set designed by Michael Yeargan, which framed the action in a sort of conservatory and used placards, slogans, painted set pieces and props to recall the era. The design was amusing and fully in tune with Elijah Moshinsky's directorial concept, which was to use Gilbert's characters to illustrate "a whole society and a whole culture behind it." The tone was determinedly lighthearted throughout—a spoof of the operetta itself— so that the audience was forcibly reminded of the circumstances that compelled Lyric to scrap Berlioz for what amounted to a piece of charming fluff. Sir Andrew Davis, who conducted with great verve and absolute fidelity to Sullivan's delicious score, even added a verse to the Major General's patter song, one of the classics of the genre:

If the presence of the British makes you fear a motive sinister,
We long ago concluded you're impossible to administer.
Recolonizing's out, although I've heard a lot of silly noise,
About the possibility of just retaking Illinois.
Instead, we're here to offer with respect and with humility,
A slice of British culture in this wonderful facility.
You're saddled with the kind of debt of gratitude one rarely owes,
But, dammit, after all we're just a substitute for Berlioz!

The only trouble with this approach was that, however entertaining it proved to be, it was essentially a betrayal of Gilbert's intentions, which were to satirize the ridiculous codes of conduct by which people live. The only members of the cast who understood this fully were Gillian Knight, the D'Oyly Carte veteran; Neal Davies, whose Major General was hilarious for being intensely serious about himself, even when at his most ridiculous; and Honeywell, whose earnest and humorless Frederic was histrionically superb. He also sang very well, and his duets with Elizabeth Futral, the ex-LOCAA starlet and chorus singer, confirmed that both of them qualified as outstanding examples of what years of commitment and training at the Opera Center can accomplish for a young artist.

Pirates sold out its run of eleven performances and helped boost Lyric back into the black.

21

The Competition Blues

A S THE SEASON PROCEEDED into late January, with three operas—*Pirates, Lucia* and *Madama Butterfly*—simultaneously in rehearsal and production, the grind began to wear down a few of the young singers. Lauren Curnow was no longer auditioning because it had been decided that she was not really a mezzo but a true soprano and she was training hard with Rolandi to move into an entirely new repertory. Levi Hernandez had had to stop singing entirely for a couple of months because he'd had to undergo surgery to remove polyps dangerously close to his vocal cords. Of the others, not all were singing with their usual verve and command in the auditions that never seemed to stop. It wasn't as if they could just show up and sing at them as if they didn't matter, because basically there were possible jobs to be had and strong impressions had to be made. The Met and most of the country's major opera companies were booking singers as much as five years in advance. Fail to show up, fail to impress, display indifference or what can pass as a bad attitude, and you could be out for keeps—waiting tables somewhere or working in a bank. The singers with the big, powerful instruments in their throats—the Quinn Kelseys and the Guang Yangs—were relatively safe, but even they could not afford to let down, kick back and just coast along for a while. The competition at every level was too fierce. "Typically, most people who come through here come once a year," is the way Chris Dickerson explained it to me, "and it's hectic because so much else is going on during this period." He had made almost all of the auditions, but had failed so far to get much of a response. His smooth, beautiful lyric bass needed to become larger for him to qualify for the big roles in the major houses, according to one estimate I heard. With age and maturity it might happen for him, but in the meantime, what? More comprimario parts? After three years in the program would he settle for that?

At the audition on January 27 for Opera Pacific, in Room 550, Dickerson, cutting his usual impressive figure and dressed in a dark blue suit with a blue shirt and a red tie, led off with the *Sonnambula* aria, then followed it up with Purcell. He sang well, if not spectacularly, but seemed to make little impression on John De Main, the youthful-looking artistic director and principal conductor of the company, which puts on a season of four operas a year at its home base in Costa Mesa, California. De Main spent much of his time during the audition winking and smiling at his teenage daughter, who was sitting off to one side, as the singers came and went. "Thank you very much," was what most of them got for their efforts, the notable exceptions being Erin Wall, Scott Ramsay, Quinn Kelsey, Guang Yang, and Stacey Tappan, who opened with *Sonnambula* and then absolutely blew all of us away with the *Baby Doe* and its acrobatic vocal leaps into the stratosphere. De Main stopped winking and grinning at his daughter long enough to ask the soprano where she was living. "In Chicago, for now," Tappan answered. Was there a possible job offer hovering in the air? Who could tell? After Tappan left the room with a cheery smile and a thank-you, Pearlman, who had been sitting quietly next to De Main in case there was a question to be answered, now observed, "It's not one of those little piping sounds." He was clearly as mystified as I by the fact that no matter how well Tappan sang, no major offers were yet coming her way. When I later touted her to Ian Campbell as a possible Lucia for the production the San Diego Opera would be putting on in February 2006, all he said was, "Her time will come."

De Main chatted affably with Ramsay, who had sung for him before, and asked him if he'd ever tackled any Rossini. To Kelsey he said, "Thank you. A pleasure. A pretty voice." To Guang Yang he said nothing, but after her superb rendition of Cinderella's coloratura flourishes his jaw seemed to sag slightly in astonishment. After it was all over I had the feeling that we had all been wasting our time, but then perhaps it was impossible to tell. The managers, the agents, the artistic and general directors—they came, saw, listened and for the most part reacted like poker players in a high-stakes game. It began to irritate me after a while. Didn't these people even begin to grasp how hard it was to be judged day after day, often without even being properly acknowledged? No wonder so many of the great singers became monsters once they'd conquered an audience and acquired fans and power. They'd paid a price for their acceptance; now it would be somebody else's turn to play the supplicant.

I walked out of the audition with Eric Weimer, who had accompanied the singers, and asked him for his thoughts. "Thank God for Guang," he said as we headed for an elevator. I asked him what he meant. "She's one of only two or three in the group who sing as if they are performing," he said. "In auditions you have to perform, you have to present yourself at your strongest." He cited Yang's incredible breath control, which he thought was instinctive, not thought out, but which gave her singing a power and a thrust most of the others didn't have yet. He also stressed again the importance of giving meaning to the words, the need to stress certain syllables. He gave as an example an aria I knew well from having sung it, Alfredo's "Dei miei bollenti spiriti," from the second act of *La Traviata,* in which the youthful lover proclaims his ardor and exhilaration in his relationship with the grand courtesan Violetta. "The whole aria is set up by what Alfredo says in the recitative leading up to it," Weimer explained. " 'Lunge da lei,' " he sings. " 'Far from her . . .' The accent has to be in the right place or the emotion is not there."

Four days later I sat in on still another audition, this one for Sarah Billinghurst, the artistic administrator of the Metropolitan. Billinghurst is third in the pecking order behind James Levine, the artistic director, who, like Plácido Domingo, seems to be everywhere at once in the world of opera, and Joe Volpe, the general director, who has yet to encounter a sacred monster he can't fire, but who recently has been sounding a bit battered by the pressure of being the heavy and will soon retire.

Billinghurst is a large middle-aged woman with short dark red hair who moves purposefully through a room with the majestic confidence of a power broker well aware of her status. Dressed in what looked like overlapping layers of scarves and fluttering kerchiefs, she sailed gloriously to anchor in Room 350 to listen to eight of the Opera Center's young artists. This was an important occasion for them. After all, this was the Metropolitan Opera they were performing for, not some minor entity out in the boondocks. The importance of the occasion was marked by the presence not only of Pearlman but also of Matthew Epstein, who sat toward the rear of the room, one leg tapping nervously up and down and his hands tucked under his armpits.

As the eight young singers auditioning came and went, all of them performing with more verve and a greater sense of urgency than they had four days earlier, Pearlman contributed useful bits of information on each of his charges, all of it geared to make Billinghurst aware of what he felt their basic strengths were and what they had accomplished so far during the season. Epstein said almost nothing, never more than a terse "good" or "very good," but it was clear from his fierce concentration on the proceedings that he was rooting hard for his singers. He is nothing if not a fan, as fanatical in his devotion to opera in general as any of the groupies who follow certain favorite singers around the world just to hear them, even over and over in the same role. At every performance during the season he operated as a one-man claque, loudly applauding in all the right spots. I found myself hoping that after this audition, in which the young artists had sung their hearts out, he'd corner Billinghurst somewhere and bully her into hiring all of them. Epstein may not be a popular figure in the circumscribed world of classical song, but he is respected and feared.

In any case, after this last one, I decided I wouldn't attend any more auditions or, even worse, the vocal competitions that throw young singers together as if they're competing in a tennis tournament or a dumb TV reality show such as *Survivor*. There are dozens of these contests every year, the most famous in the United States being the Met's and Operalia. Founded by Plácido Domingo in 1992, the latter brings some forty singers from all over the world to Los Angeles for a week to compete in front of ten judges, who decide who wins and how the $175,000 in cash prizes will be divvied up—an absurd way to judge art of any kind. How absurd? In 2004, Quinn Kelsey competed, the only one of the LOCAA young artists to do so, and while he made the finals, he didn't win any of the prizes awarded. Kelsey knows how good he is, so the experience did not faze him in the least. "I know how well I sang," he told Pearlman. The only aspect of a competition that should matter to a young singer, Pearlman maintains, is the money. It can make a difference when you're struggling to make ends meet. Otherwise, the competitions are largely meaningless, designed only to trumpet the virtues of the people putting them on. Ultimately, it is the audience that will decide a singer's fate. The trick is to get in front of one just as soon as you are ready to do so.

WITH THIS IN MIND, on January 22 I sat in on a so-called Brown Bag Lunch, one of the recurrent features of life at the Opera Center, during which tenor David Cangelosi and bass Ray Aceto talked to the young singers about how to make the transition from a young artist program to a mature career. The session was held in the common room, with Pearlman presiding and six of his young singers—Guang Yang, Lauren McNeese, Patrick Miller, Wayne Tigges, Nicole Cabell and Quinn Kelsey—sitting informally around the table, munching and drinking take-out as they listened and asked questions. The atmosphere was reassuringly informal, even though Aceto, who spoke first, projects a somewhat forbidding aura, not unlike the heavies he usually portrays onstage. He's a tall man with a booming voice but also, reportedly, a dry sense of humor. Like Cangelosi, he's been around for a while and began his career, like everyone in the room, by singing small parts and covering big ones. He used the term "street smarts" to describe what any young singer needs to acquire to progress under the current system, in which, he made it clear, it is easy to become lost. He warned the singers that auditions would go on taking place right through to the end of the season, even though few managers or artistic directors would show up for the *Butterfly,* mainly because it was an old production of an opera everyone had seen and heard so often. "But you can be surprised by who shows up and when," he added.

Aceto was an undergraduate at Bowling Green, in Ohio, when he was invited to audition in New York for James Levine, who told him he'd done well and would start in the young singers program in the fall. Aceto was a year and a half short of getting his diploma, but "I said screw it and went to the Met. I was twenty-two and I spent three years there." He remembers wandering around inside the enormous opera house wondering if he really belonged there and missing his buddies at his favorite hangout back home. "I'd spot someone and think, 'Oh, shit, who's that? Pavarotti?' It was very difficult for me that first year, very rough, and I felt insecure." His voice teacher lured him back home a number of times to build up his vocal technique and confidence again. "The system here is far more supportive on a daily basis than at the Met," Aceto continued. "There every coaching session was like an audition. I even had to coach outside the Met and then bring the pieces I'd been working on in."

Matters improved for him beginning the second year, when people began to come around for him. He debuted with the small part of the Jailer in *Tosca,* with Pavarotti singing Mario, one of his best roles. After a while, Aceto was singing so many small parts and covering so many others that he was making between $70,000 and $80,000 a year, until the Met put a stop to that by setting a limit of $47,000 on what any of the company's young singers could earn annually. It was difficult for him, because living in New York was so expensive and the Met was also very strict about what the young artists were allowed to do outside on their own. Nevertheless, he stuck it out for the full three years of the program, then for two more as what the Met calls "a resident artist," during which he was free to seek outside jobs as well.

One of the biggest turning points in his career was singing an audition in Chicago in June of 1995, when Bartoletti was still the artistic director. Lyric gave him three years of work right off the bat. "Once Chicago did that for me," he continued, "agents started picking up the phone. It puts you on people's radar." He recalled that during his years in New York he'd listen to the principal singers and wonder why he couldn't step into those big roles, only to find that the Met continued to think of him as a young singer not yet ready for the majors. The late Jerome Hines, a bass whose career was shaped by his decades at the Met, once told him, "The problem with the business we're in is that when you have the voice, you need the experience. By the time you get the experience your voice may be shot."

At thirty-six, Aceto felt that Europe at least was opening up for him. He had recently sung major roles at Covent Garden and in Vienna and Verona, and he'd begun to feel he could compete with anybody. He recalled that Levine had once told him not to be afraid of saying no and that he had done just that, when he was offered a part by Levine himself in a Met production of *Lulu,*

Alban Berg's shriekfest of an opera that works wonderfully as a drama but requires the singers to perform the kind of vocal acrobatics that, repeated often enough, can end a career. It was a daring stand on Aceto's part because, as he put it, "people in this business have long memories."

When it was his turn to speak, Cangelosi informed the group that when he went to audition for Levine at the Met, the latter failed to appear. "You can't let that kind of thing screw you up," he warned them. As singers whose main concern was to get a chance to perform at the highest possible level of the profession, they would have to put such experiences behind them and go on. Furthermore, whatever slights they endured, they would have to be unfailingly courteous and responsible toward the managements and the entities that hired them. "It's very good business practice," he pointed out, "if you say you're going to do it, be sure you do it. If you have to cancel for whatever reason, call the people yourself. Don't let your agent do it for you."

What about this whole question of agents and managers, McNeese now asked. Despite her Cherubino and her Siébel, she still had no representation and wanted to know what she could do about it. After an audition, for example, should one contact these people personally or just wait for them to act?

"At some point you're going to have had many auditions," Aceto replied. "But you can only do what you can do. You have to rely on yourself." He warned her that managers generally never want to talk directly to the singers. He suggested using e-mail, informing the person about what's been happening in your career, where you're singing, what and when. You had to keep in touch. He pointed out that Matthew Epstein's attitude was "You'll get a manager when you have something to manage." Epstein's saying reminded me of the old showbiz joke about the man standing on a beach watching a swimmer desperately battling a ferocious riptide in his attempt to reach safety. When the swimmer finally does make it, crawling onto the sand and collapsing facedown, the man strolls over, leans down and says, "May I be of some assistance?" That's an agent.

"Don't be bashful about presenting yourself," Cangelosi suggested. Aceto reminded them that all these people talk to one another a lot. "Don't think that they don't watch and remember," he said, recalling that Epstein would telephone him from time to time. "I never got anything from him, but he did keep track."

Cangelosi reminded McNeese how great it had been for her to be able to step into a major role and the fact that Ramsay had gotten to sing Edgardo at the *Sitzprobe*. "Don't ever look too lightly on covers," he said. "I've seen disasters here." He cited the example of a woman brought in to sing a major role who didn't know it.

"What's the single most important thing to watch out for with an agent?" Patrick Miller asked.

"Never pay a retainer to one of them," Aceto answered. He urged Miller to seek out the person more than the organization and not to bug him all the time. "I'm not a high-maintenance guy," Aceto said. "I don't need to be called every day, but maybe just once a week." He also advised exploring the prospective agent's roster, because he might be representing several other singers already more established in their category. "I found myself on the same roster as Sam Ramey for fourteen years and I never got a scrap, because Ramey never cancelled or got sick. But you do get smaller roles that way."

"The big agents don't guarantee work," Cangelosi said, "so I'm with a smaller one. Trust your instincts, don't be afraid, look at the roster—are they good artists?"

Pearlman intervened at this point to tell a story of a young singer who signed with an unscrupulous agent. Pamela Rosenberg, then the artistic director of the Stuttgart Opera, in Germany, urgently needed an artist for a particular part. The agent felt he had Rosenberg over a financial barrel and exploited the situation to secure a big contract for his client. Unfortunately, the woman showed up not knowing the role. "That singer was never heard from again," Pearlman concluded. I had a vision of her disappearing like Mephistopheles, through a trapdoor in the floor, to resurface later as an employee in an escort service.

Because all the young singers in the room were understudying other parts as well as interpreting smaller ones, they discussed aspects of covering. "If you step in from day one, you can have your own ideas about a role," Cangelosi observed. "If you step in in mid-role, you pretty much have to follow what the director wants. Some people make a career out of covering and are perfectly happy to do that."

"They don't like the pressure of 'I'm going on,'" Aceto said. "But, you know, if any of you are good enough to be here, you're good enough to sing in the major houses."

"Making a living and longevity are what should concern you," Cangelosi said. He reminded them that his years at LOCAA had led not only to his being hired elsewhere, but also, during the current season, to fifteen weeks of guaranteed work at Lyric.

"It's up to your agent to get you in the front door the first time," Aceto added. "The second time you have to get in the door on your own."

All this practical advice from these two young artists seemed to me to be enormously useful, but it was also faintly depressing. For instance, it had taken Aceto fourteen years to arrive at a spot in his career where, in the United States at least, he had still not quite broken through into the major bass parts. Would he ever? Who knew? Cangelosi, on the other hand, like Anthony Laciura at the Met, would remain in the character parts, content with the Normannos and Spoletas and Goros, with the occasional triumphant Mime thrown in. Both men were having good careers, but what had clearly come across from their counsel was how hard it was merely to get along in their chosen profession. No one, for instance, had asked about the money involved, not until Cangelosi said toward the end of the session, "I'm surprised there have been no questions about the money aspects."

"Be ready," Aceto told them, "to give away at least half, usu-ally as much as fifty-five or sixty percent of what you're paid. There are taxes, expenses, agency fees, outside coachings. In Eu-rope they take taxes right off the top. In Italy it's a third, in Paris thirty percent, Germany forty-eight percent. You can deduct those taxes paid there from your U.S. ones."

This seemed to cheer nobody up. Singing for your supper these days, unlike the old Rodgers and Hart hit, doesn't guaran-tee you'll be dining with wine of choice.

22

It's in the Details

*T*HE *MADAMA BUTTERFLY* that ended the 2003–2004 season at Lyric confirmed everything I had hoped to find when I first showed up in Chicago. Not because it was an unusually brilliant production (it wasn't) or because its two leads were great singers (they weren't) or because it shed new light on Puccini's melodic and sentimental score (it didn't). Not even because the conductor was Bruno Bartoletti, for thirty-five years (until 1999) the artistic director of the company and famous worldwide for his Puccini interpretations. Nor because the entire production was a revival of the one conceived and staged by Harold Prince, recipient of twenty Tony Awards for his work on Broadway. In some ways this *Butterfly* was just another in the nearly endless line of competent but not thrilling versions that grace the opera stages across the world every year. Sylvie Valayre, the French soprano singing Cio-Cio-San, and Roberto Aronica, the Italian tenor portraying Pinkerton, sang well enough, but relied exclusively on the composer to make us care about what happened to them.

What lifted this *Butterfly* out of the ordinary were the portrayals of the minor characters, especially Guang Yang's Suzuki and baritone Kim Josephson's Sharpless. These secondary roles are often sung by artists whose vocal resources are not up to the big parts. Josephson, however, is the kind of artist who not only can sing beautifully—and already has, in a number of major roles at the Met, Lyric and elsewhere—but also disappears into the characters he interprets. Sharpless, the American consul who is supposed to care enough to shed tears when Cio-Cio-San reveals that she has a son by Pinkerton, is usually just required to stand around looking skeptical at first and then faintly distressed as the action unfolds. This Sharpless came across as a fully rounded participant in the drama, the powerful American voice of decency that compensates for Pinkerton's self-serving shallow-mindedness.

As for Guang Yang, her Suzuki, a small part with no arias and only one duet to sing, became the character who made the tragedy believable. Every time she opened her mouth that rich, full, expressive voice soared over the orchestra, and her meticulously detailed, utterly convincing interpretation of the perfect devoted servant moved many of us in the audience to tears long before the catastrophic final scene. I had never before sat through a *Butterfly* in which Suzuki stole the show from Cio-Cio-San, and not because she tried to, but because she had become the most believable link between the drama and its audience.

In addition to Guang Yang, five of the other performers in the opera were either current LOCAA members or graduates of the program, and all of them would have made Frank Corsaro proud. Cangelosi's Goro was wickedly sinister, all the more so for being sweetly sung; Tigges was a properly outraged Bonze, his booming bass-baritone dominating the one scene he was in; Kelsey's Prince Yamadori was vain, self-important and, as usual, vocally impressive; Dickerson's Imperial Commissioner, a tiny part, nevertheless made an impression; and Lauren Curnow's Kate, the American Mrs. Pinkerton, who often comes across as a Stepford Wife, cut an unusually sympathetic figure and was sung with the soprano's customary grace. They all contributed to making this *Butterfly* one of the most rewarding I'd ever seen. Furthermore, the last two Cio-Cio-Sans of the season were sung by Maria Kanyova, another Opera Center alumna whose career, like Erin Wall's, seems destined to take off. I didn't see these last two performances, but the Chicago reviewers were unanimous in their praise of them both vocally and dramatically. Basically, what this production proved was that every singer, no matter how secondary his part, can make an impression. The score, if it's a great one and adequately sung, can carry you along, but often it's the details—the characterizations, the effective bits of business and interpretation—that will bring the performance to life for you and make it linger in memory. That's what these young artists had now accomplished, and it was a tribute to all those hours they had spent getting there.

NOT LONG AFTER the *Butterfly* premiere, I went home for a couple of weeks before returning for Rising Stars in concert, which would formally conclude the season for the LOCAA singers in early April. I got back to San Diego in early March, just in time to drop in on the fifth day of rehearsals for the local company's production of Verdi's *Don Carlo,* the composer's great, sprawling masterpiece of a lyric drama purportedly about the impossible love affair between Don Carlo, the royal prince and sole heir to the throne, and his stepmother, the Queen of Spain. The time is the sixteenth century, when the Spanish empire dominated on two continents and the Inquisition flourished. Verdi's chief concern was not the thwarted love affair, which historically never took place, but the larger, very real drama of the human yearning for political freedom in an era in which even the power of a king had to yield to the crushing weight on mankind of church dogma. The expression of that yearning for freedom and justice is encapsulated in the character of Rodrigo, Marquis of Posa, Don Carlo's best friend (and the only man at court whom the king trusts), who ultimately lays down his life for him and his cause. Some of

Verdi's most beautiful and impassioned music was written for Rodrigo, and in this production it was to be sung by the American baritone Rodney Gilfry, in his first interpretation of the role.

I'd been following Gilfry's career for years, ever since I first came across him in Los Angeles, where in 1993 he sang Papageno for the Los Angeles Opera in a spunky production of *The Magic Flute* directed by Sir Peter Hall. In rehearsal Gilfry had had trouble relating to the role. "I know what's there," he said to Hall during a break in the action one day. "I just can't bring it out. The music is so solemn it brings the energy level down."

"Well, yes, you see, the humor is in the degree of belief, isn't it?" Sir Peter said. "What is it Papageno wants here? Do you see? Now, let's try it again, shall we?" He patted Gilfry on the back, all the singers returned to their places and they ran the scene through again. I remember being struck by how gentle Hall was with Gilfry and the other young singers in the cast, of whom there were several. The Los Angeles Opera in those days didn't have a real young singers program, but it believed in hiring as many young local artists as possible in order to have a pool of good people available with a vested interest in not having to travel to get work. Of that group, Gilfry had gone on to have the most successful career, without ever being signed up for a specific program or winning a contest.

A native of Claremont, California, he had been singing professionally for only about a year and a half when Peter Hemmings, the general director of the L.A. opera, hired him to portray the four baritone villains in the company's 1988 production of *The Tales of Hoffmann.* This was the sort of assignment usually undertaken by an established bass-baritone, not some dewy-eyed kid fresh from playing much less demanding parts in smaller venues. I remember thinking to myself that Gilfry would never get away with it. But he did and it launched him into bigger and better things. Now in his mid-forties, tall, with a full head of wavy brown hair and leading-man good looks, he's an opera star, in demand in major opera houses all over the world.

The scene being staged in Niebelheim, the underground rehearsal room, when I arrived was the one in the second act that culminates with a public confrontation between King Philip and his son, which sets up the tragic denouement of the opera. Onstage, in addition to the chorus, were the five principals—soprano Sondra Radvanovsky, mezzo Mariana Pentcheva, tenor Sergej Larin, Gilfry and bass Ferruccio Furlanetto—two Americans, a Bulgarian, a Latvian and an Italian. The director was Lotfi Mansouri, a native of Iran, and the conductor was Edoardo Muller, an Italian, each of whom had zigzagged for decades across the operatic firmament like an erratic meteor. Here was an international complement of artists worthy of any opera company in the world, so clearly this was going to be a *Don Carlo,* one of my favorite lyric dramas, to treasure. The three male leads seemed especially promising, with strong manly voices in roles, as is usual with Verdi, that required them. When I asked Mary Peters, the production stage manager, during a break what she thought, she said, "When these three guys showed up, the testosterone level in the room got so high it knocked two months off my menopause."

The first thing that struck me as I watched Mansouri work is what always astonishes me during the production of any lyric drama, which is how in the world are they going to have this thing ready to go before an audience in just twelve more days? This was obviously the first time this complicated scene was being blocked, and there wasn't going to be much of an attempt to deal with subtleties of interpretation and vocal nuance. Mansouri, a bald, heavyset man wearing horn-rim glasses and dressed in an open-necked tan shirt and black trousers, energetically and good-humoredly maneuvered chorus and principals about while holding an open vocal score in his left hand. Like all good opera directors, he was patient and open to suggestions. Meanwhile, at a table facing the scene, Mary Peters periodically asked the singers to keep quiet, especially when Mansouri had to herd the chorus and supers about the set. It was a chatty group and a relaxed one, probably because Mansouri's approach was obviously conservative. We were going to get Verdi's *Don Carlo,* not some inflamed avant-gardist's inspired vision, say, of the court of King Philip as Hitler's bunker.

Several of the singers had worked together before, and most of them were marking, but even under these stop-and-go conditions the glory of Verdi's score flickered occasionally into life. Gilfry sang full voice, and it was evident that vocally he was perfectly suited to the lyric demands of Rodrigo. His baritone wasn't as smooth or as beautiful as I remembered it—it was somewhat dry in the middle register—but it was powerful and well focused. I didn't realize exactly what was missing, however, until Furlanetto appeared on the scene. Even though this was basically a blocking rehearsal, with everyone informally dressed and only a few props, such as capes and swords, being used, the bass stepped into the action totally in character. He marked every phrase, but in his bearing and his attitude he *was* King Philip—the troubled and lonely ruler of a vast empire, the angry father of a rebellious son, the anguished and unloved husband of a beautiful younger woman. Here was an artist at work, one who exemplified everything I'd been hearing for months now from Pearlman, Rolandi, Weimer, Rutenberg—all the coaches and teachers who had been working so hard to make the Opera Center's members not merely singers but artists. It was a question not only of talent but of fierce commitment. Maybe, however, what Furlanetto exemplified couldn't be taught.

I asked Gilfry about that when we met a couple of days later, in a backstage administrative office, and he recalled that while he was still in Los Angeles he'd been offered a chance to join the Merola young artists program in San Francisco, but had declined. "I didn't want to do it," he explained. "I was married and I already had a kid and Merola meant having to tour around in a bus.

Besides, I wanted to take a chance, to see if I could survive. In a way, it was a more intense kind of training." He went to sing in Frankfurt, Germany, where in his first season he sang a variety of leading roles in seven different operas, learning what it was all about as he went along. "I would certainly have benefited from a program like the one at Lyric," he admitted, "instead of having to learn by necessity. When I began, I'd been in college for six years and had a master's degree, but I was really green. I could have used more technical study. Learning it along the way, you pick it up, but I'm still surprised by how much I don't know."

At the time of the *Hoffmann,* he was back in L.A., where he'd been engaged to sing the part of Silvio in *Pagliacci,* a lyric role perfectly suited to his voice at the time. Because of a casting problem, the *Pagliacci* was canceled, which was when Hemmings offered him the *Hoffmann.* Gilfry bought a recording of the opera, with the great bass Norman Treigle singing the villain roles, and was appalled. "I couldn't imagine how I could do that," he said. The range he'd be required to sing was huge, culminating in a high G-sharp in the diamond aria. When he was told that the aria would be cut because Offenbach hadn't written it, he reluctantly consented. "I learned the parts and then sang them, but if I had realized then what a stretch that was for me," he said, "I'd never have done it. Not knowing is what enabled me to get through it."

In looking back on his career and the choices he'd made, Gilfry seemed undecided about young singers programs in general. About his time in Los Angeles, he said, "I was a big fish in a very small pond," implying that as just another member of a group he might not have moved ahead as quickly and that after the first year he might have become bored. Still, he realized that he might have benefited greatly from the kind of coaching young singers now receive, especially at the Opera Center. When he went to Frankfurt he had had one year of studying German at Berlitz and had had to pick up Italian and French very quickly on his own. "Generally, your colleagues and directors don't say anything to you," he declared. "So I'd have been one or two steps farther ahead and much more sure of what I was doing." He saw this first Rodrigo as a career breakthrough, a part perfectly suited to him histrionically, visually and vocally.

Over the next few days of rehearsals, whether in Niebelheim or onstage, what struck me most forcibly was the continued rather casual manner in which most of the singers approached their interpretations. It wasn't a question of whether or not they were marking, but quite simply of whether they really understood, or cared, what this drama was about. The only members of the cast who were consistently in character and constantly responsive to both Mansouri's direction and Muller's musical suggestions were Pentcheva and Furlanetto and two singers in smaller roles—Louis Lebherz, the American bass playing the fearsome Grand Inquisitor, and Laura Portune, a young American soprano interpreting the cheery but clueless page, Tebaldo. While the others simply went through their paces like athletes jogging on a track, these four were intent on developing and improving their interpretations.

During a break one afternoon I asked Mansouri about singers in general. "Well, there's no formula for doing this," he said. "Most opera singers don't get it together until their late thirties. There are others, of course, who make it as kids, but not most. Every singer must find a home and try to connect. And the people in charge of singers' programs have to be incredibly sensitive to the needs of the individual artists." He compared them at this stage of their development to interns in medicine, on the brink of their careers. They needed to have someone around to check on their vocal development. "The vocal help is vital; the casting is also vital. You mustn't use them for what you need, but for what *they* need at this stage of their vocal careers. You have to stretch them in the right way, according to their development as artists." When Mansouri was in charge of the young singers program in San Francisco, he would bring in famous old artists such as the soprano Graziella Sciutti and the baritone Renato Capecchi to work with the young artists on language, makeup, dress, "even how to fill out their tax returns."

On the negative side, Mansouri felt that many young American singers, having been sheltered and coddled in conservatory and college programs, tended to become "like cookie cutters, very generic. I'd hear wonderful voices that needed training and then I'd encourage them to develop their own individual styles, so that one soprano's Mimì wouldn't be just another Mimì but *her* Mimì." The first thing a singer does, he pointed out, is to go to the score for the notes. "While studying it, you have to ask yourself, 'What did the composer do here?' Then you go to the libretto to master the words—what are these people saying?" Mansouri would often play his singers a video of Maria Callas singing "Una voce poco fa" from *The Barber of Seville* to show them how each word, even repeated once, twice and more, seemed spontaneous, delivered with incredible technique and intelligence.

I realized that this was exactly what I wasn't getting from watching this *Don Carlo* cast approach its opening night. With the exception of the singers noted earlier, what I was getting was a generic performance. In the case of Gilfry, for instance, a nice, big, good-looking American guy singing well enough but with no fire in his belly and apparently no idea about Rodrigo other than that he was the prince's buddy, someone to share a couple of beers with while waiting for the game to start.

It wasn't until the *Sitzprobe,* on March 23, that parts of this great opera began to glimmer into life, thanks to Furlanetto. The Italian bass is not the most vocally tremendous of singers—someone on the order of James Morris or the late Nicolai Ghiaurov— nor is he physically an imposing presence, being neither very tall nor athletically built, but in performance he is so totally the part he plays that he invests it with authenticity and a kind of grandeur.

For the early part of this rehearsal Furlanetto sat quietly in

the audience listening to his colleagues work through their interpretations. Nothing much was happening, beyond a reading of
the score being tweaked from time to time by Maestro Muller for
tempi, attacks, subtleties and clean phrasing from the orchestra.
The singers mostly sat on their chairs facing the empty auditorium, sometimes rising to sing or, in the case of Larin, staying
put. The tenor had a big, not particularly beautiful instrument
that he seemed able to command without bothering to uncross his
legs. I was still wondering how he managed to do this when I noticed that Furlanetto had arrived onstage and that we were now
into the great duet between the king and Rodrigo. In this scene,
the latter, given permission to speak freely, urges the monarch to
grant freedom to the oppressed Flemish people and create an empire that history will recall as enlightened and not one of desola-
tion and oppression. Does the king want to be remembered as
another Nero? The tortured monarch replies that these are the
dreams of youth, while warning Rodrigo to beware of the Grand
Inquisitor. This is one of the great confrontation scenes in all
opera, musically magnificent and deeply moving. What Furlanetto now also accomplished was to galvanize Gilfry, who for the
first time seemed to grasp who he was and what was going on.
Rodrigo, after all, is not just some good-time Charlie, but a passionate, dedicated Spanish nobleman risking not only his standing at court but also his very life in pursuit of his and his prince's
ideals. As always happens to me when something genuine and
moving occurs during the course of a fine performance in a great
drama, I found myself riveted to my seat, thrilled, excited, as if
experiencing it for the first time. Viva, Furlanetto!

After the rehearsal I went to talk to the bass and thanked
him. He was standing backstage, chatting with friends, his coat
loosely draped over his shoulders like a cloak, Italian-style. "It's a
privilege to interpret these roles," he said, then told me that his
favorite three parts were this one, Boris and Don Quixote in
Massenet's very rarely performed opera of the same name. Each

role posed to the singer interpreting it the challenge of creating a believable, highly complex, tortured character whose emotions had to be expressed in a medium that could be unforgiving—far more so than, say, on the legitimate stage, where the actor merely has to speak his lines.

When this *Don Carlo* opened on March 27, it failed to excite the local critic, who led off her review by warning her readers that the opera lasted three hours and forty-five minutes, but even she had to admit that it was pretty good. It was better than that, thanks to Furlanetto, to a lot of good, if uninspired, singing by the women and to an elegant, convincing interpretation of Rodrigo by Gilfry. The baritone looked terrific and sang forcefully, though during the run he experienced some vocal difficulties. I had worried about him, because all during the rehearsals he had never marked and every time I passed his dressing room I heard him singing at full voice. During the course of the third performance he lost his voice almost completely and had to pretty much fake his way through the rest of the evening, but by the end of the five-performance run he was all right again. A curious lapse, but one he obviously needed to pay some attention to. It was too early in his career to be experiencing vocal difficulties. In a bigger company such as Lyric or the Met, he'd have had a cover on hand to step in for him. Another hazard mere actors don't have to face.

23

The Glory of Their Singing

B Y THE TIME I got back to Chicago at the end of March, rehearsals were well under way for Rising Stars in concert, scheduled for the afternoon of April 4. The musical preparation had been in the works for weeks, but the selections, to be presented with a minimum of furniture and props in the Civic's enormous empty space, needed to be staged. When I showed up in the middle of this process one afternoon, in Room 200, I found Pearlman working with Ramsay and Curnow on two linked scenes from Massenet's *Werther,* that tale of two bourgeois lovers that ends in the needless but dramatically satisfying suicide of one of them. As the singers went through their paces, mostly singing full voice, Pearlman stood off to one side making useful suggestions and quietly motivating their every action. Also present in the room were Billingham at the piano, Rolandi (who seemed to be hovering over the edge of her chair, giving a great imitation of a mother hen), stage manager John Coleman, Phil Morehead and conductor Stephen Lord.

When the scenes ended and Pearlman had finished giving his notes, Lord gave his—mostly comments on musical interpretation and French pronunciation. A hefty-looking middle-aged man, Lord was bearded and bald, wore glasses and was dressed in light-gray slacks, a gray shirt and a bright green bowtie as cheery as his whole attitude toward the proceedings. He struck me at once as a great singer's conductor—energetic, meticulous, but always upbeat. He had been brought in to conduct the concert by Epstein, who knew his work well as music director for both the Opera Theatre of St. Louis and the Boston Lyric Opera, companies that often hire young American artists.

Next up was the act-one duet "Si, fuggire," from *I Capuleti e i Montecchi,* Bellini's version of the Romeo and Juliet legend, in which the part of Romeo is sung by a mezzo, another of the so-called trouser roles for women in the bel canto era. It was still hard for me to believe in McNeese as a boy, but that's hardly her fault. She and Cabell, as Juliet, sang the scene beautifully and looked stunning onstage together. Pearlman suggested they end the scene holding hands, rather than standing awkwardly apart facing the audience, after which Lord noted that their pickups were tentative in a couple of places and asked them to emphasize more strongly some of the phrasing to stress Bellini's typical melodic thrust. He asked McNeese to repeat several opening phrases for emphasis, and when she did this to his satisfaction, he said, "Good! That's fine!"

Pearlman now went to work staging the entrance for the comical duet "Ai capricci della sorte," from Rossini's *L'Italiana in Algeri,* sung by Guang Yang and Levi Hernandez. It's the scene of a quarrel between a fearless, determined woman and her fussily reluctant companion. There were little bits of business—hand gestures, body movements—a perfect interplay between two artists who were totally into their roles and sang deliciously. Because he'd been out of action for so long, I hadn't heard Hernandez in more than two months, and I was delighted. His baritone is a clear, clean lyric sound, but what makes him an artist is his ability to become the part he's playing, which is the true test for any singer whose vocal resources are not overwhelming. In the scene that followed, also with Yang with the addition of Tigges, Hernandez proved his versatility. It was the act-three confrontation in Thomas's *Hamlet* between the Prince of Denmark and his adulterous mother. No laughs in this one, especially with Tigges standing gloomily by as the King's Ghost.

Hernandez, a native of El Paso, Texas, was in his first year in the Opera Center, having had to overcome not only a throat operation but a lot of vocal technical problems, which he had been working ferociously hard with Rolandi to correct. "I have so much tongue tension," he had told me some weeks earlier. "I got away with it for some time, developed some bad habits over the years." He was also smart enough not to be in a great hurry. "So if I miss a couple of auditions," he said, when someone asked why he hadn't showed up at one, "so what?" Good question. That was when I decided he was going to have a real career.

The longer the rehearsal went on, the more I was struck by how lucky these singers were to be receiving the kind of attention Pearlman and Lord were lavishing on them. In San Diego, and in almost every other opera company in the world, there is no time for this sort of meticulous, detailed work. The problem usually is getting the curtain up in two or three weeks, and on opening night it's sing or sink.

After a break in the rehearsal there was a run-through of the entire program of twenty-one selections from fourteen different operas—no stopping, only note-taking. Some of the singers marked, others sang out. It seemed to go off without a hitch, everyone in the right place, everyone in character. At the intermission I strolled over to chat with Erin Wall, who was sitting by herself off to one side, dressed, as usual, in her black pantsuit, her blond hair pulled back into a ponytail. She looked tired and told me she was. In the past three years she had learned at least ten roles, sung small ones and big ones and covered others. She also told me she had signed up to be represented by Andrea Anson, the CAMI agent who seemed to have the inside track on which of the LOCAA kids to pluck from the tree. She had all sorts of engagements to look forward to next season, including one at Lyric in Wagner's *Ring* cycle, but she didn't seem happy about some of her assignments. When I suggested she didn't have to sing what she felt wasn't right for her and observed that these managers and directors weren't gods, she answered, "But they have to be allowed to think they are." Get to be Renée Fleming, I thought, and they'll jump to your tune; that's how sacred monsters are made. Not that Fleming is one, since she has the reputation of being both gentle and kind, but she has the power to be what she wants to be. In what can turn out to be a cutthroat profession it is essential to develop an attitude, not unlike that of a high-salaried athlete or movie star. The people who make money off you are not necessarily your friends.

The next day I went to talk to Phil Morehead, who is so quiet and reserved that it had taken me weeks to appreciate his qualities as a musician. As the head of the Music Staff, he wields a considerable amount of power, but it is not, like Matthew Epstein's, immediately evident. A tall, bearded, scholarly-looking citizen who wears glasses, he lives with his wife, also a musician, in a wildly cluttered apartment full of furnishings covered by sheet music, scores and books. A grand piano occupies much of the space in his living room, and the walls are covered with paintings, framed photographs, posters, lithographs and concert advertisements. On the morning I walked in, the room had been set up for a chamber music rehearsal, with chairs and music stands crowded in next to the piano and blocking the way to one of the two sofas. Somehow we managed to squeeze out enough space to sit down, and I immediately asked how he thought the LOCAA year had gone. After all, he'd been around Lyric since 1981 and been involved almost from the very beginning in hiring the coaches and accompanists as well as the singers. Who better qualified to make a judgment of this year's crop?

"It's improved dramatically since I first came here," he said, "and especially recently, with Epstein as artistic director and Gianna Rolandi on staff. In the early years there were always several people who weren't really up to becoming finished artists and fell by the wayside. The prime requisite to being hired now is that you must have a career voice. Quite a few of them used to disappear into the ether."

He maintained that for the singers the auditions provided a terrific opportunity; everybody comes through Chicago, and the Rising Stars concert audience always includes people in a position to give a singer a job. I asked him to comment on the program for this year's affair, the selection of pieces from such a varied repertory by ten very different composers. I assumed that the choices had been made by Pearlman. Morehead conceded that this year's program was a tough one and singled out the three Richard Strauss numbers, two long arias for McNeese and Wall and a duet for Wall and Kelsey. "A little more economy from the composer would have been welcome," he added, in a typically dry understament. "It's very tough on the singers because there's always so much going on in the orchestrations." The program had been put together by Pearlman, Morehead told me, then added with a faint smile, "after which there's a committee that goes at it with a pickax."

Morehead's remark about singers disappearing into the atmosphere reminded me that two of this year's crop of LOCAA artists would not be appearing in the Rising Stars concert. Roger Honeywell, freed at last, like Frederic in *Pirates* from his indentures to the soft-hearted buccaneers, had fled to Vancouver to prepare for his Alfredo in *La Traviata.* From there it would be on to Glimmerglass for seven performances as the bandit hero in Puccini's *La Fanciulla del West* and then to the New York City Opera to tackle one of the two tenor leads in Richard Strauss's *Daphne,* a rarely performed curiosity in which the soprano is changed into a tree even as she goes right on singing.

The other absentee would be Chris Dickerson, the only member of the group who had departed unhappily. He could have sung in the concert, but chose not to. He had been in the program for three years and nothing about his time in it had disappointed him. "The coaches here are phenomenal," he had told me when I first talked to him shortly after my arrival in Chicago. I had sat in on one of his coaching sessions with Eric Weimer, when they were working on Raimondo, the role Dickerson was covering in *Lucia.* I remembered vividly how impassioned Weimer had been about making sure every "picky little thing" had been dealt with, from Dickerson's pronunciation of the words to phrasing to where to breathe to the use of legato to motivation to the need to differentiate even in places where the composer seemed to be repeating himself, which, Weimer cracked, was due to the librettist having run out of words. "This was the second opera I ever did when I was starting out," Dickerson had said after the session. "I don't know how I got through it. I had no vocal technique."

Nor was Weimer the only coach Dickerson had worked well with. He told me he had benefited greatly from sessions with Jim Johnson, whose working method with singers was quite different from Weimer's. "Jim first lets you get through the whole piece without stopping," Dickerson said, "then goes to work on it with you." (I had wanted to interview Johnson, an assistant conductor who lives in Paris, sneaks out between rehearsals as often as he can to smoke, has an acerbic sense of humor and looks, with a cigarette dangling out of his mouth, like Pépé Le Moko, an elusive character out of one of those old French movies in which people stand around looking sly and world-weary. Unfortunately, he slipped away from me before I could corner him.) As a conductor and prompter, Johnson is considered one of the best in the business, and Dickerson was quick to sing his praises. "I can't tell you how many times he saved our asses," he said.

What bothered Dickerson was that after three years in the company he seemed to have been shut out of any future with it. Of all the LOCAA artists, he was almost the only one not to have been offered an assignment for the following season. In his first year he had covered six roles and sung in three of the operas in the rep. In his second and third, he had been equally busy, but he had the distinct impression now that there would be no future for him at Lyric. He wasn't sure exactly why this was so, but seemed to feel that perhaps his resistance to learning one or two of the audition pieces that had been assigned to him had turned the powers that be on the artistic staff against him. In any case, he wasn't prepared to hang around where he wasn't wanted.

I was disappointed he wasn't going to be singing. I admired him and I liked the manly, straightforward way he sang, letting that smooth, clean bass of his pour out of his athletic six-foot-six frame with the confidence and joy of someone in control of his own talent. Dickerson was raised in Abilene, Texas, in a family that had no musical background. He studied the violin for six years, sang in the choir, played basketball and other sports—"did a little bit of everything." He liked to sing, even though at first he couldn't hit anything above a middle C. His first contact with opera was when he came across a score of "Il lacerato spirito"—Verdi's gorgeous lament by a grieving father for his dead daughter—and learned it. "Hey, this stuff is pretty good," he said to himself. When he got to Texas Tech, in Lubbock, he began to study seriously, and in the summer of 1996 he went as an apprentice to Santa Fe, where he sang in the chorus and covered a couple of roles. It was his first experience in a professional opera house. He then spent three years with the San Jose Opera, a small company where he sang a number of major and minor roles before being summoned to Chicago. He had sung for Pearlman when he was only twenty and gotten "a wonderful handwritten letter" saying he was too young, but to keep in touch. He kept in touch, went to Santa Barbara in the summer of 1999, then came to audition in September 2000, on the main stage of Lyric for Mason, Epstein, Pearlman and others on the music staff. Halfway through his second selection, Colline's aria from *La Bohème*, Epstein jumped to his feet and shouted, "Oh, that's fine! Go sign a contract!"

I thought it was sad that he wouldn't be singing as one of the Rising Stars, surrounded onstage by his colleagues in what should have been a climactic farewell to his three years at the Opera Center. Unlike Roger Honeywell, Dickerson was departing on a low note—but then low notes are what basses specialize in.

AT AROUND NOON on the day of the concert, I showed up backstage, happy to find the area inside and around the Rehearsal Department again full of light and activity, as it had been for the whole run of the season, which had ended with the last *Butterfly* on March 21. Amy Bishop was sitting alone behind her desk as the singers, who had begun drifting in one or two at a time, stopped by to drop off their lists of invited guests to be allowed backstage afterward. Scott Ramsay's was the longest. "Cute hair, cute hair! The best yet!" he said to Bishop as he handed her his roster. How many were coming, I asked him. "Too many," Bishop cracked. Two of the tickets he'd left at the box office to be picked up, Ramsay told me, were for a long-time Lyric subscriber and her husband. After Ramsay's Edgardo, the subscriber had written to Bill Mason to tell him how well Ramsay had performed. Mason had passed the note on to the tenor, who had then written to the woman to invite her and her husband to the concert. She had called to thank him personally and had expressed astonishment that he had actually taken the trouble to write to her.

I took a stroll around the corridors, gratified to find on each dressing room door a card formally announcing by their last names only the presence of the young singers. Behind one closed door I could hear Wayne Tigges warming up. Out of another suddenly popped Lauren McNeese, barefoot and clutching the guest list she had just made to hand in to Bishop. Guang Yang and Nicole Cabell smilingly hurried past to get ready. Quinn Kelsey moved grandly toward his quarters, looking as confident and cool as if he already had a long career behind him and this was going to be just another performance. Here they all were, in fact, stars at last, if only for a day.

Back outside the Rehearsal Department, Gianna Rolandi, looking exquisite in a bright red suit and high-heeled Italian pumps, appeared to be about to bounce off the walls. "Oh, I'm so nervous," she said. "I hope somebody's going to bring me a tranquilizer." Matthew Epstein appeared, bundled up in his usual black, all of his facial muscles in constant motion, his eyes looking huge behind their thick glasses. Richard Pearlman, a study in cool, strolled up to Amy Bishop. "Are all the people in?" he asked. "Good, then I'll do my tour." And he set off toward the dressing rooms to speak to each of the singers individually. We were twenty minutes away, and by this time I was so nervous myself that I went to stand in the wings for a few minutes, listening to the comfortingly friendly buzz of the audience.

At two o'clock sharp Bill Mason opened the proceedings by walking out alone onstage to introduce himself and to welcome everyone to the concert. Then he named and thanked all of the main sponsors one by one, with each name greeted by applause, before turning the proceedings over to the artists.

Patrick Miller was the first to appear, strolling out to stand all alone on the empty stage, an inoffensive abstract backdrop behind him, the great orchestra at his feet and Stephen Lord facing him at the podium, baton upraised. Miller sang "Questa o quella," the aria in Verdi's *Rigoletto* in which the handsome Duke of Mantua cheerfully describes himself as a ruthless seducer. Miller looked the part and sang the aria, with its soaring top notes, as effortlessly as if he were standing in his shower stall.

That was only the beginning. The rest of the afternoon flew by for me, as if I were attending a gala put on just for my benefit to celebrate a centuries-old tradition of great singing. The young artists seemed to feed off one another, displaying a commitment and an enthusiasm that usually characterizes successful sports teams. All season they had worked together and rooted for one another and it showed. By the intermission the audience seemed to be totally captivated, and when I went backstage I found Epstein there, more excited than I'd ever seen him, congratulating everybody and pouring out words of encouragement and praise. It was the sort of moment he clearly lived for, and it filled me with admiration for him. A love of great singing is what animates all of us who are involved with this curious art form.

I HUNG AROUND BACKSTAGE for quite a while after the concert, until long after most of the singers and their entourages of relatives and friends had left. I realized that I didn't want to go. I had been living my own past vicariously through the ups and downs of these young artists over the season, and this event itself had brought back so many memories. I wandered out onto the huge stage of Lyric and gazed out into the vast void of now empty seats stretching back in serried rows and then up to the balconies rising toward the ceiling. It was utterly daunting. How in the world had I ever imagined that I could stand on such a stage and sing to an audience that had heard the best? Then I told myself it didn't matter; my own career in song had never amounted to much, but it had deeply enriched my life.

Some years ago, back in Rome, I had gone with my wife to a performance of Donizetti's *Lucrezia Borgia* at the Teatro dell'Opera and spotted my old friend and fellow voice student Vittorio. He was sitting with friends in a parterre box on the side. At the first intermission I stood up in the aisle and waved to him. After the performance he drove us out to his penthouse apartment overlooking the Tiber, where he poured us stiff cognacs and we began to catch up with each other's doings; we hadn't seen each other for more than a decade. He was still a doctor, specializing, he told me, in rich Americans. After a while, he reminded me of the fun we had had trying to become great opera singers. "Now look at us," he said. "You are just another journalist and I am just another doctor." He waved an arm around to indicate his luxuriously furnished living room and suggested that we quit everything to go and sing in the Rome opera chorus. He then put on his stereo an old recording of Gigli and Caniglia performing the last-act love duet from *Andrea Chénier,* in which the two protagonists are whisked away in a tumbril to perish gloriously together, bellowing full-throated fortissimo high notes, on the guillotine. What better way to go?

High Notes

THE DAY AFTER RISING STARS in concert, I had tea with Gianna Rolandi in the upstairs lobby of a luxury hotel on Michigan Avenue. I found her irritated by the review of the event in the *Sun-Times*, which, though very favorable to all the singers, had referred to them at one point as students. "That's a no-no and it really pisses me off," she said. These singers were not students, she pointed out, but young artists building careers for themselves by refining their techniques and interpretations of major and minor roles.

Fine, I wondered, but what about the year as a whole? What would linger longest in her mind about it? "I just feel really proud to play a part in their careers," she said. "They're babies when they come here." She cited McNeese and Wall as examples. "And then they become artists. It takes a couple of years to get solid technically. It took Erin and Lauren and Scott three to get where they are. Scott's top notes were very small and falsetto-ish." She recalled the struggle over Roger Honeywell. "I must have done that *Pirates* duet with him a hundred times, he was having such trouble with it. And then there's Guang Yang, who did a very brave thing to come here, because she could already have had a big career. And Lauren Curnow, now having the potential to become another Patricia Racette, a great acting singer. She's such an artist herself." She paused a moment and glanced briefly away from me. "But who knows?" she added. "You get 'em to sing correctly, then you hope for the best."

After I had gone home and over the next few months I kept track of what the young singers were up to. In late June, in Room 200, five of them—Tigges, Kelsey, Miller, Curnow, and Cabell—sang in an in-house performance of *Don Giovanni.* Pearlman reported that it had been a huge success, especially for Kelsey, a charismatic and majestic Don, and Lauren Curnow in the often thankless part of Elvira. Kelsey had been expected to shine in the title role, but as Elvira, the wretched and abandoned victim of the great seducer who often comes across as a laughable dupe, Curnow, in her first soprano outing, not only sang brilliantly but, in Pearlman's words, "established the essential nobility of the character."

Over the summer months there was a *Fledermaus* produced by the Northwest Indiana Symphony, in which Miller sang a graceful Alfred, the tenor boob in love with the heroine, Rosalinda, and Guang Yang impersonated Prince Orlofsky, a comical mezzo trouser part. Pearlman, who directed the piece, reported that Yang not only sang magnificently but, to the audience's delight, made herself up to look like "Chairman Mao in drag." In early August, the LOCAA singers appeared at the Grant Park Music Festival in Puccini's farcical one-acter, *Gianni Schicchi.* "The entire cast was . . . excellent," reported the *Sun-Times,* going on to single out Levi Hernandez in the comedic title role, Guang Yang, Ramsay and "the extraordinary baritone of Quinn Kelsey."

Then, on Saturday, September 18, Erin Wall became a full-fledged star. It happened on the opening night of the company's fiftieth anniversary season, in a *Don Giovanni* featuring three of opera's biggest names—Bryn Terfel as the Don, Susan Graham as Elvira and the Finnish soprano Karita Mattila as Donna Anna. At ten o'clock that morning Mattila announced that she was too sick to perform. Wall had been covering the part and so it was she who went on instead. "It was a once-in-a-lifetime chance to do such a plum role," she informed an interviewer a few days later. As they say in show biz, she knocked them dead. After her opening highly dramatic aria, "Or sai chi l'onore," she received a huge ovation. She sang so well throughout the evening that at the curtain calls the whole audience rose to its feet to applaud her. Mattila, considered today one of the great sopranos of our era, showed up for the second performance and also received raves from the critics, but even more than with her Marguerite the year before, Erin Wall had now established herself prominently in the operatic firmament. "Oh, sure, I wouldn't mind singing Donna Anna again," she told the reporter. One of her specialties, I had long ago decided, is understatement.

Over the ensuing weeks, as I was writing this book, I kept track of all the major developments in the careers of the young singers. Only Erin Wall had so far emerged as an important artist soon to be in demand everywhere, but all of them were still working hard at their careers. Roger Honeywell was out in the world making a name for himself, while the rest of them were busy, either still at Lyric singing mostly small parts and covering major ones or performing elsewhere with regional companies. Most had also acquired agents, who were setting up auditions for them and getting them jobs.

Before leaving Chicago, I sat down for one last interview with Lauren McNeese and her husband, Michael Mayes. Even though the future was still uncertain for them and neither had yet secured representation, they were upbeat about their careers; they both had bookings in the coming months that would pay their bills, but, as usual, they would be spending long periods apart. McNeese would be working mainly at Lyric, while Mayes would be busy in Santa Fe and at the Michigan Opera, in Detroit, singing comprimario parts. They'd been together for five years and had become accustomed to long separations, but they admitted it was hard. The dream they nurtured of having a small ranch in their native Texas, where they could spend part of each year and raise a family, seemed a distant one. Still, they were not about to give up. "We have friends who own houses and are doing very well," McNeese explained, "but not something they love."

Even if you achieve stardom and ultimately become by choice and caprice a true sacred monster, your life as a professional opera singer will be lived out of suitcases. You study seemingly endlessly, you practice, you work out, you come, you perform, you hope it's a success and that the public loves you, you pack your bags and you move on. When Wagner wrote *The Flying Dutchman,* the musical saga of the poor ship's captain doomed to wander the earth endlessly in search of a woman selfless enough to throw herself off a cliff for him, he must have had an aspiring opera singer in mind.

ACKNOWLEDGMENTS

THE IDEA FOR THIS BOOK originated in a luncheon conversation with Pete Fornatale, then my editor at Crown. Another senior editor, Doug Pepper, also supported the project and helped get it off the ground before leaving to return to his native Canada, where he now heads another publishing house. I miss them both, but their successor, Genoveva Llosa, has proved herself to be a treasure, an editor of great skill and dedication who helped in many ways to bring this narrative to life. Everyone at Crown has been supportive and I thank them all.

When I was sniffing around for the right American opera company to approach with this project, one name kept coming up—Lyric Opera of Chicago. My friend Craig Rutenberg, one of the finest vocal coaches and accompanists in the world of opera, steered me toward Richard Pearlman, who runs the program for the young singers there. Craig told me there was no better person for that job anywhere and he was right. Pearlman believed it was important that this backstage story of young artists trying to launch their careers be told and he immediately gave me his full backing. With it I wrote to William Mason, the general director of Lyric, who agreed and opened the doors of the company to me, making it possible for me to sit in on rehearsals, meetings, coaching sessions, master classes and performances, and to interview anyone and everyone I wanted to talk to. It was courageous and admirable of him to do so, as I had only my reputation to guarantee my integrity as a reporter. I am deeply grateful to him—as I am to every other member of this remarkable opera company. During all of the months I was there, roaming around backstage, sitting in on events and talking to people, no one barred the way to me or refused to be interviewed, not even Matthew Epstein, then the outspoken and willful artistic director, who prides himself on never giving interviews or providing access to reporters. (Epstein has since moved on.) Sir Andrew Davis, the company's music director and principal conductor, could not have been more gracious and understanding.

It would take much too long to list every member of the Lyric staff who helped to make this narrative possible, but I have to single out a number of people who went beyond the merely helpful. Susan Mathieson Mayer is the best promotion and marketing director I've ever met and, like me, loves the ponies almost as much as opera singers. Danny Newman, the cheery octogenarian who has been promoting the company since day one, was a joy to talk to. Magda Krance is the superwoman of PR, mistress of a thousand disciplines and a damn fine writer to boot. So is her colleague Jack Zimmerman, who can placate any subscriber or audience, often just by falling back on his favorite word, *nevertheless*. Roger Pines, the company's dramaturg, is a bottomless well of information on singers past and present and on opera in general.

In the Rehearsal Department, the backstage heart and soul of the company, Marina Vecci and Josie Campbell can solve more problems than Figaro, especially with helpers such as Amy Bishop, Greg Henkel and Sarah Olender on hand. In Education, Jean Keister Kellogg enlightens with her radiant personality everything she turns her hand to. Stage managers Caroline Moores and John Coleman and their staff were patient and understanding in allowing me to hang around even when the backstage action was at its most frenzied. And the Tech guys and dolls were awesome.

From the music staff, no one was more fun or enlightening to talk to than Eric Weimer, but also on hand to make my note-gathering easy were Bill Billingham, Betty Buccheri, Tim

Shaindlin and others. Philip Morehead, who runs this show, has an understated style that at first disguises what turns out to be an enormous musical knowledge and awareness of what's going on. Donald Palumbo could probably teach the tone-deaf to sing in tune, and no one tells a better story than Jim Johnson, who from his prompter's box has saved more singers from straying than the Salvation Army has souls.

Inside LOCAA, just getting to hang around and talk to and become friends with Richard Pearlman has made my time in Chicago more than merely worthwhile. Gianna Rolandi is like a fresh, clean wind blowing across the open ocean; there's not a whiff of bullshit to anything she says. Dan Novak has also become a good friend. He runs very efficiently what amounts to a business operation, but he has the soul of an artist and behaves accordingly. Thanks, too, to Dan DiLuciano and especially to Alicia Takushi, who piled extra work on herself on my behalf.

And again my thanks to everyone else at Lyric, all of whom contributed to making this project so rewarding and so much fun.

I am also very grateful to Elizabeth Kaplan, my agent for many years, for her support and commitment. I could not have written this book at all in the time allotted to it by contract if it hadn't been for Frank Scatoni, who gently tugged me into the late twentieth century by teaching me how to use my now indispensable laptop. (My next step will be into the twenty-first, when I embark reluctantly onto the Web.) And thanks, too, to Jennifer Thornton, proofreader and editor extraordinaire, for help and advice on literary stuff in general.

My wife, Alice, had to put up with me while I disappeared periodically into my work. Her support and love has, as usual, been invaluable.

$\mathcal{A}$BOUT THE AUTHOR

WILLIAM MURRAY was the author of more than thirty books, including *City of the Soul* and *The Last Italian*. He was a staff writer for *The New Yorker* and contributed to *The New York Times Magazine, Opera News, The Nation* and *Esquire*. He lived in Del Mar, California.

A NOTE ON THE TYPE

This book was set in PAVANE, an old-style serif font created by Lars Bergquist in 1997. The font is a modernization of a Garamond-style typeface based on Jean Jannon's *Caractères de l'université* of 1621.